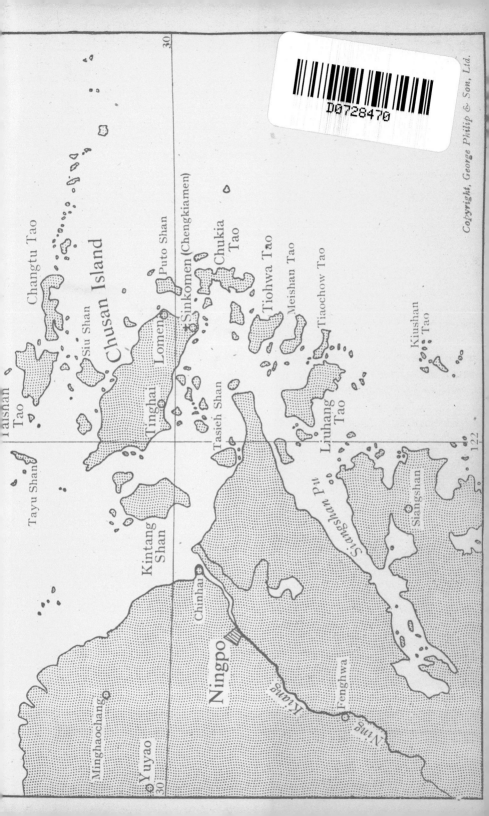

Copyright, George Philip & Son, Ltd.

Changtu Tao

Chusan Island

Siu Shan

Puto Shan

Sinkomen (Chengkiamen)

Chukia Tao

Tiohwa Tao

Meishan Tao

Tiaochow Tao

Kiushan Tao

Taishan Tao

Lomen

Tinghai

Tasieh Shan

Liuhang Tao

Siangshan Pu

Siangshan

Tayu Shan

Kintang Shan

Chinhai

Ningpo

Minghaochang

Fenghwa

Yuyao

Kiung

Ning

30

30

122

Gift of Mrs. D. M. O'Brien

SISTER
XAVIER
BERKELEY

SISTER BERKELEY—AGED 71 YEARS

SISTER
XAVIER BERKELEY

(1861-1944)

SISTER OF CHARITY OF ST. VINCENT DE PAUL: FIFTY-FOUR YEARS A MISSIONARY IN CHINA

by

M. L. H.

With a Foreword by
HIS EXCELLENCY MR. JOHN C. H. WU
Chinese Minister to the Holy See

LONDON
BURNS OATES
1949

NIHIL OBSTAT: PATRICIVS MORRIS, S.T.D., L.S.S.

CENSOR DEPVTATVS

IMPRIMATVR: E. MORROGH BERNARD

WESTMONASTERII: DIE XV OCTOBRIS MCMXLVIII

PRINTED IN GREAT BRITAIN BY
THE GARDEN CITY PRESS LIMITED
LETCHWORTH HERTFORDSHIRE FOR
BURNS OATES AND WASHBOURNE
LIMITED
28 ASHLEY PLACE LONDON S.W.1
First published 1949

To
ALL MISSIONARY SISTERS IN CHINA
THIS BOOK IS DEDICATED
BY ONE OF THEM

FOREWORD

By John C. H. Wu

Chinese Minister to the Holy See

"My heart is fixed there where Jesus hath wished it to be fixed." (St. Gertrude.)

ONE of the most interesting visits I have received since my coming to Rome was from an old French priest, Father D. Maximilien Hérault. He had come from the San Pietro in Vincoli to ask for a few copies of my booklet on *The Science of Love*, a study on St. Thérèse of Lisieux, for, he said, he had use for them in the direction of souls. During the interview our conversation turned to the missionaries in China. To my greatest pleasure I discovered that he was a boyhood friend of Father Vincent Lebbe. He told me that when Lebbe was a little boy his father asked him, " What would you like to be in the future ? " The answer was, " I want to be a Sister of Charity "! From this incident one can easily imagine what a deep impression the Sisters of Charity had made on the little boy who was one day to become a great missionary in China.

A little after Father Hérault's visit I received a letter from " M.L.H." telling me that she had been writing the Life of Sister Xavier Berkeley. I was very happy to learn of this, because although I had heard about the good works of the Sisters of Charity I did not have an inside knowledge of them. How glad I am, then, to receive from the publishers the advance proofs of a book which I had been waiting so anxiously to read!

Now I have read it. My impression is too deep to be made explicit. All that I can safely assert is that the boy Lebbe was not far wrong in wishing to be a Sister of Charity. I myself have the same wish. I want to be a Sister of Charity *in spirit*.

The most important thing in life is to have a proper ideal to live for and to die for. This is why the great educator Confucius used to discuss ideals of life with his pupils. Once when Yen Yuan and Tsu Lu were waiting upon him he said to them, " Come, let

each of you tell his ideals." Tsu Lu said, " I wish to have carriages
and horses and light furs, to share them with my friends, and to
feel no resentment if they should spoil them." Yen Yuan said, " I
wish never to vaunt of my goodness, nor to make a display of my
merits." Then Tsu Lu said to Confucius, " May we hear your
ideals, sir ? " The answer was, " To comfort the aged, to be
faithful to my friends, and to treat the young with fostering
affection and kindness."

It is no exaggeration to say that the life of Sister Xavier Berkeley
has realized all these ideals of Confucius and his pupils. In truth,
with the Sister these ideals were further ennobled by the fact that
they were but streams flowing directly from the Living Source
of Divine Love, the Sacred Heart of Christ. To be a faithful
follower of Christ is to be another Christ; and to be another
Christ is to be filled with the Holy Spirit, and to be sent out to
announce the glad tidings to the poor, to heal the broken-hearted,
to deliver man from the thraldom of sin, to give sight to the blind,
to set the oppressed at liberty and to usher in the Kingdom of God.
What a mission this is! Sister Xavier Berkeley certainly did more
than her share in carrying out the mission, which is common to
all Christians worthy of the name. And it is precisely because she
was so faithful to her mission as a Christian that her life was such
a perfect fulfilment of the Confucian ideals; for Christianity has
come to China not to destroy Confucianism but to enliven it and
bring it to a greater perfection.

This book is more interesting than any novels that I have read;
for truth is more romantic than fiction. The Sisters of Charity
are in the very thick of the battle of life. In season and out of
season, they fight with the Devil over the souls of the sick, of the
dying and of the prisoners. To all appearance, they are feeble
beings and weak vessels; in reality they are invincible soldiers of
Christ, armed as they are with the breastplate of faith and love
and the helmet of hope.

I deeply regret that I did not come to know Sister Berkeley,
although I was born and grew up in Ningpo. But as a child I did
occasionally see the white-cornetted Sisters walking in pairs on
the streets of Ningpo, going about doing good. To me they looked
more like fairies than human beings. Little did I suspect what
mortifications and trials they had to undergo in their strenuous
pilgrimage through this valley of tears. I remember once our

house was honoured by the visit of two elderly Sisters. They had a conversation with my mother; they must have spoken the Ningpo dialect, as my mother knew none other. I don't remember for what purpose they came; probably it was for soliciting alms for the poor. But that is beside the point. The point is that all of us were deeply impressed by their angelic purity and radiant kindness. I have forgotten their faces now; but my heart thrills with joy when I reflect that perhaps Sister Berkeley was one of them! Did they suspect that thirty years later our whole family would come to the fold of the Good Shepherd? Or did they even then pray for our conversion? Well, such things will only be known in Heaven.

Ever since I became a Catholic my ideal has always been to do the work of Martha with the spirit of Mary. This is what I wrote years ago about the Little Flower of Jesus: " If Thérèse had been a member of the home in Bethany she would have served Jesus as carefully as Martha did and at the same time cast furtive glances at Him to see whether He was completely happy with Mary sitting at His feet." This seems to be exactly what Sister Berkeley did throughout her busy life in China. Her life was full of activities, to such an extent that her last words were: " Oh, I am so weary, so weary. I can do no more! " But at the centre of her being she was continually united with Our Lord. Having embraced the One, she could never be distracted by the many. In such a soul Love transforms every action into contemplation. In fact, so long as one's love of God is genuine, one can engage in contemplation without stagnating into a quietist, and one can be active without degenerating into an activist. Such a soul enjoys the liberty of the children of God, and obeys the authority of the Church as the dictates of her own heart; for the same Spirit that guides the Mystical Body guides also the individual member. This is the reason why such a strong character as Sister Berkeley was also one of the most obedient daughters of the Church.

One of the charms of this book is that the graphic account of the Sister's activities is interspersed with her retreat notes, thus bringing into relief the source from which she constantly drew her strength. Æsthetically, the effect is somewhat like that made on me when I read Tolstoi's *War and Peace*, where in the brief lulls between the breath-taking battles the general would lift his eyes to the blue sky where everything was so calm and peaceful.

This book is all the more charming because the author is unconscious of her art.

No one can read this book without desiring to become a better Christian and without winning a deeper insight into the words of Christ. Like the lives of the saints, this Life makes you realize that every word of Our Lord is a cheque that will be honoured at the Bank of Reality. Has He not said, for instance, " I promise you, . . . everyone who has forsaken home, or brothers, or sisters, or mother, or children, or lands for my sake and for the sake of the gospel, will receive, now in this world, a hundred times their worth, houses, sisters, brothers, mothers, children and lands, but with persecution; and in the world to come he will receive everlasting life " (Mark x. 29-30: Mgr. Knox's version). Has this promise ever failed anyone ? Never! In the case of Sister Berkeley, the reward was more than a hundred times; for when she came to die, thousands of people in Chusan and Ningpo wept as children mourning their much beloved Mother. The Chinese are a grateful people; they never forget benefits received from a loving hand. But woe to the missionaries, if there be any, who go out to any country without a genuine love for God and for the people to whom God has sent them!

Happy are they who, like Sister Berkeley, have left all, including their self-will, for the sake of Christ; for by leaving all they shall find all. In her spiritual notes we read: " Above all, keep the gaze of your soul fixed calmly on God alone, trying to view all things as He views them." " Confide entirely in Our Lord, He will never fail you." " Welcome any little sufferings that come your way as precious jewels to be offered to Our Lord while waiting till you have the privilege of offering Him your life's blood." " You *must* be a Saint; only will what He wills and you will be a Saint." Here, as Father Denis Nugent so well puts it, " we get a glimpse of the intense spiritual life of union with Our Lord that pulsated beneath the simple, even-tempered, kindly Sister of Charity, as she went on her way doing good ".

The trouble with the modern world is that there are too few men and women of true ambition. The ambition to be a saint is the only one that makes life worth living. For a saint, even in this life, can honestly say with St. John of the Cross, " The heavens are mine, the earth is mine, and the nations are mine; mine are the just, and the sinners are mine: mine are the angels and the

Mother of God; all things are mine, God Himself is mine and for me because Christ is mine and all for me." To choose less than All is to be satisfied with the crumbs that fall from our Father's table. And yet how many wretched people are wasting their lives for a few millions of dollars when they could possess the whole universe if only they would! And how many are hankering after the vain glories of the world when by a change of heart they could have the true glory of being the children and heirs of God. It is my hope and prayer that this book will lead many a prodigal son, who would fain feed himself with the food of the swine, to return to his Father's house to enjoy the wonderful Feast of Life.

JOHN C. H. WU.

ROME, *November 15th*, 1948.

PREFACE

By Father Denis Nugent, C.M.

IT was a happy decision of the Superiors to have permitted that the noble figure of the Pioneer Missionary Sister of Charity be presented to Catholic readers in 1948, the year which marks the centenary of the arrival of the Sisters of Charity in China.[1]

Like the sun radiant and warm after the storm clouds have passed, Sister Xavier Berkeley comes to us, just as the smoke of the world's most terrible war has lifted, to offer to our war-tired eyes the beauty and grandeur of her long life, all consecrated to the work which the Son of God came on earth to perform.

St. Thomas of Aquin teaches us that God's Love is the cause of the goodness which is found in His creatures, and that no one of them would be better than another unless it were more beloved by God.

Very early in the life of Sister Xavier Berkeley we perceive this divine predilection singling her out for the vocation to which God had destined her. The outward sign of the intimate promptings of God's Grace is very often a slender thing—for little six years old Agnes Berkeley it will be the picture she received the day she and her little brothers and sisters were enrolled in the Association of the Holy Childhood. That picture spoke to her soul. The sight of two Sisters of Charity in the act of saving little Chinese babies thrilled her, and she said in her heart that she, too, would be a Sister of Charity ; that she, too, would one day go away and do the same.

At that moment she could only foresee the salvation of little babies, but God had mapped out for her a programme that would include the relief of every human affliction.

To that end, God created and poured in abundance into her heart the charity and goodness which is associated in the minds of all who came into contact with the name of Sister Berkeley.

The gripping story of her life is the unfolding of charity in continuous activity during the long fifty-four years in which, as

[1] For various reasons the publication of this book was unavoidably delayed.

daughter of St. Vincent de Paul, she radiated his spirit of love and compassion in China. The words of St. Paul the Apostle, like a ballad burden, ever rang in her heart—" The Charity of Christ urgeth us "—and with the ardour of an athlete she ever pressed on to attain the reward attached to God's Call to the missionary life, which for her consisted in souls in ever-increasing numbers.

In Ningpo city and on Chusan Island the thought of the multitude of souls who were waiting to be saved haunted her, and her rich and fruitful mind was ever active in finding ways and means of attaining sublime ends.

Though she concentrated her best energies to the duties which obedience laid upon her, she did not live in a " tower of ivory", unconscious of the needs of God's Church in other places.

From her House of Mercy on Chusan Island her charity radiated to all the stations in the vicariate. She had a predilection for the Chinese priests, most of whom she had known as students, as they trod their anxious way during the long years of preparation for the priesthood. It was for her a real joy to help them in their efforts to build up their Mission stations.

The necessity for having English-speaking priests in China was a thought which occupied her mind from the first day that she set foot on the soil of China. Not that she believed naïvely that the English language, like a charm, would christianize the land; but she knew that America and England and Ireland could send apostles to take a hand in the harvesting for Christ of the enormous country of China. She knew, too, that the presence of English-speaking missionaries would help to eradicate from the minds of the natives the belief that the Catholic Church was only the French Church, and that the great Anglo-Saxon nations were completely Protestant.

For long years, by her prayers and her correspondence, Sister Berkeley encouraged the Founder of the Maryknoll Foreign Missionary Society, when, as Director of the Society for the Propagation of the Faith in Boston, he had begun the arduous work which God had inspired him to do. She became a fairy godmother to the infant community that had, on the banks of the Hudson river, begun life so humbly less than forty years ago, and lived to see it grow and prosper, and send forth its priests and Sisters, who now, with God's blessing, labour for the conversion of pagan souls in several vicariates of the Far East.

With the same zealous interest and sympathy Sister Xavier followed the modern gigantic missionary movement which within the past thirty years has stirred the soul of Ireland. In the " Maynooth Mission to China " she saw a revival of the spirit which, in the past, sent hosts of Irish missionaries, who, as exiles for Christ, planted the Cross over Europe and brought the proud victorious barbarians to the feet of the humble Saviour of mankind.

Such is the enchanting figure which the writer of the life of Sister Xavier Berkeley holds up to our admiration. The youthful reader will be captivated by the romance of this noble lady, in the flower of youth, casting aside the good things of this life, as an athlete does a garment which impedes his action, leaving home and friends and country, and setting out for far-off China in quest of souls.

" *Exempla trahunt.*" May we not hope that more than one, touched by this noble generosity, may feel the call of God to do what she has done and to follow whither she beckons on ?

All will discover, with edification for their souls, in this captivating story the secret of Sister Xavier's long life of persevering goodness. From the beginning, with simple faith, she paid attention to, and took her directions from, her Divine Master, who had Himself told us what are the conditions of our success in His service. " He who abides in Me ", He tells us, " and I in him, he bears much fruit, for without Me you can do nothing."

From her spiritual notes we get a glimpse of the intense spiritual life of union with Our Lord that pulsated beneath the simple, even-tempered, kindly Sister of Charity, as she went on her way doing good. Like St. Paul, she could say in all truth, " For to me, to live is Christ " (Phil. i. 21). She found Him everywhere —in her Sisters, in the tabernacle, in the poor. He appeared to her in the hungry, thirsty, in the homeless stranger, in the naked, the sick and the prisoner. That is why even the most wayward could say that she treated him like a mother, and that she was no respecter of persons.

The memory of this great holy Sister of Charity will remain in the hearts of all who knew her and especially in the hearts of countless Chinese who knew no other mother-love but hers.

DENIS NUGENT, C.M.

ST. PAUL'S SEMINARY, NINGPO, *December 8th,* 1946.

CONTENTS

LIST OF ILLUSTRATIONS

B

AUTHOR'S INTRODUCTION

"My son, let me do as I have a mind in your regard; I know what is best for you." (The Imitation of Christ.)

IN one of Sister Berkeley's earliest spiritual retreat notebooks we find these words from the *Imitation* : "My son, let me do as I have a mind in your regard; I know what is best for you." We may surely think that she heard God's voice and invitation in very early youth and took them to her heart. She never spoke of her first desire to "give all and receive all", but she certainly chose her path of life when very young.

This made no obstacle to her frank enjoyment of the many years she passed in her beautiful Catholic home. She herself related that when she was about fifteen, their chaplain spoke to her very solemnly, telling her that at her age she should really be more serious and not always be scampering about like a boy and thinking only of enjoying life. She replied with a smile, "When I am twenty, I am going to run away and hide myself in a convent, but until then I am going to have all the fun and enjoyment I can get in life."

An Englishman, a relative of one of her Sisters in China, visited Sister Berkeley's house on Chusan Island in 1932. He spent some days in this rather primitive Chinese Mission in the middle of the Chusan Archipelago, often passing through the big House of Mercy (*Tzong-ze-dong*) with its orphanage, homes for old and infirm men and women and hospitals for the sick poor of the islands, established in 1868 and served by the Sisters of Charity of St. Vincent de Paul. He drank in the spirit of the works, wondering at times at the joyful whole-hearted devotion to God and the poor seen on all sides in spite of the poverty and difficulties of the pagan surroundings.

On his return to England he went to Worcester to visit Sister Berkeley's relatives, telling them all that he had seen in Chusan. He was taken to Spetchley Park, the family home of the Berkeleys, and passed through the rooms, round the gardens and park, with its beautiful trees, and down to the little Catholic graveyard.

After this visit he wrote a long letter to Sister Berkeley in Chusan, and in it we read:

"Does it bring it all back to you, over sixty years ago ? I seemed to see the child who ran about those gardens and through those rooms and up those nursery stairs. I pictured also the girl who began to face her vocation, and who achieved a new intimacy with things unseen as she prayed in the Chapel, an intimacy which took the place of the child-like awe with which she started. No, it did not take its place; it deepened and enriched it, and it is still with you in your Chinese home.

"I looked at the picture of you as a young girl, and it seemed to me that the look on your face was of one set to go forward on her Lord's path, gallantly and with fortitude. It is good to think of you after all these years able to testify to the truth by which that young girl determined to live those many years ago. The fidelity of God is as great as His Love, and by fidelity, I mean the utter trustworthiness of God and His conquering grace."

The birth of Sister Berkeley's special vocation for Foreign Missions in China is well known. At the age of six, with her elder brothers and sisters, she joined the Society of the Holy Childhood, the work of which is the salvation of pagan children. She received as membership certificate the famous picture of the Sisters of Charity in China rescuing abandoned babies. The little girl of six, studying this picture, said, "When I am older I shall go to China and save babies like those Sisters." She never wavered in this vocation and throughout her long missionary life the work nearest and dearest to her heart was that of the Holy Childhood.

We find an interesting note in the English Annals of the Holy Childhood, which we have permission to quote:

"Over a hundred years ago an Englishman, Mr. Ambrose de Lisle Phillips, and his wife were visiting a friend, Mr. Kenelm Digby, who with his family was living in Paris. Through him, they were introduced to an old French Bishop, Mgr. de Forbin Janson, who was then developing a scheme to link up Catholic children with the poor pagan children in far-away lands, by means of a league of prayer and sacrifice which was to be put under the patronage of the Holy Child Jesus. He laid his plans before the Holy Father in Rome, and then consulted Pauline de Jaricot, who had established the Association for the Propagation of the Faith.

"On his return to Paris, the Bishop made his scheme known to the Digby family, and thus it came about that some English children were the first members of the Holy Childhood Society, as it came to be called. The story is told by Marcella Digby, who became a Sacred Heart Nun and a Missionary, for she opened a convent in Peru in 1899. She says : ' I can only remember that we were the first to give our alms for the little Chinese children. In accordance with the wish of the saintly Bishop, our childish hands were the first to put a small sum of money into his hands, so we became the founders of the Holy Childhood.' "

The promoter of the local branch of the Holy Childhood Society in England of which the Berkeley children became members was a good old lady living in their own village of Spetchley. It is interesting to know that she was the aunt of the venerable Arch-bishop Redwood of New Zealand, who died at the age of ninety-four in 1935.

Sister Berkeley remembered that, as children, she and her brothers and sisters gave their pocket-money and made little sacrifices to collect money for saving Chinese babies. Sixty years later, the membership picture of the Sisters of Charity and the babies was still in her prayer book, worn and faded. It must be confessed that it was then stolen by one of her companions and sent to England to be reprinted and used as her Golden Jubilee picture, a memorial of fifty years' vocation as a Sister of Charity, September 8th, 1882, to 1932. This increased to sixty-three years, of which fifty-four were spent in the China Mission.

In an appreciation, written after her death, by the Canadian Holy Childhood, we read:

" The greater one's love, the more willing is the spirit of sacrifice. Such was the love of Sister Xavier Berkeley ! May her story urge others to accept the challenge her life inspires."

AUTHOR'S NOTE

Sisters of Charity are not writers of books; they have other things to do. The author makes apologies for the many shortcomings in this book from a literary point of view, due perhaps to her having spoken mainly French and Chinese for the past twenty-three years. It is not strictly a biography, though it traces the life of a Sister in the China Missions. It is rather a story of the works God did through a Sister of Charity who was faithful to the spirit and obligations of her much-loved vocation.

The author's grateful thanks are due to many friends who gave valuable help and encouragement. Amongst them stand out Lady Winefride Elwes, Sister Margaret Egerton and Mr. T. F. Burns.

In obedience to the decrees of Pope Urban VIII and other sovereign Pontiffs the writer declares that the graces and other supernatural facts related in this volume as witnessing to the sanctity of Servants of God other than those canonized or beatified by the Church rest on human authority alone; and in regard thereto, as in all things else, the writer submits herself without reserve to the infallible judgement of the Apostolic See, which alone has power and authority to pronounce as to whom rightly belong the character and title of saint or blessed.

I

EARLY DAYS AT HOME

AGNES MARY PHILOMENA BERKELEY was born on June 1st, 1861, at Overbury Court, Gloucestershire. She herself said, " I was the first of the second half-dozen." There were twelve children in that family and all grew up. Sister Berkeley also said, " My mother always did everything very correctly; it was a girl, a boy, a girl, a boy, a girl, a boy, two girls, two boys, a girl, a boy "—six sons and six daughters !

Her father was Mr. Robert Berkeley, J.P., D.L., of Spetchley Park, Worcester; her mother, Lady Catharine Berkeley (*née* Browne), second daughter of the Earl of Kenmare of Killarney. Among the many stately homes of England, especially those for which Worcestershire is famous, few can rival the beauty and charm of Spetchley Park, for over 400 years the seat of the Berkeley family. This beautiful Catholic home is situated in a widespread park with magnificent trees, two large lakes and many glades, stocked with red and fallow deer. There is one especially noble oak tree, the girth of which is so great that a grotto has been built in the boughs, overlooking a cricket ground.

The first recorded ancestor is Earl Ralph Berkeley; he married a sister of Edward the Confessor, who was in the habit of spending Christmas at Berkeley with his court. In a succeeding generation the Berkeleys sided with King Stephen against Henry II, and their estates were confiscated and granted to Robert Fitzharding, grandson of the King of Denmark, whose family had come over with William the Conqueror. However, a union was effected between the two families and Fitzharding's son assumed his wife's name of Berkeley, which is derived from the Saxon " berk " (birch tree) and " ley " (place).

Later we read of Lord Thomas Berkeley, who settled in Worcestershire and was the founder of the Spetchley branch of the family. Charles II stayed in the old Manor House at Spetchley and escaped from it during the battle of Worcester, when Cromwell captured the city. The people of Worcester suffered much for their loyalty to their king, among them Sir Robert Berkeley, grandson of Lord Thomas and Judge of the King's Bench, who had succeeded to Spetchley.

The old Manor House was burnt by the Presbyterian troops, and when Cromwell announced his wish to go and see Sir Robert the Judge arrayed himself in his robes, and sat on a bench in the garden, saying that as he had no house in which to receive him he must do so in the open. He then fitted up his stables, and lived there for some time.

There are many evidences at Spetchley of the favour of Charles I, among them an exquisite miniature of His Majesty and two beautifully illuminated books, a bible and a prayer book, on which are the royal monogram and arms.

The present noble mansion of Spetchley was built by Sister Berkeley's great-grandfather and his portrait and that of her great-grandmother, " Appolonie Lea ", hang in the spacious hall. Her grandfather built and endowed the Berkeley Hospital for old men and women in Foregate, Worcester.

Over 400 years have elapsed since the Spetchley branch of the family separated from the parent stem at Berkeley Castle, Somersetshire. The Barony of Berkeley is one of the earliest creations, and in its pedigree the family trace three royal descents, those of England, Scotland and France, and the arms of England are quartered on their shield. But, living among their own country people as the Worcestershire Berkeleys have always done, no title is dearer to them than the " Squire of Spetchley ".

Above all, they held the Faith, the ancient Catholic Faith of their forefathers, for which many of them had suffered cruelly. They were staunch supporters of the Church, and founded monasteries, convents, chantries and hospitals. At the time of the French Revolution, the Berkeleys of Spetchley gave hospitality to three different refugee Communities for many years—Benedictines, Dominicans and Poor Clares, with their chaplains.

" Mr. Robert Berkeley [our Sister's father] filled many public offices of trust, he was always to the fore in promoting everything that tended to the welfare of his neighbour and his county. He carried a single-mindedness of purpose and devotion to all that he undertook which won for him the respect and admiration of all brought in contact with him.

" He was widely and deeply respected as a man who had the interests of his neighbour at heart, and he worked and toiled and gave the best years of his life for them.

" There was another side to his character; he was a man imbued with a deep spirit of faith and religion. His faith was the root of all the good actions of his life. He looked beyond the things of this world and kept his thoughts on Heaven. He had a wonderful gift of prayer; his whole soul was filled with the spirit of prayer. He found in the silent friendship of God the greatest joy of his life.

" The private chapel at Spetchley was maintained at his own expense for the Catholics of the neighbourhood, and he was often seen praying quietly there. When all had retired to rest, Robert Berkeley would steal alone to the little chapel and offer his last thoughts to God.

" Because his life was filled with prayer, he was a man of the deepest humility, of the greatest resignation, and of the sweetest affability."[1]

Lady Catharine Berkeley was the second daughter of the third Earl of Kenmare. She was born in the reign of George IV and served her Church and country for ninety-five years under five sovereigns—George IV, Victoria, Edward VII, George V and Edward VIII. The best of these years she gave to the bringing up of a family of twelve children, six sons and six daughters, all of whom have testified by their good lives to the excellent training under their mother's influence.

Lady Catharine's early childhood was spent in her beautiful home at Killarney among the lakes and the lovely surrounding scenery. The year of her birth saw the passing of the Act of Catholic Emancipation, which greatly ameliorated the lot of Catholics and allowed them to build public churches, but when in London Lord and Lady Kenmare and their children frequented the Bavarian Embassy chapel in Warwick Street. On weekdays they heard Mass in the mews attached to the Jesuit house in York Place, which had been transformed into a chapel, and was the forerunner of Farm Street church. Lady Catharine used to describe a Midnight Mass at which the *Adeste* was sung by an old lady, Lady Nugent, who accompanied herself on a harmonium in the sacristy.

In 1851 Lady Catharine was married in Chelsea Old Chapel by Cardinal Wiseman to Mr. Robert Berkeley of Spetchley Park, this

[1] From the sermon preached at his funeral, Spetchley Park, September 13th, 1897.

being the first marriage performed by a Cardinal in England since the Reformation. The early days of their married life were spent at Overbury Court and there Cardinal Wiseman came as their guest to open the Benedictine Church of St. Gregory at Cheltenham.

In Lady Catharine's *Memoirs* we read :

" Robert escorted the Cardinal to Cheltenham in an open carriage with four horses, postilions and outriders, and we all followed in open carriages. People were a little doubtful of the reception the Cardinal would get, as feeling had run high and the windows of the church had been smashed. Precautions were taken, but all went off very well, and he was greeted most cordially."

His brilliant intellect and charm of character had won their way to men's hearts and had disarmed the animosity with which his advent in England had been viewed.

We read again, on the occasion of this memorable visit :

" Running down to Mass at Kemerton on one of the mornings of the Cardinal's visit, I met him in what was then called the Filbert Walk, returning from saying his Mass in the little church. I thought to myself that never again would a Cardinal be met in that way on that spot." (It was to the little Kemerton Church that the baby Agnes was taken to be baptized in 1861.) " Thursday, May 28th, was my birthday, and the Cardinal came down to breakfast with a charming sonnet he had composed for me, and which he presented with a bouquet of flowers. I have treasured the sonnet all my life."

The Berkeleys were much attached to Overbury Court and its beautiful grounds, but when in 1864 the rightful owners desired to take up their residence there the ever-increasing family of Berkeleys was obliged to move, first to Wolverton and then to Wootton Hall, Warwickshire. Finally, on the death of the old Mr. Berkeley, the family took up their residence at Spetchley Park in 1874; the little Agnes was then twelve years old.

" Here," we are told,[1] " in Spetchley, as in other places, Lady Catharine was always ready in her kindly charity to come to the help of those in need, but above all she was devoted to her holy religion. Born of good Catholic parents, she kept her Faith as the greatest treasure God had given her. In the early days of her life this was a matter of considerable difficulty, very different from what it is to-day. At that time, the Catholic religion in England was suspected, despised, and even hated.

[1] Quoted from the sermon at her funeral, Spetchley Park, August 28th, 1924

" Lady Catharine did what she could to spread the knowledge of the truth, and assisted converts and poor Missions which were struggling against enormous difficulties and opposition, and she had the great joy of seeing all the members of her family grow up believing and practising that Faith which she had taught them as little children. Surely such a long and consistent life of fidelity to God and His holy religion must have had a great share in bringing about that great Catholic revival which took place during her lifetime. In her youth, Catholics were scarcely known in England, Wales and Scotland, and churches were few and far between.

" To-day the Catholic population exceeds two millions, and there is hardly a town of any importance which does not possess a Catholic church to bear witness to the ancient Faith of our fathers. This change has taken place, not only through the influence of Milner, Wiseman, Newman, Faber, Manning and the Vaughans, but surely also to the holy, unobtrusive and consistent life-work of women like Lady Catharine Berkeley.

" She was in the best sense of the words, *Grande Dame*, with all the dignity and graciousness which those words imply. She belonged to the nobility, but retained the simplicity of the ' Faith of a Breton Peasant'. Yet Our Lord tells us that riches and high station are obstacles to faith and virtue, only to be surmounted by His help. ' With God all things are possible.' In the simplicity of her faith, Lady Catharine continued through the ninety-five years of her life the prayers and pious practices she had learned at her mother's knee.

" In England we owe a deep debt of gratitude to the old Catholic families for their heroic defence of their religion through three centuries of fines, imprisonment, torture, death and galling persecution. With Catholic Emancipation came, in many cases, a decline in fervour, as had been in the early days of Christianity. Once it was the joy of a noble Catholic family to give a child to God; not so now when worldliness has crept in. Lady Catharine was true to the old type, and it was her great consolation in her declining years to have given from her children a priest and a Sister of Charity to do God's work. She taught her children, as she herself had been taught, to turn first and foremost to God.

" Her simple faith, her zeal for God's honour and the spread of His Kingdom, and her devotion to God's greatest gift to us— the Blessed Eucharist—these were the distinguishing characteristics throughout Lady Catharine's long life. Her fourth son, Oswald, became Dom Oswald Berkeley, O.S.B., and led a life of heroic work and devotion in the Mission of Whitehaven, where he is still loved and remembered. It was his mother's great consolation in her last years to think that her priest son would be at her side when God's call came. Alas, this great sacrifice was asked of her; Dom Oswald died in April 1924, just four months before his saintly mother.

" She had, however, the great joy and consolation in 1923, the year before her death, of seeing again the other child whom she had given to God, the Sister of Charity. Sister Berkeley was called to England to represent the Holy Childhood of China at a big Missionary Exhibition in Birmingham, and she was sent to visit her aged mother. They spent many hours together and there was a family gathering before her return to China.

" The following year death claimed four members of the family, among them the saintly mother of ninety-five years. On the morning before her death, she heard Mass and received the Viaticum. This noble Catholic lady had the privilege in her last years of having in her home a chapel in which the Blessed Sacrament was reserved. The last words she said were those repeated after the priest, ' Blessed be Jesus in the most Holy Sacrament of the Altar.' She then literally fell asleep, yielding up her soul to God without a struggle."

The little baby born on June 1st, 1861, was, as we have already said, carried to Kemerton Church to be baptized and named " Agnes Mary Philomena ". Her godparents were the Countess of Denbigh (née Mary Berkeley, her father's sister) and Mr. John Herbert of Llanarth. She was named after her aunt, Agnes Berkeley, who had been a professed nun in Mother Margaret O'Hallahan's Dominican Community at Stone. Known as Sister Mary Philomena, she had entered in 1853, and two years afterwards was made Novice Mistress, in which office she remained until her death in 1860. She was one of Mother Margaret's most valued subjects, and she spoke of her death as an incomparable loss to the Community. She wrote: " We may truly call her a Saint. I never saw anything like her, and out of Heaven I don't suppose I ever shall."

The little Agnes spent only three years at Overbury Court. In her mother's *Memoirs* we read: " Agnes, aged three years, fell off a little bridge into the stream which passes through the Eystons' grounds next door to Overbury, but she was pulled out and was none the worse."

In later years Overbury Court was again to let and the Dowager Duchess of Norfolk thought of taking it for her orphaned grandchildren, the Hopes. But it was represented to her as being a very dangerous place for children—two lakes, so much water! The Duchess considered for a moment and then said, " Well, the Berkeleys lived there a good many years and there were twelve little Berkeleys and I never heard that one of them was drowned! "

In their next house, Wolverton, Lady Catharine complained that " there was no elbow room ", the rooms were so small, and her great consolation was her pony carriage with a pair of spirited ponies, in which she drove herself and the children about the country, even following the hunt. The Berkeleys were always great hunters and Spetchley Park was often the " Meet of the Hounds ". In 1869 they moved to Wootton Hall, which they liked very much, for it had a big lake and beautiful grounds. The family was now complete, the last member, Wolstan, being born in 1870, and that same year the eldest daughter, Augusta, was presented at Queen Victoria's Drawing-room.

Lady Catharine, in her *Memoirs*, gives a very interesting account of a royal visit to Killarney in 1861. The Prince Consort's birthday occurred during this visit, and, according to their custom on that day, he and the Queen sat side by side at dinner. It was his last birthday, for he died the following December. The Queen so enjoyed the beauties of the scenery and the lakes at Killarney that for almost the only time in her life she was unpunctual for her engagements, and remained an hour longer on the water than had been arranged.

Agnes was a very strong, active and healthy child and seems to have had only one illness, a light attack of scarlet fever when she was ten. She never went to school, though her two elder sisters received part of their education at the Dominican Convent, Stone; the second sister, Minnie, made her First Communion at the Assumption Convent, Kensington, and Maud also went to school for a time. Later, they were all educated at home under a very capable French governess.

In a picture of her old home, Sister Berkeley once pointed out three windows in the front of the house on the first floor: " That was our schoolroom," she said, " next to my mother's room." She added, with a twinkle in her eye, " I used to think I would rather like to go to school, just to have the fun of running away! "

At schoolroom tea their French governess always read aloud to them in French, and Sister Berkeley remembered, when she was about seven, the reading of the French Annals of the Propagation of the Faith, and the account of the Mongolian lama who made a pagan pilgrimage in China on his knees. He afterwards became a Catholic and a priest; Sister Berkeley met this converted lama in the Kiangsi in her first year in China.

She made her First Communion on her birthday, Whit Sunday, June 1st, when she was twelve. She spoke of kneeling between her mother and her father in their own chapel, but she said no more. She was one who kept her secrets for God alone.

The Berkeleys led a quiet and very simple family life, though full of fun and enjoyment of country activities in the beautiful park at Spetchley, whither they had moved in 1874, and the lovely Severn country around, riding, fishing and boating on their own big lakes, which, when frozen, were generously thrown open to the public for skating.

Picnics, too, were numerous. Sister Berkeley said, " We always went for a picnic on my birthday; we were a very homely family, not visiting much. In my young days, families kept much to themselves, not all this running about and visiting, even with children, as in these modern days." In her old age, her brother Hubert recalled to her the family joke of the " poy " for the picnic. When an impromptu one had been arranged suddenly, their old cook was heard to lament, " Ah, now, if ye had only 'a' told me before, I would 'a' made ye a poy [pie]! "

There was daily Mass, said by their own chaplain in the Spetchley chapel, and rosary and prayers at night for the family and servants. There was no lack of boys to serve on the altar, for from five years of age the six brothers were in the sanctuary. Another touching Catholic custom in that family was that every night after dinner the father and mother visited the children in bed, the mother spraying each one with holy water and saying, " Give your last thoughts to God, my children, and your first thoughts in the morning." Sister Berkeley said, " We were sometimes very naughty and used to duck under the bedclothes because my mother gave us such a drenching with holy water! "

A Chusan Sister says, " I have in my possession a little picture which Maud Berkeley sent me some years ago. It is a small print of the Child Jesus, mounted on a card and surrounded with an illuminated design in gold and colours, evidently done by a child's hand. On the back of the picture is written in a child's handwriting, ' To darling Papa on his birthday with love from Agnes '." She was then ten.

That picture did good work sixty-eight years later. During the years of war and the Japanese occupation of Chusan, the Sisters withdrew their children from the little sanatorium, " Lorette ", which they had on the mountain outside the North Gate, because the going and coming were often difficult and disagreeable when passing the Japanese sentries. Hearing a rumour that Lorette was to be occupied, everything was hastily packed up and brought into the city house by the canal; the children were evacuated and gardeners and women left to guard the house and land. The little birthday picture of the Child Jesus was placed in a frame inside one of the windows that He might take charge. He did so, for no Japanese or Chinese guerrilla soldiers took possession of this house.

.   .   .   .

The year 1877 saw a very joyful event in the Berkeley family—the double wedding of the two elder sisters, Augusta and Minnie, in the chapel at Spetchley. Augusta was married to Viscount Campden and Minnie to Mr. Fitzherbert Brockholes of Claughton Hall. Alas, eighteen months later the family was plunged in great grief, for Augusta, the eldest, who had always been idolized by her parents and younger brothers and sisters, died shortly after the birth of her first child. Her husband was inconsolable, for in those short months of married life the young Viscountess had made herself much loved in her new family and by those living on her husband's estates. Sister Berkeley once said, " My eldest sister was a wonderful person, loved by all; she always did everything with a smile and she went to God with a smile." The little motherless baby grew up as Lady Agnes Noel; she was the godchild of Agnes Berkeley, the future Sister of Charity.

Many celebrated visitors were often guests at Spetchley, among them Archbishop Ullathorne, a great family friend. Sister Berkeley remembered the fascinating tales he told them of his early life in Australia, but the Berkeley children often had hard work to hide their smiles at the many " aitches " dropped and the broad Yorkshire accent of the good Archbishop.

The laws of the Church were kept strictly in that family. Sister Berkeley related: " On fast days there were no dispensations for a hundred and one reasons as nowadays. My father and mother fasted, my elder brothers and sisters fasted, Catholic visitors fasted; no one thought of not doing so. Collation (the light eight-ounce meal allowed on fast days) was governed by our old butler. My brothers and sisters used to say to him: ' Well, now, do you think I have had eight ounces ? ' and he would reply,

' No, I think you can have a little more.' Presently he would say,
' Well, now, I think that is eight ounces; you had better stop '."

Archbishop Ullathorne was very anxious to get this promising
subject in the old Catholic family for the Community he had
founded, the Dominicans at Stone, under Mother Margaret
O'Hallahan, where her aunt had been a nun. He arranged with
her mother, when Agnes was nineteen, that she should visit Stone
and stay for a while in the convent, but this had no effect in
changing her vocation. On his next visit to Spetchley, the Archbishop called the young girl and said to her, " Well, so you have
quite made up your mind to be a Sister of Charity ? ' " Yes,
my Lord ", she replied. " I have quite made up my mind to
be a Sister of Charity."

During her last year at home her parents took her for a most
delightful tour of France and Italy, including a visit to Rome,
where she knelt at the feet of His Holiness Leo XIII and received
his blessing on her vocation, together with a relic of the True
Cross, which she wore to the end of her long life.

On May 9th, 1882, three weeks before her twenty-first birthday,
Agnes Berkeley left her beautiful home for ever and went to the
house of the Sisters of Charity at Bullingham, Hereford, for
postulation, the three months' probation required of aspirants
before entering the seminary or novitiate.

Among the books found after Sister Berkeley's death was a
plainly bound Latin Missal, on the fly-leaf of which is written:

<blockquote>
Spetchley Park, May 9th, 1882
Agnes Berkeley from her affectionate sisters
Maud, Constance and Etheldreda.
" Leave all and find all."
</blockquote>

Also a small, plainly bound New Testament in which is written:

<blockquote>
Spetchley Park, May 9th, 1882
Agnes Berkeley from her affectionate Mother
M. Catharine Berkeley.
</blockquote>

The date on which she left home was May 9th, the same as that
of the double wedding five years before.

Throughout her long community life Sister Berkeley spoke
rarely of home and personal affairs. We find written in her
spiritual notes: " Never think or speak of myself, my family or
my private concerns unless necessarily to Superiors and before

ROBERT BERKELEY

LADY CATHARINE BERKELEY
AGED 93 YEARS

SPETCHLEY PARK, WORCESTER

THE BERKELEY FAMILY, 1867

The last two members had not yet arrived; Agnes, aged six, is seated at the extreme left. " I came," she said, " at the top of the second half-dozen."

Our Lord." But in her last years of life, as is often the case in old age, childhood's memories seemed to revive and were gathered by one who lived with her.

Her mother's privately printed *Memoirs* gave many details of the old Catholic family life, and a favourite cousin, Lady Winefride Elwes, has given her memories of one to whom she was warmly attached, and whose missionary life she followed closely with deep interest and generous help.

Some later notes have been given by a religious of the Sacred Heart, whose family was a near neighbour of the Berkeleys, living on the other side of Bredon Hill. She wrote:

" My earliest memory is of going with my sister, when we were quite young, to strew flowers in the Corpus Christi processions at Spetchley. I remember the whole-hearted devotion with which everyone worked ; the whole household had only one thought, that of the Procession. Afterwards Sister Berkeley's elder sisters showed us a picture of their young ' Nun sister'. I remember the love and reverence with which they spoke of her, and there was no repining in their gift. They were proud to have her on the Chinese Missions. I asked what a nun was, and from that moment I date my own vocation.

" The old-world atmosphere and deep Catholicity of the Spetchley Park home always struck me; it reminded one of penal times in the steadfastness of its inhabitants. A great friend of ours, Lady Agnes Noel, was daughter to the eldest of the Berkeley girls, and through her we learned more about the loved ' Chinese Nun'.

" The inspiration of that Catholic home has remained with me ever since, and in that impression was the ever-present memory of the Missionary. That is very long ago but I owe it much."

It was this Catholic home of strong faith and piety which produced the Sister of Charity who did great things for God in the pagan land of China.

C

II

THE SISTERS OF CHARITY OF ST. VINCENT DE PAUL

WHEN Archbishop Ullathorne gave Agnes Berkeley his blessing on her vocation, he did not add, as some bishops and priests do when their spiritual children announce to them their desire to serve God as a Sister of Charity, " God help you, my child ".

It is supposed to be a very hard life physically, with little time or encouragement for the development of the interior, spiritual life of the soul. A French Sister, over forty years a Missionary in China, relates that when she told a priest, a family friend, of her desire to follow this vocation, he said sadly, " *N'y allez pas, mon enfant, là-bas; ce n'est que bras et jambes !* " The true life and spirit of the Sisters of Charity are little understood in the world. What does St. Vincent, the Holy Founder, say of it ?

> " The life of a Sister of Charity is a hidden and laborious one, a life led in company with Jesus, Mary and Joseph in the Holy House of Nazareth, one of daily toil, consecrated to the Divine Master by prayer and union of hearts. To be a Sister of Charity is to be a daughter of God, for God and all that belongs to Him is charity, so to be in charity is to be in God and God in you.
>
> " Your life," he tells the Sisters, " is a very trying one; flesh and blood have no part in it, and if you do not gather strength from prayer, it will be very difficult, nay, impossible, for you to persevere. Do you think that Martyrs went through greater suffering than a Sister of Charity who acquits herself perfectly of her obligations ? "

Fr. Joseph Leonard writes in his translation, *St. Vincent de Paul and Mental Prayer*:[1]

> " One of the best-known names of modern Catholic saints is that of St. Vincent de Paul. It is, at least, doubtful if the real man is as well understood. The serious student of the history of social reform is acquainted with the manifold activities of this seventeenth-century French priest. . . . Men and women inspired by his example

[1] Burns & Oates, pp. 1, 14.

and teaching have for the last three hundred years devoted their lives to carrying out the schemes he devised for the relief and succour of the poor and suffering, and at the present day one of the spiritual families he established (the best known of his foundations, the Sisters of Charity) counts more than 40,000 members scattered over the entire world. . . .

" The idea of a body of women, wearing the ordinary costume of the period, moving freely through country lanes and streets of cities, not to speak of appearing on battlefields, yet bound by the vows of religion, was an idea utterly foreign, and perhaps even repugnant to the ordinary Catholic man or woman of his time. The sight is so common nowadays that one is apt to lose sight of its daring originality, and to forget what qualities of tact, persuasive power, sagacity and vision were needed to carry out such a project.

" The seventeenth-century layman and ecclesiastic firmly believed that the proper, and, indeed, the only suitable place for a woman who had taken religious vows was within the walls of a monastery, and yet St. Vincent succeeded in his attempt at bringing women outside convent walls and in opening up new fields to their devotion and self-sacrifice in the care of Christ's suffering members—the poor and afflicted."

In the same work there is a letter of the Very Reverend Francis Verdier, Superior-General of the Priests of the Congregation of the Mission and the Sisters of Charity, written to Fr. Coste, C.M., in April 1923, from which we quote:

" The external works of this great Saint [St. Vincent de Paul] are known and admired. . . . But the interior life such as he conceived, preached and practised it, has hitherto remained almost entirely unknown. Vincent de Paul is known as a Saint, and it is freely granted that he is a great Saint. But had he a spiritual doctrine, a doctrine of holiness ? And if so, where is it to be found ? What are its characteristics ? . . .

" The two spiritual families who are the heirs of his spirit of charity, and carry on his fruitful and manifold activities, may be seen at work. But have these two families, priests and sisters, an intense, interior life, capable of satisfying souls enamoured of devotion and self-oblation, of a devotion that is concealed, which perhaps may be the best, of a hidden self-oblation tending towards perfection ?

" Are they enamoured of virtue, of a generous virtue directing all the soul's energies and activities towards God, enamoured of sacrifice, of a daily, total and irrevocable sacrifice, of a two-fold love of God and souls, or better, of a great unique love embracing both God and souls ? Are they enamoured of a life of union with God, of consecration to Jesus Christ—in a word, of perfection ? . . . If St. Vincent's spirit is understood, the real spring of his marvellous activity will be revealed and we shall learn from him that an active and laborious life is conditioned precisely by the intensity of its interior life."

On November 29th, 1633, a widowed lady living in a retired quarter of Paris received into her house four young peasant girls, whom she intended to train in caring for the poor of Paris under the guidance of the Ladies of Charity. As the little group knelt that night to pray, they had no thought of the mighty work they were quite unconsciously inaugurating, for this was the beginning of the Community of the Sisters of Charity, which is now spread in almost every part of the world where the Gospel has been preached and which numbers to-day over 45,000 members.

The Ladies of Charity was an association formed by St. Vincent de Paul of charitable women of the peasant or middle class, who cheerfully assisted their poorer neighbours in times of sickness. When the ladies of Paris heard what was being done in the provinces, they wished to do likewise, but in spite of their generosity and goodwill difficulties arose. They were often not able or permitted by their husbands to go and give personal service to the poor and suffering.

St. Vincent de Paul and St. Louise de Marillac, the noble French widow, known also as Mademoiselle le Gras, gathered together a few pious peasant girls to be trained to help the Ladies of Charity to visit the poor and distribute their bounties. Amongst them was Marguerite Naseau, who had taught herself to read while minding her flocks, and who afterwards had gone from village to village teaching little girls and doing all the good in her power to her neighbour, living herself in such extreme poverty as to find herself frequently without food. She also collected alms to defray the expenses of poor students who desired to become priests.

Marguerite Naseau was the first Sister of Charity, and it is said of her that everyone loved her, for everything about her was lovable. She died very young, a martyr of charity, having taken a poor plague-stricken woman into her own little room and laid her on her own bed; then having caught the disease she cheerfully made the sacrifice of her life.

This little beginning developed and increased, and the humility of their origin is as dear to the Sisters of Charity as the seal of God on their Institute. St. Vincent often said to the first Sisters,

" God alone has formed your company, for I never thought of it, neither did Mlle le Gras. God alone thought of it for you." Mme Goussault, the first Superior of the Ladies of Charity in Paris, who was always a warm and constant friend of the Sisters, said to St. Vincent, the day before her death, " All night I have seen the Sisters of Charity before the throne of God. Oh, how greatly they will be multiplied in numbers. What good they will do and what happiness will be theirs! God showed me great things with regard to them."

The first work of the Sisters trained by Louise de Marillac was that of visiting the sick poor in their own homes, and this has always remained one of the most important, but others have been added. The care of the foundling children was so dear to St. Vincent that he used to say that if there were angels among the Sisters they should be chosen for this work. The education of the poor became one of the Sisters' duties, and to this was soon added the care of the sick poor in hospitals.

St. Vincent also sent his daughters into loathsome dungeons to care for the poor convicts, and later to nurse the wounded soldiers on the battlefield. From that day to the present time, the Sisters have followed armies of many different nationalities; during the two Great Wars, 1914-18 and 1939-45, thousands of Sisters of Charity nursed the wounded in hospitals and ambulances and even on the field of battle. Last, but not least, the Sisters do not hesitate to leave home and country to go to the uttermost parts of the earth, to China, to Persia, to Poland, among the lepers of Madagascar, and to the great lands of the Western seas. The device emblazoned on their coat of arms is:

" The Charity of Jesus Christ urgeth us."

The spirit of the Sisters of Charity is founded on the three virtues, humility, simplicity and charity. Charity is the guiding spirit of their works—charity, that love of God and man which presupposes forgetfulness of self, personal abnegation and consequently humility and simplicity, with the sole desire of pleasing God, by doing good to their neighbour. Hence the depth of their spiritual life, which alone is capable of sustaining their tireless and disinterested zeal for the relief of every kind of distress, and which demands a perfection at least equal to that of the cloister. Hence the considerable share allotted in their existence to the

building up and perfecting of their spiritual life—Morning and
Evening Meditation, Daily Mass and Communion, the particular
and general Examens, Spiritual Reading and so forth. In a word,
their aim is to unite the duties of a contemplative with the toil
of an active life.

The works of charity of the Sisters are merely the outward sign
of their spirit, the translation of that ardent love of the God of
all charity. St. Vincent tells the Sisters that " they will be in the
world but not of the world, they will be seen practising all the
virtues of religious without bearing the title, in the sight of God
and for His Love, in a cloister made, not of stone, but of their
own free will, by obedience ".

The portion of the Sisters of Charity is to labour for the poor
in whatever manner these may need their help from infancy to
old age, at home and in foreign lands, instructing, nursing, visiting
—from innocent children to poor prisoners. The poor have always
a right to their love and service, and the Sisters speak of them as
their " Lords and Masters the Poor ". Fr. Bernard Vaughan said
that the Sisters of Charity are to the poor as an eye, a foot, a hand
and a heart—everything.

St. Vincent tells them in the first chapter of their Rules that
God instituted their Community " to honour the Charity of Jesus
Christ, the source and model of all charity ". They are to have
no cell, but a hired room; no cloister but the streets of a city, or
the wards of a hospital; no enclosure but obedience; the fear of
God is to be their grating and modesty their veil.

The " hired room " means that the Sister is not to look for a
fixed abode; wherever obedience places her, she must say, " Here
will I labour for God and the poor as long as it is His Will, but
I must be prepared to go elsewhere at any moment that He makes
known to me that it is His Will that I leave everything in obedience
to my Superiors." The noisy streets of the city, the slums and
crowded haunts of poverty and, alas, often of sin—these are the
Sister of Charity's cloister. Here is she to go up and down, seeking
to bring souls to God, and relief and consolation to those in
greatest need of both spiritual and temporal help. There is she
to find God, for, as St. Vincent said, " You go ten times a day to
miserable hovels but there ten times a day you find God."

Their enclosure is to be obedience. Souls consecrated to God
are bidden to go forth and mingle to some extent with the world,

not to shrink from entering the prisoners' cells or from approaching the wounded soldier on the battlefield or in the ambulance. The Sister is to go amongst Turks and heathen, and what is to be her safeguard ?—obedience, an enclosure she is never to leave and from which she can never be forced. " My children," said St. Vincent, " keep your Rules and they will keep you." The strong barrier placed between the Sister and the world is the " Fear of God " and she is ever to draw around her the protecting veil of " Modesty ".

Speaking on Detachment, the Saint says:

" To be a true Sister of Charity you must leave father and mother and everything of this world; you must, moreover, leave yourself, for if you give up everything else, but not yourself or your will, you have done nothing. You belong entirely to God; the soul that lives in charity lives in God and God in her. Your Community has been instituted to honour Our Lord Jesus Christ, the source and model of all charity, serving Him corporally and spiritually in the person of the poor. It is Jesus Christ you serve in the person of the poor convicts in their chains, as well as the little children; you go to miserable hovels but there you will find God, who receives as done to Himself all you do for the poor, and these poor will open the Gates of Heaven for you and intercede with God for you. How much you should love your vocation ! I know nothing greater in the Church of God. By it you devote your life to your neighbour for the love of God."

St. Vincent never wearied of assuring the Sisters that they were called to become souls of prayer, and that they could not persevere in their vocation without mental prayer; that prayer is the life of the soul, and that as a body without a soul becomes a corpse without life or movement, so a soul without prayer is without motion or activity in the service of God.

" Take, then," he tells them, " the resolution of making meditation every day. Let us never leave off praying; let us constantly raise our hearts and minds to God and keep ourselves in His presence, sending forth our sighs and aspirations to Him. If you knew the pleasure God takes in beholding a poor Sister of Charity who prays with childlike love and reverence, if you knew the treasures of grace He prepares for her, it would not be necessary for me to exhort you to pray. To be faithful to your duties you must lead an intense interior life."

From God alone comes the call to such a life and those who would learn whether God calls them to it should above all pray for grace and light. A candidate accepted passes three months of " postulation " in one of the Sisters' Houses, that she may see the life and works and that her own dispositions may be studied. She then enters the Novitiate or Seminary, as it is called, where for about twelve months she is trained in the interior life, dividing the time between instruction, study and manual work.

When she has received the habit and cornette which distinguish the children of St. Vincent, she begins the active life for the poor, but five years elapse from the time she enters the Seminary before she is allowed to take the simple Vows of Poverty, Chastity and Obedience, to which a fourth is added—" to serve the poor corporally and spiritually ". This fourth Vow is especially dear to the Sister of Charity as being her chosen lot bestowed on her by God. These Vows bind but for one year, not with the idea of making it possible for Sisters to leave their vocation—on the contrary, it was to strengthen them in it that St. Vincent gave them the joy of renewing their offering of themselves to the Divine Spouse every year on the Feast of the Annunciation, the happiest of days for a Sister of Charity. He also wished that the fear of being unworthy of renewing their Vows would make the Sisters strive with greater fervour and generosity to be faithful to their holy vocation.

The great devotion of the Sisters of Charity and a most marked characteristic among them is love for Mary Immaculate. From the beginning of the Community the following prayer was added to each decade of the Rosary, which is said to be the " Office " of a Sister:

> " Most Holy Virgin, I believe and confess thy Holy and Immaculate Conception, pure and without stain. O most chaste Virgin, through thy virginal purity, thy Immaculate Conception, thy glorious prerogative of Mother of God, obtain for me from thy Divine Son, humility, charity, great purity of heart, mind and body, holy perseverance in my dear vocation, the gift of prayer, a good life and a happy death."

It is remarkable that this prayer was in use in 1633, more than 200 years before the dogma of the Immaculate Conception was defined. Great though the devotion to Mary Immaculate has always been in the Community, it has certainly intensified since 1830, when Our Lady appeared to Sister Catherine Labouré, a Seminary Sister, in the chapel of the Mother House in Paris and commanded her to have a medal struck, which has since been known throughout the Catholic Church as the "Miraculous Medal", on which is inscribed the prayer, "O Mary, conceived without sin, pray for us who have recourse to thee."

Every Sister of Charity who is faithful to her vocation enjoys the hundredfold promised by Our Lord. Her life may be humble, laborious, hidden and unnoticed, but it is spent in union with Our Lord, imitating what Jesus Christ did on earth when He went about doing good. She can confidently hope that she will realize the promise of St. Vincent, which she has seen fulfilled in those of her companions who have gone before, namely that "those who have loved the poor will meet death without fear".

In a Sister's heart is kept ablaze the same fire of charity which consumed Sister André, who, on her death-bed, was asked by St. Vincent if there was anything in her past life which gave her fear. She replied: "No, Father, nothing at all, except perhaps that I have taken too much pleasure in serving the poor. When I used to pass through the villages going to attend the poor sick people, it seemed to me I did not walk; I thought I had wings and could fly, such joy I had in serving them."

An English secular priest, Fr. Holden, who had been educated at Douai with a view to working in the English Mission, in a letter to Louise de Marillac wrote: "Heavens, Mademoiselle, I wish your daughters realized the greatness of their vocation! If the world were capable of understanding it, you would not have room for all the princesses who would join their ranks."

. . . .

Three weeks after the new postulant, Agnes Berkeley, arrived at Bullingham, she celebrated her twenty-first birthday, June 1st, 1882. Forty years later an old Irish Sister who was present in the house at that time said: "On that day, the Berkeleys came from all the four quarters of the globe to visit her, and the house had a never-to-be-forgotten feast."

The postulant was brimming over with energy and ready for all kinds of work. We hear that she had sometimes to be sent for long country walks "to work off steam"! On one occasion, when she returned, the Sisters said to her, "How did you go over the stream, Miss Agnes? There is no bridge." She replied with a smile, "I took off my shoes and stockings and waded across." "Ah," said the Sisters delightedly, "we knew you'd get across that stream."

The first week in September she joined a party of other postu-
lants at the Central House, Mill Hill, and was sent to the Paris
Seminary, for the English Seminary was not yet opened. It was
curious that the Sister in charge of the party was Sister Ryan,
who was called to the China Mission. An account of her life and
work is found in *Tipperary's Gift to China*. When Sister Berkeley
arrived in Shanghai, in 1890, she was greeted by Sister Ryan.
" Do you remember me ? I took you to the Seminary."

In the big Paris Seminary, among over 300 young Sisters of
different nationalities, she found her cousin, Sister Feilding, who
had preceded her by a few months. Having a very good knowledge of French, they found little difficulty in adapting themselves
to their new life, and drank in and appreciated the beautiful
instructions of Sister Verot, the First Directress. They were both
generous souls. In Sister Feilding's Life[1] we read that she said
it would give better example, besides being a little mortification,
for them not to be too much together even in their free time.
She also said, when there were distasteful things to support, " We
have had so much of the good things of this world; surely now
we can do a little bit of penance." Lord Denbigh, Sister Feilding's
father, brought his friend, Don Bosco, to see them in the Seminary,
and they received the blessing of this great Saint.

In Sister Berkeley's spiritual notes of her Preparatory Retreat
we read:

" Try always to keep myself in the presence of God in a bright
happy manner, making little invocations as I walk about.
" Recollect myself on the way to the chapel; make an act of contrition on entering and remember I enter the presence of God.
" Always use a book at vocal prayer and follow all the words."
(This habit she continued to the end of her life, always having a
book before her during Community prayers.)
" Often make spiritual Communions; a Spiritual Communion
is to plunge myself into the grace of God like a bee into a flower."

During her first long Retreat:

" Go to humility by the road of great simplicity. Each morning
see what occasions to guard against pride and to practise humility.
" Do all your actions simply under the eye of God, looking neither
to the right nor to the left.
" Keep and treasure up your own and God's secrets.

---

[1] *Edith Feilding, Sister of Charity*, by Lady Cecil Kerr. Sands & Co.

" Say your Rosary with your Angel Guardian or some Saint to make up for your distractions. The Rosary is the chain that draws us to interior life; we study Our Lord's interior life and use the words spoken to Our Lady when she crushed the serpent's head, pride.

" For humiliations make an ejaculation and go simply on."

Perhaps a fit of home-sickness brought the following:

" Go bravely on, doing your best, keeping your superior will firm in your resolutions, though the inferior will flinches and fails. Throw yourself into Our Lord's arms, like a weak child into its mother's; trust entirely to Him and continue fearlessly afresh for He is with you."

The Seminary Directresses liked and understood this big, active English Sister. She was seldom sent to sit quietly sewing in the Seminary, but to tasks which sent her running to the top of the house or up to the roof. Sister Berkeley said that she was always received with great kindness by Sister Verot, the First Directress, who became her lifelong friend.

With her youthful, energetic *savoir-faire*, Sister Berkeley was ready for anything, but the first Saturday in the Paris Seminary, when the Sisters descended to the basement for the weekly cleaning and polishing of shoes, she confessed that she was utterly at a loss. " I had never seen it done," she said, " and I did not know how or where to begin." A kind French companion came to her help and initiated her into it, and one may be sure that very soon afterwards no shoes shone like those of Sister Berkeley. Forty years later, when she visited the Mother House in Paris, an elderly French Sister accosted her, smiling, " Do you remember me, Sister Berkeley? I was your *professeur de cirage* in the Seminary."

A new family grief came to her in the first months of her Seminary; her elder sister, Minnie, the second of the two brides of the double wedding, Mrs. Fitzherbert Brockholes, died unexpectedly. She was a very holy soul, a real Child of Mary, born on the Nativity of Our Lady and living a life of great piety. Sister Berkeley made no note of this sorrow; she surely took it to Our Lord's feet and sought consolation from His holy Mother in the chapel.

In September 1883 she made her Retreat of the *Prise d'Habit* (Clothing), and we see by her notes that she concentrated on the four points, Regularity and Obedience to Rule, Fidelity to Prayer, Charity, Purity of Intention, especially dwelling on the need of humble prayer and preparation of daily meditation.

" Remember you are now the *fiancée* of Jesus Christ. Keep for Him your body, your soul, and especially your heart with great care and vigilance.

" God alone! Seek nothing else, not even sensible consolations in prayer, for they are not God, but rather natural pleasures that He gives, because you are too weak to love Him alone and solitary on the Cross.

" The Charity He asks of you is a firm unflinching will to do His Will without consolations in spite of what it may cost nature.

" Trust in Him alone and if you fail, humble yourself, tell Him you can do nothing without Him, then start bravely afresh. Each fresh struggle brings its own reward.

" *Notre Très Honoré Père* [the Father General] told me to have great devotion to Our Lady, to behave always like a daughter to my Sister Servant,[1] and to be very prudent in my intercourse with externs, as otherwise St. Vincent *sera mécontent de vous et nous!* "

After the *Prise d'Habit* Sister Berkeley offered herself for the China Mission, but she was sent back to England and placed at Plymouth in charge of the Orphanage School.

---

[1] The Superiors of the houses of the Sisters of Charity are called the " Sister Servants," the name given to them by St. Vincent, based, as he said, on the words of Mary, " Behold the handmaid of the Lord."

III

PLYMOUTH

PLYMOUTH was a very poor House, founded by a French lady married in England, Mrs. Falcon. After her husband's death she became a Sister of Charity. There was a small orphanage and the usual works connected with the visiting and care of the poor in the parish. Sister Berkeley had the great privilege of having Sister Howard as her Sister Servant during the first two years, and we may surely believe that it was Sister Howard who instilled into her the great love and devotion for the work of the children which was so marked a feature of her own life.

In Sister Berkeley's spiritual notes of those early days, we read:

" In devoting yourself to the children, you devote yourself to Our Lord, so never tell them they give trouble or speak to them sharply.

" Be grave, quiet, firm and devoted to the children. Let each child know that she is loved, above all never let them make you lose your peace of mind. Do your best and leave the result to God; failure may be for your own spiritual advancement and therefore His Holy Will.

" Say an *Ave Maria* for the children every time you go to the chapel."

Sister Howard's advice: " Teach the children to have a great horror and dread of sin, not to go as near to it as possible, but to avoid all occasions—not to do things because others do them."

In Plymouth in those days life was hard on nature. Sister Howard in her early years was very austere and expected all to follow generously in the great road of mortification. The food was very different from that to which Sister Berkeley had been accustomed; her health failed and in those first years one heard of constant fainting fits. The older Sisters in the house sometimes good-humouredly teased her, saying, " How will you ever go to China if you are always fainting on the stairs ? "

It must be said that when Sister Howard became *Econome* and Seminary Directress at the Central House, Mill Hill, she changed her views very much and realized the necessity of plain but abundant good and nourishing food for the Sisters, so that they should not break down under the heavy works of their vocation.

Many years later in China when Sister Berkeley was once discussing the question of how to build up the health and strength of her Sisters, especially the young ones, a work to which she gave great thought and care, one of her companions asked what was the cause of the fainting in her early years. Sister Berkeley paused a minute, smiled, and then said rather apologetically, " Well, you know, it was the funny food! It took me some time to get accustomed to it."

She found the children very difficult to manage, and she once said in her old age, " The Plymouth children were terrible! " Possibly they were no worse than all institution children, poor little souls, the greater number of them orphans from very poor families with inherited bad instincts, hardened by having already had their share of suffering in the world. The very gentleness and loving care of the Sisters often seem to bring out their bad qualities; they respect and obey harder treatment. Sister Berkeley had had no experience of schools or children outside her own home and she had everything to learn; but she set to work courageously and with prayer and zeal succeeded remarkably well. Years later, old Plymouth children often wrote to her in China.

Sister Howard's brother, the Duke of Norfolk, often sent beautiful gifts for the children, and once he brought his yacht to Plymouth Sound and invited the Sisters to bring the children on board for the day. We read in a letter from Sister Howard to her mother: " The children wore your red dresses, white neckties and gloves, and looked very nice; they ran all over the yacht and the sailors helped them to climb the riggings. Sister Teresa [Berkeley] looked as if she would like to go up with them and Henry begged her to do so! " She certainly would have done in her worldly days.

Her intense love for her family, which was a very united one, seems to have given her anxiety in her early days as a Sister. We read in her notes:

" Do not let your love for your family take away a hair's breadth of your love for God.

" Every legitimate love that interferes a particle with Divine Love must be cut off.

" Let them seek you, not you them, and if you are forgotten, so much the better; do for them what is kind or necessary when it in no way interferes with duty or love of God, to give them pleasure, not seeking your satisfaction at all.

" Take pleasure in their company as God lets you have it, but never throw yourself into it heart and soul.

" Make little acts of love of God in your heart while they are with you."

She finished her first Retreat in England with, " I *MUST* be a Saint so I must begin at once. Above all, be very faithful to prayer."

We see her fighting against her quick temper and want of consideration for others, caused by too great eagerness to go ahead and follow and develop her own ideas. We read in her notes:

" To give up my own ideas directly my Superior has spoken and never discuss; obey promptly, cheerfully and simply.

" Yield if possible to the ideas of other Sisters; in obeying them you have the merit of humility and obedience.

" Be as tender to them as you are to yourself, and, above all, mind your own business. Why lose your peace of mind for that for which you will not have to answer ?

" Above all, be peaceful; otherwise it is a sure sign that there is more self than God in the matter; never hurry, for when you hurry you are only hurrying to do your own will. Remember Our Lord is never in noise and confusion; His Will is generally found in the Rules and the will of others, for then at least you are trampling on self.

" Always yield and agree if possible."

In her third year of vocation Sister Berkeley was named by the Paris Council for the China Mission, and she arrived at Mill Hill to prepare for the departure. The English Superiors regretted that she should have been called before she had made her Vows, and when the news was sent to her family her parents represented their desire that one so young should not be sent to such a far-off Mission before her Vows. The call was cancelled and Sister Berkeley went back to Plymouth, after having exacted a promise from her parents that they should make no further objection. She had to wait another five years for the second call.

In the meantime she worked at the spiritual foundation of her vocation and the development and strengthening of the interior life of prayer and virtue, without which, St. Vincent so often said, it would be impossible for a Sister to persevere in her vocation. She devoted herself also to the school and the children, raising the standard of their education, and sending her young under-mistresses to be trained. Her great aim was to give the children a happy life and she organized plays, picnics and excursions, also boating on a large stretch of water. One of her children in later life said, " We had the time of our lives with Sister Teresa [Berkeley]." We read in her notes:

" Try and be a mother to the children; be very patient and gentle with them; think before you speak and then never change. Show them that you love them and that their concerns interest you, but no familiarity on either side.

" Train up the children for God; formation to virtue comes before every lesson. Remember you will have to answer for their souls."

For her own interior life she writes :

" Silence and recollection are the only means of preserving and entertaining your Divine Spouse in your heart; dissipation and thinking of the past, two great enemies.

" You are specially the child of Divine Providence. As far as possible do your best in daily duties, then leave the result of every-thing and even your formation to virtue in God's Hands.

" God works wonders on nothingness."

In July 1887 Sister Berkeley had the privilege of going to the Mother House in Paris to make her Vow Retreat. She concen-trated on Mental Prayer, Preparation for Meditation, and Holy Communion, and writes:

" Have a firm determination to be all His Own and prove your love at every Communion by some real sacrifice. The more acts of virtue (faith, etc.) you make, the more grace you prepare yourself to receive. Never mind feelings, they are nothing."

She studied and prayed over the obligations of the Vows:

" Poverty: Keep only what is strictly necessary. Be very careful of clothes, mend or take out stains at once yourself; poor people have no servants. Always take the trouble to be poor, to use things and mend things in your work as long as possible.

" Chastity: Exteriorly, by the simple, dignified, but bright and joyous recollection of the Spouse of Christ, even in the midst of hard work, not expending yourself entirely exteriorly, but remem-bering who you are, Who is within you and for Whom you work. Give up all worldly, schoolboy, childish ways and expressions; they are unworthy of you. Chastity is preserved by prayer, humility and vigilance, by making Our Lord the centre of all your affections and all your thoughts. Prove your love for Him by mortifications;

AGNES BERKELEY—AGED 17 YEARS

SISTER BERKELEY, AGED 22 YEARS,
at her clothing

never do any single action for praise or notice; walk on human respect, seeking God alone; crush self in little daily actions, such as comfortable positions, senses, curiosity, humiliations, and try to do each action for God alone.

Obedience: Always ask permissions in particular. Try to obey the other Sisters' wishes when it does not entail harm to the children or breach of rule. Never discuss others' concerns, above all your Superior's decisions.

" Service of the Poor: Be grave, quiet, firm and devoted with the children; never speak when angry. Don't be so weak as to mind what they say or think; be independent of all opinion and work for God alone. Never give to yourself a minute of the time that belongs to the children. Do not pass your guards or work on to other shoulders, unless with permission. You are not worthy of your glorious vocation if you give up its duties so easily. Remember you will have to answer for the soul of each child who goes into the world unprepared and uncorrected of her faults; you are responsible for each grace or merit forfeited, or sin committed through your fault."

On her Vow Day, in Plymouth, September 8th, 1887, she wrote:

" See the Will of God in each circumstance and action of the day. Do each one to please Him alone; never be so weak as to mind what people think. Practise great purity of intention by Silence, exterior and interior, Regularity, Prayer and Mortification. Drive thoughts of self away with *Ecce Ancilla Domini.*"

Her thoughts were always turning to her future Foreign Mission and she was evidently reading and studying the Life of Blessed John Gabriel Perboyre,[1] for she wrote in 1889:

" How beautiful is the Cross planted in the midst of a heathen land and watered with the blood of the Apostles of Christ (Blessed Perboyre).

" The cause of God articulates itself as before in minute observance, so now, so under conditions of colossal warfare, but the battle has already been won and the altered circumstances are not required to make the Saint, but only to proclaim him. ' I have lost the race I never ran', is the cry of the despiser of little things, whereas the Saint has many times over won his martyr's crown in the hour of peace (Blessed Perboyre).

" Blessed Perboyre spoke often of God, rarely of others, and then always to their advantage, never of himself."

She resolved to persevere in cheerfulness as it is the true way

[1] Blessed John Gabriel Perboyre, C.M., was martyred at Ou-tchang-fou, in Honan Province, China, 1840.

D

to advance in every virtue and she reminded herself of Sister Verot's words, " Work out your salvation with joyousness of spirit, for God loves the cheerful giver." Again she urged herself to greater effort to obtain the true spirit of prayer and she wrote, " We cannot be true Sisters of Charity without being Sisters of prayer, for prayer keeps alight the furnace of charity."

Again we read on the Vows:

" Poverty: Be large-minded and generous towards companions and the children, tight-fisted towards self, withholding even allowable comforts in a spirit of poverty and to please Our Lord.

" Chastity: The simple dignity of a Spouse of Christ, avoiding childish, masculine ways, strict mortification of senses to bring them subject to God's Will alone. Remember that every movement of mind or body belongs to God; a chaste soul only lends herself to creatures as charity or the works demand, she gives herself up entirely to God alone, and His Love brings her continually back to Him in the interior retreat of her soul. Castles in the air and thoughts of the past increase self-esteem and human respect and are great obstacles to interior life.

" Obedience: Ask permission in detail so as not to run the risk of breaking your Vow.

" Service of the Poor: Learn from the Sacred Heart His tender charity, devotion and compassion for souls; every moment of time is vowed to them; never retake what is given. Let each child know that your aim is to make her as strong and virtuous as possible. Always pray before dealing with the children; one requires to lay in a good stock of virtue during morning prayer to pass the day well with them. Bring up your children to be pure, pious, obedient and charitable.

" Treat your Sisters with a bright and gentle charity, ever remembering the dignity of a Spouse of Christ. Never fear a snub, accept it joyfully and send it heavenwards as a jewel.

" Sister Howard told me to aim at obtaining humility by mortification of the eyes (reading), mortification of the imagination, exterior self-restraint (still too much *la tête en l'air*), and that my unrestrained reading had caused me to forfeit many graces."

We read in Sister Howard's Life that she said of herself that if she had stayed in the world she might have lost her soul through her love of novel reading. One remembers that St. Teresa said that her passion for light reading kept her for many years from close union with God.

. . . .

In August 1890 Sister Berkeley went to Mill Hill for her

annual Retreat, and found there in the infirmary Sister Edith
Noel, her sister Augusta's sister-in-law. After many years of
devoted service of the poor, Sister Noel's health had broken down
and she was dying of consumption. Sister Berkeley visited her
several times; she knew that Sister Noel was praying to Our Lady
to take her to Heaven on August 15th, the beautiful Feast of the
Assumption. On the last morning, when she went to say good-
bye before returning to Plymouth, she asked her, " When you
get to Heaven, will you do something for me ? Ask that I may be
sent to China, and quickly." " I will surely do so," replied
Sister Noel, and the two said their last good-bye on this earth.

Sister Noel died on the Assumption, and two days later the
funeral procession went down the hill to the little graveyard in
the fields at Mill Hill. When the coffin was being lowered into
the newly made grave, a telegram was handed to the Superiors.
It was a call from Paris for Sister Berkeley to go to China and to
come without delay. Sister Howard said, " I wonder, did she
ask Sister Noel to do that for her ? " The next day Sister Berkeley
arrived and Sister Howard greeted her with, " What did you ask
Sister Noel to do for you ? " " To send me to China, and quickly,"
was the prompt reply. " Well, here is the answer," said Sister
Howard, handing her the telegram.

Sister Berkeley left the next day for Paris. The call was urgent,
for the party for China was leaving in a few days' time. There
was no chance to say good-bye to her family, but the day after
she left England a crowd of brothers and sisters followed her to
Paris, and invaded the parlour of the Mother House in the Rue
du Bac, much to the amusement of the French Sisters.

The departure was unexpectedly delayed so there were many
visits and shopping expeditions to supply the needs of the future
Mission. Among the gifts was a harmonium. Sister Berkeley
had a great taste for music and was accustomed to playing in their
family chapel, but when asked once why she never did so in
China, she replied, " Well, you know, there are always so many
others who do it better than I do."

On the evening of the departure, the brothers and sisters hid
behind a wall and listened to the farewell ceremony and singing
of the Missioners' hymn at the Mother House. Then they followed
the party to the station, bringing big baskets of fruit for the hot
night journey to Marseilles, also purchasing pillows, but at that

proceeding the Sister from the Mother House protested, " *Elles sont les Sœurs Missionaires*," she said, " *et les Sœurs Missionaires n'ont pas besoin d'oreillers !* " But Maud Berkeley had an answer as usual, " *Mais, ma Sœur, les Sœurs Missionaires ont aussi les têtes et elles ont besoin de dormir.*"[1] The Sister laughed and gave way.

Good Fr. Meugniot, C.M.,[2] who was in charge of the party, returning to China as Father Director of the Sisters of Charity in the China Province, was much interested in this big English family, was introduced to all, and invited them to come and visit their sister in China. Sister Berkeley's last words as the train steamed out of the station were, " God alone! that is it now, is it not ? "

One cannot help thinking of the father and mother, alone in the big home, praying in the chapel for the child they would probably never see again on this earth.

---

[1] " They are Missionary Sisters, and Missionary Sisters don't need pillows." " But, Sister, Missionary Sisters have also heads and they need to sleep."
[2] Father Meugniot, C.M., was the nephew of Saint Catherine Labouré.

IV

CHINA—FIRST MISSION

WHEN St. Vincent sent his daughters on Foreign Missions for the first time, he seems to have foreseen they would spread throughout the world. He told them of the vast fields of labour, not only " from the East to the West ", but from time to eternity, Divine Providence would one day open to them. He said that when the time came, he hoped there would be found in their midst those who would cross the seas and generously devote their lives to pagans. Perhaps, as they listened to the words of their holy Father, the Sisters wondered who would guide and guard them in those far-off lands. If so, the question was quickly answered, for Louise de Marillac, their holy Foundress, handed them a picture of Our Lady, who, she said, they were to look on as the " true and only Mother of their Company ".

It seemed right indeed that the first Community privileged to have " the streets of the city for cloister and the prisons and wards of hospitals for cells " should also have the honour of being the first to seek for souls in foreign lands. But though the Vincentian Fathers (Lazarists) went to China in the seventeenth century, the white cornette had not penetrated farther than Constantinople until two centuries after the death of St. Vincent. When the treaty after the Opium War had been signed and it was not too great a risk to go there, the Sisters of Charity trod the path along which so many devoted Nuns of various Orders have since followed.

It was at Macao that the first band[1] of Sisters of Charity arrived in 1848 and among them was Sister Gabriel, sister of Blessed John Gabriel Perboyre, C.M., who eight years before had suffered martyrdom at Ou-tchang-fou, Honan. The Sisters landed on June 21st, but after three years' work at Macao, hampered by endless trials and difficulties, they were transferred to Ningpo and given charge of the Holy Childhood Orphanage, hospital work

[1] Sr. Louise O'Sullivan and companions.

and the visiting of the poor. Their arrival at Ningpo was again on June 21st, the anniversary of the day on which they had landed in China, and on which, nineteen years later, in 1870, the Sisters of Tientsin suffered martyrdom, ten of them under frightful conditions. Among them was Sister Louise O'Sullivan, an Irish Sister,[1] who for many years had worked in China.

Since then it is remarkable to notice the number of new Missions whose opening has fallen on June 21st, by no human arrangement. The Sisters of the American Eastern Province arrived unexpectedly at Kanchow, Kiangsi, and opened St. Margaret's House, their new Mission, on June 21st, and many extraordinary events for the Sisters happen on this date. No wonder the feast of St. Aloysius, June 21st, is specially kept by them in China, and that they look on him as one who opened to them the door of that immense Empire.

.   .   .   .

On the long sea voyage Sister Berkeley prepared herself for her future Mission life, renewing the Retreat she had just made. In her notes, we read:

" God seems to demand the blood of martyrs as the price of Faith.

" God helps those who, for His sake, undertake great things, and He never fails those who put their trust in Him alone.

" I am much inclined to tepidity in my spiritual life, and if I do not tackle it at once by prayer and silence, I shall most likely have great temptations later on.

" In Plymouth I failed principally in prayer, rule, charity and order. Our Lord has brought me to China to become a Saint by the perfect and joyous accomplishment of His Will in the smallest things, especially with regard to rule and the saving of souls. Devote your life to souls on earth and those in purgatory.

" *Fiat Voluntas Tua* in suffering and in action. Try and obtain the great grace of martyrdom, that greatest proof of love you can either give or receive, by the perfect practice of Charity.

" What can you give Him more than your blood ? How can He love you more, after giving His Life with such terrible torments for you, than by giving you the wish to make Him as far as you can an equal return, helping you to accomplish it, and then rewarding you eternally for a little suffering ? "

On the sea, she writes:

" Fr. Meugniot told me to be faithful to prayer; to have great purity

[1] *Cf. Pioneer Sisters in China*, C.T.S. of Ireland.

of intention and never give way to discouragement; with regard to my Superior, to assist her as much as possible in the difficulties of her work; to be very careful about permissions; and always to put her first.

" With regard to my companions, to be an angel of peace and take all remarks in good part; to answer them joyously, but go my own way with great simplicity and charity.

" With regard to the doctor, to be cordial and on good terms with him, but not his slave; not to make myself necessary or familiar; to imitate the modest dignity of Our Lady, and have great, fearless simplicity in thought and word.

" For myself, to shake off depression and fly to the Holy Eucharist in all trouble; to work out my salvation in joyousness of spirit, simplicity of word by saying at once what I think; of thought, by avoiding *arrières pensées* and castle-building; of action, by fearlessly trying to do my duty, heedless of what others think or say.

" In my work, to learn from the Sacred Heart His tender, zealous, self-forgetful charity for the poor, His representatives, our Lords and Masters; never to retake one minute that is vowed entirely to them: always to pray before dealing with them, and never to show disgust or repugnance in word or action.

" Prayer: The success of mental prayer consists in the way I prepare overnight, and in keeping my thoughts fixed on the subject from the moment I rise. Make the acts with fervour; you will conquer at last. Make a resolution, choose an ejaculatory prayer, and have some thought to dwell on during the day. Say at night three Hail Marys to Our Lady of Perpetual Succour to beg the spirit of prayer and recollection during the next day.

" I must try to have a more delicate conscience and not such a *demi-volonté* for perfection. The principal reasons of my troubles in the past have been my want of condescension to the wishes and opinions of others, saying biting things. I will try and give in gaily to others in everything that is not breach of rule or cause of injury to the poor. Not for all the world would I pierce Our Lord's Heart, yet that is what every biting word said to a Sister does. Charity is the flame of the love of God. If you do not love your neighbour, you do not love God."

At Singapore, Sister Berkeley had the great pleasure of meeting her younger brother, Captain Hubert Berkeley, who was stationed in the Malay States. Kind Fr. Meugniot, with his usual large-mindedness, told the young soldier to take his sister where he liked for the day, so the two drove off gaily to visit his friends, many of whom were in convents and religious houses.

There are many extracts of Sister Berkeley's letters during her first twelve years in China collected by her cousin, Lady Winefride

Elwes, and published by the Boston office of the Propagation of the Faith. In one she describes the beauty of Singapore and the harbour of Hongkong:

> " The sight of the Highland Tartan made my heart bound, though it was not the ' Black Watch ' [her brother Mowbray's regiment]. . . . I was agreeably surprised with the Hongkong Holy Childhood children, from a few hours old to eighteen or twenty years old, so clean, bright and intelligent, It was too amusing to see the mites of six and eight flying about, doing their morning housework better and quicker than children many years older. Their embroidery and needlework are beautiful.
>
> " When eighteen years old, they place high pieces of wood under their heels and their feet are wrapped up tight, for without these precautions no husband would be forthcoming. The Missionaries send the gentleman to call; the affair is settled, and these marriages often turn out very well, the contrary is the exception. The difficulty is that the Chinese like their boys and often make presents of their girls, so there are not sufficient Christian men for the requirements of the maidens. This overcrowds the orphanages with big girls; a certain number get vocations and after a long trial turn out useful members of Communities."

On October 26th, 1890, came the long-desired end of the journey:

> " What we felt when at last we set foot on Chinese soil and for the first time knelt before Our Lord in our new home, it is easier to imagine than tell. God grant we may do all the work He has in store for us here and win many souls for Heaven."

All arrived safely, including the harmonium, which it seems gave much amusement—" *La Sœur anglaise, qui arrive avec son piano !* "

October 30th: " My destination is Kuikiang, Kiangsi Province. My business will be the hospital and dispensary, for the Chinese of course. It is three days' journey from here, and we go up the Yangtse Kiang in a steamer. It is the house which is the farthest in the interior in the southern division and the nearest to the site where Blessed Perboyre was martyred. I hope we shall make a pilgrimage there. We start to-morrow."

The next letter, dated November 15th, gives a pretty description of the three-days' journey up the broad Yangtse Kiang, " a river worthy of the name ":

" For many hours the banks could be seen only as a line on the horizon, the river being about ten miles broad. After a long stretch of country, which was as flat as a pancake, we came to lovely scenery, with mountains rising up one behind the other, villages nestling at their feet round picturesque pagodas, the river looking almost like a sea in the foreground, and the whole lit up morning and evening by such brilliant lights.

" Kuikiang was reached late on Monday night. The Sisters at the Hospital heard the steam whistle and came on board to welcome us. There are four Sisters here, three French ones and myself. It is for the Hospital that an English Sister is required, as the doctor, Dr. Underwood, is a Scotchman, and most of the Europeans on the Concession are English-speaking.

" Every morning for a couple of hours the dispensary is thronged with every species of human misery, which the doctor, a very kind and clever man, sees *gratis*. The most fearful legs and eyes are what principally appear. Really the unfortunate Chinese have marvellous powers of endurance, for they allow themselves to be cut, their eyes to be turned inside out with hardly a shudder. One man actually held the basin while the entire half of his lower jaw was being drawn or rather broken out.

" Operations take place nearly every day and are, as a rule, very successful. It is terrible to see the misery and suffering around, diseases brought on by their poor food and filth, and yet their souls are in a worse plight. Nearly all we receive are pagans. We have the consolation of baptizing those who are dying and also any very sick babies brought to the dispensary."

The next sentence alludes to one of the prevalent beliefs in pagan China, that Christians cut out the hearts and eyes of children and young people to use in charms and medicines:

" Others are beginning to realize that we do not cut out hearts and eyes, but not much can be done to their dull pagan minds during the short stay in the Hospital. It will require some generations of Catholicity to put religion into them. The hope of the Mission is in the children though they say the Hospitals do more towards killing prejudice.

" This Hospital has been established only about eight years. It was a missionary architect's first trial and unfortunately is built of wood, which lets in the heat in summer and every draught in winter. It is very picturesque with its verandahs, under which the Sisters sleep in summer, the heat is so great. At present it is just like May or June in England.

" We are just off to Benediction at the Parish Church which is at our gate, and oh, the singing! During the whole of Mass the uproar goes on. Everyone has his own key; he who squalls loudest, prays best, and some devout women keep up a high soprano through their nasal organ. The first Sunday I spent in one convulsion, this species of devotion was so unexpected. The Chinese sing all their prayers in this way, and they seem to be able to go on like wound-up machines.

" In the Hospital their meal time is rather like the feeding hour at the Zoo. Now I am up to them, so two faithful satellites barricade me in with chairs, the assault is then all in front and the poor creatures, their basins being filled, depart to their beds where they devour their food with the help of their two little sticks. Last year 23,000 people came to the Dispensary and 1,063 to the Hospital which has to have very elastic walls."

Sister Berkeley now received her name " Xavier " which she kept throughout her long Mission life. The study of Chinese, without which " nothing can be done for their unfortunate souls ", occupied Sister Xavier's every spare moment, and her " dear Chinese " were already very close to her heart.

" And oh, the state they are in, the poor creatures! Sister Superior is longing to have two suits for each patient (the Chinese in winter keep on their clothes in bed) so that on their arrival they should be washed (every rag taken off them and put away until their departure) and dressed in the hospital clothes. Every Chinaman has for winter a shirt, plain trousers and padded trousers over them, a padded long coat and a plain coat on top. They may not have a bowl of rice to eat, and often do not, but they will have padded clothes which, it is said, they put on at the first frost and do not take off until the next summer.

" Sister Superior was meaning to put off the luxury of cleanliness until she had the wherewithal, but I asked her to purchase the stuff and cotton padding and I would try to get the money. We are indulging in new padded counterpanes in which they roll themselves, and it would be a pity to let them get alive as they will by delay. It was suggested, as no other means seemed available, to give the patients clean garments under and over and leave their own padded ones between, but at such a sandwich I protested!

" In this hospital, the patients get rice and vegetables daily, meat four or five times a year and fish on Sundays. In most hospitals they get the two last-named luxuries frequently but here they cannot afford it; and yet strengthening food goes much further towards curing these half-starved creatures than medicines."

March 19th, 1891: " The Chinese are charitable to each other and give beggars food and clothing for fear of a curse, of which they are terrified. Begging is a regular trade; they have a kind of king to whom some shopkeepers pay as much as ten dollars a year to keep his subjects from their door. Next to nothing can be done for the souls of this poor class, except help them into Heaven on their death beds. Of course they would willingly become ' rice

Christians' any day. The country people are of quite a different stamp, and though not converted, carry into all parts of the country the knowledge that there is a God Who loves the poor and causes them to be cared for. If a missionary goes to their villages he is well received."

While the poor country people were carrying this message of love and charity to their distant homes the troubles of the summer of 1891 broke out, and Sister Xavier wrote many interesting letters. In June she wrote:

" Thank God, the city Sisters are all here. There may be burning, for the people are so excited, but we have three men-of-war in the river, a French, an American, and a German." Later: " Everything is quiet at Kuikiang now and there is better news from the interior, where the Mandarins are doing their best to prevent trouble, and punish. We see a good deal of them and they are very amusing. They are on the most friendly terms with the Sisters. They enter in an easy fashion, seize chairs, and over tea and biscuits discuss Orphanage news, the health and ages of the Sisters, etc. They are talking of building a small barracks near the Sisters' house, to afford permanent protection. Some more French sailors are being brought to us to be nursed; we have a large room for Europeans."

August 6th: " It is gratifying to see how anxious the authorities are to keep our heads on our shoulders, but since our Chinese friends have taken it into their heads to be so fond of burning places, one is slow to buy or make improvements. Anyhow, before they began, a nice little wash-house with bath places was finished, and good cement put down in the Hospital to keep off the damp. It is to be hoped that all will not come to an untimely end; we hardly expect it, for the Kuikiang people have no real dislike for the Sisters.

" There is some danger perhaps for the Sisters in the city, though the commander of the *Aspic* is mounting guard and would be over the walls at the first sign of trouble. He even has ladders ready. Here, there is no danger except from fire, and that is not likely; Chinese soldiers as well as Europeans guard the Concessions at night. Besides, could we be safer than in the arms of Providence ?

" Rocked in the arms of the ' cradle of the deep ' comes into our minds when we go to bed at night."

During her first summer Sister Xavier was attacked by a terrible Chinese fever which threatened her life—a temperature of 107 which no remedies or treatment could bring down until the English doctor ordered her to be put into a ' cold pack ' and that saved her, though she said, " It nearly killed me. I thought I should die of weakness." When the French Sisters asked the doctor what they should give her, he replied bluntly, " Tea and toast!'' so, Sister Xavier related with a laugh, '' I got tea and toast at all hours! ''

She was called to Shanghai and a letter from the Central House there, dated October 4th, 1891, says:

'' We are expecting to hear of further trouble in the interior as several hundred men from Honan, one of the worst Provinces in China, are said to have entered the Kiangsi, bent on mischief. Well, I shall see none of their doings as I am not returning to Kuikiang. Ningpo is my destination and Sister Visitatrix will take me there on Thursday. I am replacing an English Sister who died there last April, and who acted as interpreter. We hardly expected two English Sisters to be left long together, we are precious from our rarity out here.

'' Maison Jésu Enfant, Ningpo, will now be my address. It is the oldest Sisters' House in China. I believe they have been in possession over forty years and there is still among them one old Sister who was at the foundation. They have all the works there, dispensary, Hospital, Catechumenate, Orphanage, and they also visit the poor. It is only twelve hours' voyage from Shanghai, so if the war takes place the Sisters will have to abandon for a time other houses, but not Ningpo.''

At Ningpo, Sister Xavier found herself in a quieter district, the Province of Chekiang being more advanced in every way. Its inhabitants, after forty years' contact with the Sisters of Charity, treated them with respect, and allowed them in all safety to go about visiting the sick and baptizing dying babies. Many of Sister Xavier's letters are now written on board the native '' sampans '' (punts) as she does her visiting of the riverside villages.

All the Sisters in those days took their turn for this privileged work, the first given them by St. Vincent. Sister Xavier related that her good, kind Sister Servant, Sister Solomniac, always said with joy, '' Monday is my day '', and in spite of her many other duties she rarely missed setting off early Monday afternoon for several hours of visiting the sick poor in the city. She often came back, drenched with perspiration, thoroughly tired out, but her face beaming with joy over the contact with the poor and the harvest of Baptisms gained.

Sister Xavier wrote most of her letters while the sampan jerked and rolled the Sisters up the river to distant villages. We read:

'' This river-travelling reminds me of the picture of the Sisters of Charity and the babies by the water side. It is much the same in reality, though the babies are not actually exposed to die among the rushes; but they are often put outside the door to die, poor little things, as death brings bad luck into a house, and sometimes they are summarily put an end to.

" We have had a fair day, twenty-four Baptisms in about eight or ten little villages, dotted among the rice fields. We take women with us, go in different directions, and meet the boat at a certain hour. They speak here quite a different language from the Kiangsi dialect, and it is rather a curious feeling being quite alone among a people one can hardly understand or make understand."

The isolation in which the small band of Sisters lived at Ningpo was extreme, for they were in the very heart of the Chinese quarter, far removed from the European Kampo. They were the only Europeans who lived in this quarter and in the early days the roofs of the houses almost touched across the narrow streets, paved with cobble-stones. At Kuikiang, lying on the high road between Shanghai and Hankow, they knew more or less what was happening around them.

When rare visitors did come, they brought disquieting news and forecasts which were to prove true, though the word ' Boxer ' does not yet appear in Sister Xavier's letters.

V

THE NINGPO NURSERY — MEDICAL
MISSION WORK

FOR some time in her early years Sister Xavier had also charge of the tiny babies in the nursery, and like all newcomers to China she was horrified at the high rate of mortality amongst them. She set to work with her devoted companion, Sister Germaine Doverschaun, to try to save the lives of these poor little derelicts by all possible care.

A cow was bought and there is an amusing photograph of the cow being milked in the garden of the nursery. Sister Xavier also appealed to her mother and friends at home for help in this work of rearing the babies, and big cases of Allenbury's Food and babies' feeding bottles arrived. Every morning at five o'clock Sister Xavier supervised the making of the food, and she sometimes rose in the night to visit her beloved babies and see if the night nurse was doing her duty.

However, she was eventually forced to admit that Chinese babies do not thrive on artificial feeding, and the only way to make them live was to put them out with wet-nurses in the country. She and Sister Doverschaun organized a good service of these nurses, putting respectable Christian women in charge of districts to supervise them. Every month the babies were brought in to be inspected and the nurses paid, while the Sisters often made surprise visits to see them.

Little " trousseaux " of clean clothes were given to them when they were sent out, though there were many criticisms that these would be stolen or given to the nurses' own children. Sister Xavier always spoke rather indignantly of the babies being received with the remark: " Another little angel for Heaven! " Certainly a large number arrived in a dying condition, yet she always insisted that it was the law of God that everything possible should be done to save their lives and rear them. She carried on this work of devotion to the babies to the end of her long life.

It is interesting to see from her notes that she did not expect to live long. We read in 1892: " You have to become a Saint, and you have only probably about two or three years in which to do the work."

In her old age she said that the Sisters, in those early days, died like flies. The fatiguing work in the hot summers took a heavy toll of health and strength, and they had neither lighter habits nor closed mosquito curtains. Such dispensations were gradually given and more precautions taken to preserve life, when it was realized how valuable their services were and how difficult it was to replace the generous workers.

Sister Xavier's notes say :

" We must not expect to go to Heaven on a feather bed. Our Lord Himself went to Heaven by suffering and the servant must not look to be in better case than his Master (St. Thomas More)."

She adds:

" St. Thomas More possessed that nobleness of mind, that generous unselfishness of spirit which shrinks from no earthly sacrifice, even from the rendering up of dear life itself, and which considers loss as gain, so that the path of duty be rigorously followed."

Most Europeans suffer from boils in the hot climate and Sister Xavier was no exception; from her first year in China she was nearly always covered with them during certain months. When home in 1923 she received injections which cured them. Life was not easy for one with such overflowing energy and youthful enthusiasm. These exposed her to criticism from those around her of different nationality, but she bore it all, outwardly smiling, and went her way; she certainly suffered, but her devotion to the Holy Eucharist saved her. In her old age she said that during her first years in China she often went to the chapel and said, " If *You* were not here, I would go home by the next boat! "

We read in her Ningpo Retreat Notes:

" Fly to the Holy Eucharist in all troubles, expecting to be tried and strengthened by the Cross, let storms pass over your head in peace and joyousness, then go quietly on your way.

" In Holy Communion try to be very intimate with Our Lord, telling Him all your difficulties and listening to what He has to say. Always try to bring some present to Him and renew your Vows at each Communion.

" It was owing to the careful offering of the day's first fruits to his God, which shed so much peace over the life of this great good man (St. Thomas More).

" Treat your Sisters with bright and gracious charity and fearless simplicity, do numberless little acts of kindness to them as to Our Lord's Spouses—that they are not returned makes your intentions all the more pure. When spoken to unkindly, answer with calm, modest and fearless simplicity and all charity; do not keep silence, for silence generally comes from cowardly want of simplicity and for fear of losing self-control and is followed by internal boiling! "

How often one reads those words " fearless simplicity " and how characteristic of her. The Superior of those years, the kind Sister Solomniac, understood her, had a great affection for her and evidently gave her fairly wide permissions to go ahead. In Sister Xavier's notes we read:

" Have a great spirit of faith with regard to your Superior; treat her as a dear, kind mother; be full of respect and affection for her; never say or do anything that would pain her, ask her the necessary permissions very quietly; try and lead her gently to see what is for the best, then in her decision see God's Will, above all, show great charity and spirit of faith in speaking of her."

Later we read :

" God, the Poor, and the necessary permission; then go ahead and never mind what people say."

She quotes the advice of Sister Visitatrix:

" Love the poor Chinese, speak of them with respect and affection. How is it possible to have come so far and to have given up so much for them and then to speak of them in terms that should never be heard from a Sister of Charity to her ' Lords and Masters the Poor ' ? All a Sister's joy, all her delight, is in the service of the poor, every moment of her time, her whole person is vowed to their service. It is a kind of profanation to devote either to another occupation."

In December 1891 the charge of the Hospital for Women and Children was given to Sister Xavier and she set to work with characteristic energy. The hospital was in true Chinese style of those days—open wooden framework for windows, to be stuffed with rags on cold nights. Her Superior, though her purse was continually drained by the orphanage, had the buildings repaired and Sister Xavier assured her that she would see they were not summoned for debt.

Though not a trained nurse, Sister Xavier showed great aptitude for this work and nursed her patients very well. She trained

"A NURSE IN THE COUNTRY," NINGPO
Mother is washing clothes in the river, so big foster brother minds the baby.

THE ARRIVAL OF A BABY, NINGPO

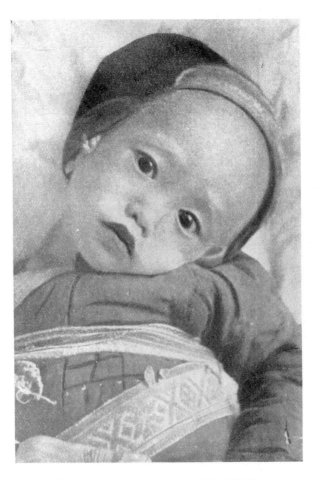

" PLEASE WILL YOU ADOPT ME ? "

herself by accepting instruction from all sides and by study. Medical books of all kinds arrived from England and she made a really good library, studying in her spare moments. We see big notebooks which she filled in those days, writing details of her cases, the prescriptions given and their effects. In these note-books are many letters from her aunt, Lady Denbigh, a great authority on sick nursing, and many recipes for cookery for invalids. Sister Xavier related that she made all kinds of things over little Chinese charcoal stoves, beef tea, barley water, etc. She grasped very early in her medical and nursing work that half the illness in China is due to want of strengthening food, and many who were nursed by her have spoken of her devoted care and the interest she took in their recovery.

In those days the foreigners in Ningpo were on very friendly terms; Protestants and Catholics of all nationalities were good friends and met together to discuss difficult affairs. Often the British Consul would send a rickshaw into the Chinese city to the Sisters' House, begging that Sister Xavier should be allowed to come and act as interpreter. In this way she gained many friends among them, and was much appreciated by the Consuls, to whom she often rendered valuable service.

The Protestant doctors generously gave their services for the Sisters' orphan children and poor patients, often receiving them in their hospitals for operations or special treatment, *gratis*. The well-known Dr. Grant of the North Gate Hospital, Ningpo, was a valued friend of Sister Xavier; he took great interest in her babies and sick people. After her death, in one of her medical notebooks was found a characteristically kind letter from Dr. Grant, which we quote:

" Dear Sister Xavier,
" I am very very sorry that I cannot get into the city to-day but I have promised to see the sick Father again at Kampo. We operated on the glands of your little one and she is doing nicely. Syrup of Ferri Phosphate will be good for her.
" I am glad to hear that Sister Superior is better but I am sorry that Sister Madeline is so poorly.
Yours sincerely,
John Grant."

Over forty years later, on a journey to Shanghai from Ningpo, an old gentleman rose up from an armchair in the saloon of the

E

Tsin Pekin and approached the Sisters. " Is it Sister Xavier ? " he asked. " Dr. Grant ? " was her reply, and the two renewed their memories of the good old days, when all worked together as friends.

It is amusing to relate that she kept her friends the doctors up to the mark. On one occasion an appointment had been made to see a poor woman from a far-off country district. The doctor arrived two hours late. " I blew him up," said Sister Xavier, " and he understood that the poor must not be kept waiting."

She had many friends among the Ningpo foreigners and their children adored her. Major Watson's two little girls, Minnie and Jessie, became life-long friends and later always visited Sister Xavier when she came to Shanghai. She gave them good advice for their future lives and always spiritual help for their souls. A little Catholic English boy, whose adopted father, a man in the Customs, died, was left in the guardianship of the British Consul, who insisted that Sister Xavier should also act as guardian.

With the permission of her Superiors, she placed the little lad with the Marist Brothers at St. Francis Xavier's College, Shanghai, who accepted him at the tender age of five years, and he was cared for by the good Brother Antonin. Sister Xavier followed the boy until he had a good situation, and, years later, he always brought his wife and family to see her when she came to Shanghai. This young Englishman died of consumption and Sister Xavier followed up the little family and placed the eldest boy with Brother Antonin, asking one of her own brothers to pay his school fees. This lad, Dick Simmonds, enlisted with the British forces in Shanghai in 1941, was taken prisoner at Singapore, and died in the Sarawak camp two days before the Japanese surrender in 1945.

It is edifying to note that she had a very delicate conscience with regard to these extern friends; we read in her notes:

" Treat externs with a bright and gracious charity and fearless simplicity, utterly heedless of what people say or think as long as you please Our Lord and do good to souls. Never enter into discussion with them, but turn it aside with some quiet straightforward remark. Example and prayer do more than words, with less risk to modesty and humility. In talking to externs, speak of outside subjects only for the sake of charity, never ask questions for personal pleasure and always try to see things from Our Lord's point of view. I am so often unable to answer worldly remarks through my negligence at mental prayer, and therefore I am not enlightened by the Holy Ghost."

August, 1891: " The Holy Childhood is our principal work. The children are brought to us when only a few hours old, usually because the parents are too poor to rear them. We put the mites out with nurses for two or three years, and they are then brought in here and kept until a marriageable age, say sixteen or seventeen years. They see their bridegrooms at the altar steps for the first time; the poor children peep over their shoulders to get an idea of the man they are to be united to for life. (This custom is changed now.)

" To-day one of our girls was married, her husband paying twenty dollars for her. Among the Christians they are not allowed to pay more than fifty dollars, which must be spent on the trousseau, to break them of this idea of selling. Some of our children turn out really well, though this early married life, surrounded with pagans, is full of difficulties. The other night, returning rather late from a distant village, it was quite dark, when far along the river we could hear the *Ave Maria* being chanted. On coming up to a little fishing boat moored to the bank, we found that it was one of our girls and her husband deep in their Rosary and quite heedless of passing pagan boats. One thing, all fairly good Chinese Christians have a great devotion to Our Lady and I think she gets them to Heaven in spite of their faults."

So great an influence does the Chinese woman possess, when once the novitiate of suffering and slavery of her early life is over and she has given birth to a son and is the mistress of the house, that—

" If she becomes a Christian ", writes Sister Xavier, " she generally draws after her the husband and children, but if the man comes first, he often remains a tepid kind of creature and the house is pagan. Many Missionaries will not baptize a man unless the woman is also a Christian to keep the house and the husband straight. It is extraordinary what influence the Chinese woman has, although everything is done to lower her. She has not even a name, but is called by the name of her son, e.g., ' Lipah Ahm ' (Lipah's mother).

" An example of that dreadful foot binding among the women was brought to us last Friday—a little girl of ten years with both feet dropping off. All we could do was to cut the tendons and the feet dropped off and she is left with two stumps. When healed, she will probably have two wooden feet and get about like several of our cripples do here. Our Holy Childhood children do not now have their feet bound, but the extern children do and it is quite an undertaking. At the Kuikiang Orphanage the orphans have to have small bound feet as otherwise husbands could not be got for them."[1]

[1] The custom of binding women's feet is now entirely abolished in China.

July 1893: " We are having a roasting summer. People say that for years it has not been so hot. We were a couple of months without rain, rivers were dried up and drinking water most precious. Fasts were prescribed by the ' Tao-Tai ' (Mandarin), pigs were not allowed to be killed. The ' Tao-Tai ' had to go down on both knees before any reptile caught in a spring, in order to make the divinities propitious. Daily we met processions of idols all over the town.

" Meanwhile we were reaping a harvest of souls, for the poor babies cannot support the long continued heat. We have over thirty or forty or even fifty baptisms in a day or in an afternoon. Really God's Providence is wonderful, over and over again apparent chance leads us to some out-of-the-way nook or hamlet not visited for ages, to find children simply waiting to die, dressed out in their smartest clothes according to Chinese custom. We almost hurry out of the house so as not to be present at the last moment, our work is done and the soul safe.

" On more than one occasion the Sisters have been hailed by the father who declared that his child had been dead for hours and was just come to life again. Could it be saved ? Of course, the little one had had a long faint or stupor before drawing its final breath which Our Lord seems to have delayed for hours until the waters of Baptism had flowed over its head. We don't care to have such cases often. Though the child may be at death's door, if we have entered the house and looked at it, we have killed it. If we tell the parents there is no hope, it dies because we have decreed it, and therefore at our next visit, all the babies are hidden away. We prefer that children should linger or revive for a time.

" The other day, regular tropical torrents of rain made us take refuge in a den and gave us time to take an inventory. It was about half the size of our study and made two rooms. In the parlour were two tables, three benches and a heap of rubbish, a grandmother, a mother, two children, five hens and eight pigs. Through the litter we made our way to the youngest baby who has now taken flight to Heaven.

" The belief is that until they, the babies, are a month old, they have no souls, so it does no harm to let them die and saves them much misery. One poor little baby we met when out the other day was wailing in a corner; the mother declared, ' Why, that baby costs a penny a day to feed, so now I let it cry away and it has gone to skin and bone.' She would not give it to us to rear, so Baptism at least secured for it a happy eternity after such a little life of suffering.

" Another mother had a little boy, a fortnight old, for sale; her husband, an opium smoker, had sold the first and kept the money, so she meant to be beforehand with him this time. The children they wish to bring up, they are foolishly fond of, giving in to their every whim, so that the young tyrants rule the house. In many homes, you see a poor little down-trodden girl, the future daughter-in-law until her wedding day, if she survives so long.

" When one thinks, however, of these people being pagans, and of the cruelty one finds sometimes even in our Christian countries, one cannot be surprised. We get accustomed to expect very little and in consequence when traits of devotion and gratitude show themselves, they are doubly welcome. How fond one gets of them in spite of all the dirt and misery, but that, of course, is part of our vocation. Anyhow I am infinitely happier surrounded by my poor Chinese here with all their sores and miseries, physical and moral, than I should be in the smart General Hospital at Shanghai. Life will not be long enough to thank God for such a grace."

Afloat, October 1893: " In one place a picture of Our Blessed Lady is kept among a band of pagan families with the greatest reverence and devotion. The pagans declare that the ' Holy Mother of God ', as they call her, has worked wonders for those who have prayed to her and the picture is kept in the family that has last received a mark of her protection. The catechist seized the opportunity to explain who Our Lady really was. The pagans were much impressed and begged for books to learn more about the Faith. A scholar who came to the Sisters at Hangchow to be cured of opium smoking, declared that a similar picture had been treasured up in his family for nine generations.

" At Hangchow, the Sisters are rejoicing at a really wonderful cure. A Military Mandarin, twenty-six years of age, of very high position, was terribly injured by an explosion of gunpowder—face, chest, back and the left arm especially were in a frightful state. Five days after this, they sent for our Sisters, who found the poor fellow in a pitiable condition, flesh and clothes all matted together; nothing had been done since the accident. They had him brought to the Hospital and wrapped him up in a piece of Blessed Perboyre's cloak (his sister's greatest treasure). The pain from that moment ceased; he has become gradually better and at present, though still with the Sisters, there is hardly any sign left of the accident. His father, a Mandarin of high position, is loading the Sisters with presents; he brought them himself, one of the greatest marks of honour in China. Some characters traced by his orders and sealed with his seal are to be placed over the dispensary and Sister Perboyre's door— ' Skilful hand, mother of the unfortunate ' is the translation. It is hoped that this cure will do much towards killing prejudice.

" It is wonderful how the Faith is spreading in the province and sometimes there are striking examples. One pagan who acts as schoolmaster and doctor on a small island off the coast went to visit a neighbouring island; he met the Christian catechist there and became a catechumen. Shortly afterwards he had a terrible trial; his eldest son, though quite a boy, was intentionally killed in a quarrel. In China the eldest son is the idol and hope of the family. All pressed the father to avenge himself in the customary way: ruin the family of the murderer and destroy their house. The man refused, saying that he was a Christian now and would not seek revenge, but would leave the matter in the Hands of God.

" A few days later the eldest son of the murderer was killed by an accident; shortly afterwards his second son suffered the same fate, and his third and last was brought to death's door by a violent fever. The schoolmaster doctor was asked if he would come and try to save the only remaining boy. ' Of course ,' he answered, ' I will come and cure him ', and so he did. The pagans are so astonished that nearly all on the island are now catechumens and our friend the schoolmaster has just arrived for final instruction before Baptism. This is the way they are drawing one another, mostly simple folk and fishermen.

" It is delightful here, seeing the Mission work so full of life and vigour. I defy any Catholic in Europe or America to know by heart an equal number of litanies and prayers, for visits to the Blessed Sacrament and for all the Feasts of the year, for every kind of occasion, each with a particular chant, generally men and women alternately. To-morrow there is to be Confirmation, and during the week a retreat for catechists has been going on. The great cry is for priests and catechists, the priests to follow when a band of catechumens is collected. The harvest does seem ripe if only there were more labourers."

December 1894: " The extremes of heat and cold are great in China. After the scorching summer comes a severe winter. The milk in the kitchen was a hard unbreakable block, even the bread was a frozen mass. The dispensary work was very trying, the medicines were blocks of ice and had to be kept in hot water, and the ink froze on one's pen. The priests who were out in the Missions had a very hard time but they bring back most consoling news of the progress religion is making everywhere. Catechumens are coming in by hundreds and seem, on the whole, a very promising set."

Sister Xavier's letters are full of compassion for the hard-working priests of the province, a cry, almost passionate sometimes in its energy, for more labourers in this ripening harvest.

She writes in 1895 :

" It is a real comfort to do something for these poor priests in the interior. Some come here for rest, looking like wrecks. Of three at the Residence, one received the Last Sacraments to-day, another looks more like a corpse than a man, and the third can neither sleep nor eat but always has a racking headache. The last two are quite young, the great trials that they have to undergo and the bad food soon tell upon them, though of course they hold on as long as possible. They look upon this place as a sort of ' Mothers' Home ', and nearly all are from France.

" It is said of Blessed Gabriel Perboyre that shortly after his martyrdom he appeared to his brother, saying, ' My hands are full of graces and no one asks me for them.' By the Christians in China his memory is held in veneration and his intercession invoked as the following incident testifies.

" The Chinese priest I mentioned the other day, who received the Last Sacraments, is now up and, though very weak, goes about. When the end was evidently near, and symptoms of immediate death were showing themselves, as a last resource he was wrapped in the cloak of Blessed Perboyre and a relic put on his breast. Since then he has rallied in a wonderful manner and is a perfect miracle."

June 1895: " The Missionaries have suffered a great deal lately, they come back from the interior looking like walking spectres and one, alas, never arrived at all. He succumbed at Hangchow on his journey in a boat, having received the Last Sacraments. He was only forty years of age, one of the most valuable men in the vicariate, as he was such a good Chinese scholar, and overflowing with zeal and energy. He was doing wonders in a huge district, working with three Chinese priests, and hundreds of catechumens were flocking into the Church. Everywhere the cry is for priests and catechists.

" It seems as if Almighty God wishes to show He can do His work without anybody. Formerly Christians were so few, conversions so difficult, that the priests more than sufficed for the work. Now that thousands are begging to be enrolled, it is overwhelming. These good missionaries must always be prepared for death, as often a Confrère will have several days' journey to reach a sick priest. One Father died with his Christians around him, suggesting the ejaculations he had generally used when caring for their dying friends."

One is struck by the keen interest Sister Xavier took in all the Mission works, especially those of the priests in their apostolate for souls. This was characteristic of her to the end of her life; indeed, she was interested in Mission works all over the world and it gave her a very wide outlook. One may surely say that the secret of it was her passion for souls. She took her vocation in that light very seriously. We read in her notes:

" We have three vocations to thank God for: first, to Christianity, and in this pagan land, how easy it is to look upon things that surround us with the eyes of pagans and not according to the spirit of Faith, in fact to contract the faults and the spirit of the Chinese pagan. Second, to the Company of the Sisters of Charity. How do you act up to the spirit of this vocation, your Vows, your name ? Third, to the Chinese Mission. God said to you, ' Go and teach all nations, baptizing, etc.', and you went. How do you fulfil the duties of this vocation ? Remember you will have to answer for the souls God has committed to your care."

She writes again on the work of the Missionaries:

" It is strange and wonderful the way the Faith is spreading, the cry on all sides is for priests. The catechists are doing wonders, but what can a mere handful of priests do for these thousands of catechumens ? Each one is doing the work of five. Bishop Reynaud does not know which way to turn to meet the calls on all sides. He has at present only nineteen priests, all told, and, to add to his troubles, death continues its work amongst them. One received Extreme Unction to-day, three or four more seem to have one foot in the grave, but they still remain at their posts. It is a glorious work for those who hunger and thirst after souls ; they can come and gather in the harvest which others have sown in sufferings and disappointments of every description. The Faith is spreading fastest in districts where Missionaries now dead had spent their lives in most ungrateful soil without any apparent result."

Sister Xavier continued to work at her own supernatural perfection, realizing always that prayer and good works are of little avail otherwise. In her notes we read:

" Zeal and piety of no ordinary degree may labour at the work of the conversion of others with scanty success because defective in close union with God. Compare yourself with the Saints, not with one another, for it is to sanctity each one is called, what the Saints have done you can do with the help of God. Your whole life, each day, from 4 a.m. to 9 p.m., is one chain of grace, attaching the heart of Jesus to your own heart—a grace, a link, is lost, the chain is broken, with difficulty will succeeding grace reach your soul. How often, after a fervent meditation and Communion in the morning, you return in the evening to Our Lord's feet, unable to utter a word. During the day the chain has been broken, grace has been resisted."

Later letters tell of many improvements in her hospital, which is overflowing with patients. Her good friend Sister Howard often sent her big cases of medicines and medical equipment from England which helped her to do good work. One who was with her in those days speaks of her great devotion to her patients ; she was often seen sitting on a bed, bending down to try and understand what the poor sick woman wanted and where she was suffering. We read in her notes:

" Enter into all the details of your hospital work yourself ; give medicines, serve rice if possible, never let others do your duties with regard to the patients, it would show how little you realize whom you are serving and caring for. Avoid all anxiety about your patients, offer each case to Him as it comes in, ask His guidance and blessing on your efforts and remedies, then leave the result entirely in His

Hands, feeling sure that whatever happens is for the best. You only want His Will accomplished, no glory or pleasant feeling of success for yourself, but what is for His greater glory and the good of souls.

" Don't let criticism or opposition discourage or in any way disturb you. The Cross is the sure sign that the work is God's work and will succeed in His own time. You simply go on, steadily, calmly, seeing the Will of God in each action and circumstance, never flinching or growing impatient and discouraged because God tries you. He loves souls and the poor far more than you do, never fear; if His time is not yet come, if He wishes to try your persevering love, let Him do so."

About this time Sister Xavier had the pleasure of a visit from her brother, Captain Hubert Berkeley. On his way home from the Malay States on leave he took in China, so as to get first-hand news of her for the family.

Arriving on the Ningpo Bund one morning early, he left the steamer but he had no idea where the Sisters' House was situated, and not speaking Chinese could not ask anyone for information. Surrounded by Chinese rickshaw coolies and others, he walked into a shop on the Bund, sat down, took out a notebook and pencil and began to draw a Sister of Charity!

When he arrived at the cornette there was a howl of delight from the crowd of Chinese around him. He was seized on all sides by the rickshaw men and carried by one of them to the Sisters' House, " Maison Jésu Enfant ", in the city.

VI

"LA JEUNESSE OUVRIÈRE"

THE needlework of the Chinese women and children is of great beauty and perfection and is one of the chief means employed by the Sisters to gain resources to help their poor people and orphans. Sister Xavier writes with a heavy heart in 1893, saying:

> "We are obliged to refuse work from having no sale for the embroidery, etc. It has struck me that America might be a good place to dispose of some; Americans admire it very much."

She followed up this idea of getting help from America, and first of all got into touch with the Foreign Mission Aid Societies, who were delighted to receive her interesting stories of real Mission life and works. Sister Xavier opened up American alms to all the Sisters' Houses in China; she was the pioneer.

It was in these years that she first came in contact with Fr. Walsh (later Bishop Walsh), the enterprising Director of the Boston Propagation of the Faith office, who in later years founded the American Foreign Mission College, Maryknoll, New York. Fr. Walsh became a life-long friend of Sister Xavier and sent her generous help in the Ningpo days, especially for the Holy Childhood. A system of American godmothers was instituted; babies were baptized for them and adopted with yearly support. Interesting details of the children growing up, with photographs, went to the godmothers.

But Sister Xavier was not satisfied, and she wrote to Fr. Walsh in this strain: "You must not only send American money to the Foreign Missions but also train American missionaries to come out and work for souls." The seed was already sown in Fr. Walsh's heart and he needed no urging. Fr. Price and he were already putting their heads together, and the result was the foundation and miraculous development of Maryknoll, whence many hundreds of American missionaries, priests and sisters, have gone forth to pagan lands to work for souls.

Fr. Walsh spoke of Sister Xavier as the " Co-Foundress " of Maryknoll; he had a great admiration and respect for her. Many years later a Maryknoll Bishop in South China said: " In the Seminary at Maryknoll, at Spiritual Conferences, Fr. Superior [Walsh] often used to give us ' Sister Xavier Berkeley ' as an example of the life of sacrifice and zeal which God requires in those who go to work in Foreign Missions."

As all the open ports in China in those days were English in tone and language, the need of a sprinkling of English-speaking priests was very great. Against much contrary opinion, Sister Xavier always maintained that American youth, given good spiritual training and hardy formation, would make excellent Foreign Missionaries, and she lived to see this belief realized beyond all expectation.

She also kept up a good correspondence with Ireland, having a strong strain of Irish blood in her, and often saying, " The Irish will make any sacrifices for the saving of a soul." Her letters to Ireland aroused great interest in China Missions, and helped in the founding of " St. Joseph's Young Priests' Society " by Mrs. Taafe, and also in the opening of the " Maynooth Mission to China ".

In her letters to Sister Howard she represented the urgent need of English-speaking priests in Shanghai and this brought good fruit. At that time the spiritual needs of the English-speaking Catholics, of whom there were many, especially in the Customs and Police Forces, were sadly neglected and in that huge port many an unfortunate soul came to shipwreck. Her cousin, Sister Feilding, who came to China in 1903, specially devoted herself in the General Hospital, Shanghai, to these " down and outs ", who always spoke of her as the " good Sister Clare ".

Sister Howard's brother, Lord Edmund Talbot, when in Rome on his official duties, spoke of this need of English-speaking priests in Shanghai, and eventually the situation was understood. There is now, thanks to the American Jesuits, a beautiful church and large social club for English-speaking Catholics in that city.

. . . .

The Chinese-Japanese war, with its consequences of heavy taxation and trade depression, brought great sufferings to Ningpo. Sister Xavier writes in 1895:

"We know not what to do, to relieve the large number of poor, infirm creatures who are thrown on our hands. Rice is so dear. One paralyzed girl, with a rope around her neck, was being dragged to be drowned in a canal. She was rescued and brought here by a Christian. We have nowhere to put the women; it will be a terrible thing to have to refuse them admittance. Let us hope Providence will come to our aid."

The distresses of war quickened into yet greater activity the inventive charity of Sister Xavier. Through her Foreign Mission friends in America she had already begun to find purchasers for the lace and embroidery, and had in her head a scheme for opening large workrooms, not only for their own girls and women, but also for the poor pagans outside. The workrooms became a happy reality. She writes:

"You little realize what a boon it will be to these poor people and to the Mission, if we succeed in obtaining a permanent sale for their embroidery. Most of the Christians are very poor but when we can give them work, their homes are less comfortless and they have enough to eat. For a year or so they worked for a shop in Paris, but that fell through. Nearly every day now women come in for work, and yesterday, to our joy, a pagan woman came to ask to stay a little while in our house to learn to work—a very great step.

"If you only knew the terror they have of spending a night in the house, even those who receive us most cordially at home! You would be amused to see them come trembling inside for the first time, peeping about to make sure that we are not stealing their souls from them, for they are firmly convinced that we can deprive them of their souls by just looking at them and that yet they can go on living. Poor people, they are so full of these absurd beliefs and traditions that it is a real miracle when they are converted. And this miracle is being worked now without any apparent human means in all directions. The catechumens are reckoned to number between eight and nine thousand.

"But to return to the work! Fr. Ferrant, the superintendent of the business, hopes that we can open some kind of make-shift workrooms at once, and as funds come in things will settle themselves. We have a scheme for making our own satin; it could be begun on a small scale, a few looms, sixty dollars each, put up in what, in Europe, would be called a shed. We have the land for mulberry trees; large tracts were bought in the rebellion of 1861. The trees can be procured in any quantity from the Christians of Tso-fou-pang, where there are forests of them and the inhabitants live by their silk worms. We hope this scheme will be carried through."

Later, she writes:

"The embroidery is going on very well. We have just sent a

large box to England. If we had funds, we would start a place to make better satin than we can buy in Ningpo. It would pay its way and train many hands."

Under the superintendence of Fr. Ferrant and the direction of Mgr. Reynaud, Bishop of the Chekiang Province in those days, Sister Xavier started *L'Oeuvre de la Jeunesse Ouvrière*, similar to our technical schools for young workers, the object of which was to draw in pagans as well as the Christians, women and children, teaching them trades and providing them with employment. This was done quite irrespective of creed, with the result that prejudice was broken down, and pagans and Christians associated together quite happily under the kindly Christian influence of the organizers of the work.

The need for this work was felt as the Societies of the Propagation of the Faith and the Holy Childhood do not touch the pagan children. The former may only teach the children of Christians until they reach the age to learn a trade, and no pagans may be admitted to their schools, except, of course, as catechumens, the object being the direct teaching of religion and hospital work.

L'Oeuvre de la Jeunesse Ouvrière takes in pagan children and has them educated and taught to work, cares for them until their marriage and assists them in preparing for it, and is ever ready to receive them when in trouble or in want. The object, therefore, is to establish outside workrooms, giving also some education, forming what we call technical schools. It preserves the children from the dangers and miseries of outside apprenticeship under pagan masters, besides teaching them excellent trades. They are kept for the first year at the expense of the school and receive no remuneration, but at the expiration of the year they begin to earn. A small sum is then taken for their maintenance and the rest put on one side until the term of their apprenticeship has expired. By that time they are capable of earning sufficient to support themselves and their families if they are married.

The work is really for the benefit of both sexes after they have left school; it prevents Christian children, especially boys, from being ruined in pagan workshops. The pagan children, while learning their trade, imbibe Christian ideas, which bear fruit in good habits and behaviour, and even the gift of Faith when they grow older.

The trades taught are those peculiar to the town; the women and girls embroider, make lace, spin and ply their needles in any way. Pagan women are also accepted and the monetary gain which the wife is thus able to contribute adds to the comfort of the home and assures her of the affection and respect of her husband.

The boys and young men become designers and silk and satin weavers, according to their capacity. It is chiefly with them that the Christian influence bears fruit. They are more free to embrace the Faith than the girls, who are often engaged as small children to pagans, so that they cannot receive Baptism unless their future husbands also consent to become Christians. Boys have not this obstacle and pagan and Christian youths study together every evening, use the same books, say the same prayers and assist at Mass together. Thus, by degrees, the light of Faith penetrates into their souls and they ask for Baptism. This, however, is not given to them unless they have reached a reasonable age and understand their responsibilities as Christians.

Sister Xavier writes in 1896 that the satin-making scheme for boys is slowly being realized. Three or four have been apprenticed, and the eldest, she remarks with justifiable pride, " already works better than his master ". A welcome gift of £5 is invested in two cotton-beating machines, worked by the feet, and she describes her plan:

" We will get a couple of youths to work the machines to earn enough (about twenty to twenty-five dollars) to buy themselves one each, with which they will return to their villages and be replaced by other boys, who will do the same. Thus, little by little, various families will be helped; for when they have a cotton-beating machine, a good living can be earned. It is an excellent though very tiring work. A few little five-pound notes do turn out very useful, don't they ? "

Meanwhile Sister Xavier was searching for markets in which the embroidery, lace, etc., could be disposed of. Again her good friend Sister Howard came to her help, and she interested her brother, the Duke of Norfolk, in this new Mission work, Chinese technical schools. He called a meeting at Norfolk House, London, at which large numbers of leading Catholics were present. The work and objects of the schools were clearly explained and great interest was aroused.

A committee was formed, of which Mr. Leonard Lindsay was secretary and treasurer; he filled these offices with great devotion for over thirty years. Funds were collected to put the work on its feet, and to provide capital to keep it going until the pupils made it self-supporting. Sister Xavier was able to erect a large airy workroom with good accommodation for the boy designers and weavers. She took intense interest in this work, but always first from the point of view of saving souls. All her life she had a horror of Sisters engaging in commerce, and losing sight of the spiritual object of their vocation.

The launching of this work naturally brought much opposition and criticism, but she prepared herself for them. We read in her notes:

> " In the difficulties and trials of every day, see the Will of God, accept them cheerfully, because you only will what He wills. Keep your will very closely attached to His Will, doing your best not to cause Him displeasure and calmly walking over self and human respect and not heeding their outcry. Accept your Superior's wishes brightly, carry them out exactly. Don't allow yourself remarks to other Sisters. She has her manner and way of looking at things, you have yours; God wishes you to follow hers.
>
> " Above all, keep the gaze of your soul fixed calmly on God alone, trying to view all things as He views them. You fail, you are impatient, neglect duty; an act of humility, self-abasement, confidence, up and try again. You are called to an apostleship of Charity; clothe yourself with Jesus Christ, fill yourself with His spirit, His way of thinking, acting.
>
> " Your watchword, ' the Glory of God, the salvation of souls ' by work and by prayer."

The death of her much-loved father brings the following: " Be most faithful in saying your Rosary well; remember that it was dear Father's favourite devotion." In her old age, Sister Xavier related that her father always said his Rosary on his way home from hunting and she often heard her mother say anxiously, " I know he'll fall off one day! " She continues:

> " God calls you to be a Saint; the greater the difficulties, the harder the struggle, the more love do you show. Confide entirely in Our Lord, He will never fail you; He will help you to arrive at the sanctity He calls you to and perhaps to martyrdom.
>
> " Welcome any little sufferings that come your way as precious jewels to be offered to Our Lord while waiting till you have the privilege of offering Him your life's blood.

" You MUST be a Saint; only will what He wills and you will be a Saint; abandon yourself to Him with perfect confidence in this life and He will grant you the grace of martyrdom at the end—blood for blood if such is God's will."

The work of the technical schools progressed well under the zealous direction of Fr. Ferrant, who, after having been the heart and soul of the work at Ningpo, was made Vicar Apostolic of the Kiangsi Vicariate. As soon as he arrived in his new district he set to work to establish it there. The generous spirit of Sister Xavier took great interest in his efforts, and she recommended his needs to the London Committee, which, according to her plan, was to help establish technical schools in many parts of China.

One cannot but admire her energy and zeal in founding this work and carrying it on; she got into contact with many large shops in England—Maple's, Liberty's and others. Through an agent in Hongkong large boxes of work were despatched regularly and paid for by him. At that time the work was so much appreciated that all was willingly accepted. Chinese coloured embroidery on satin was much in fashion then for curtains, wall panels, cushion covers, etc., and the work done at Ningpo was very beautiful, the shading of colours being exquisite. Sister Xavier related that the Chinese were wonderful imitators; they could copy anything, even a living bird or flower, but she did not succeed in getting them to do original work. However, in modern days Chinese artists are showing great talent in original work.

While the commercial side of the work was succeeding, education was also making good progress, bringing Christian and pagan children into continual contact with the Sisters and overthrowing all prejudice. Sister Xavier writes:

" Many homes are entirely kept by the work they get from us. In some cases they would be actually starving except for this, women are so badly paid, as a rule. One sees these poor girls sitting together, working away, hardly lifting their eyes, yet very happy over it as it means so much to them, and raises their position. A rice winner is a person to be considered and respected; even in matrimonial arrangements it has its weight and wins for the girl a better match. If you could but hear them in the workroom after the day's labour is over, the noise and almost screams of laughter of all those young people! It makes one thankful that they have some happy days in their otherwise very dark lives."

Sister Xavier is particularly interested in the boys, and writes:

THE NEW EMBROIDERY WORKROOM OF THE CHINESE TECHNICAL
SCHOOL, NINGPO, 1897

CHUSAN : VISITING THE SICK AND POOR IN THE VILLAGES
One sister is baptizing a dying baby.

THE ARRIVAL OF BABIES, CHUSAN

" There seems to be a real blessing on our little weavers. We picked out the children in the greatest peril, some poor little fellows with very doubtful characters. But the result is more than we could have hoped for. These small boys, who were on the high road to becoming a disgrace to society at large, are now perched by their looms, as serious as judges, working like men and doing so well.

" It is true, once the work is over, they are regular little *diables* for noise and pranks! But they are practical in their way all the same, and duly informed the priest that if in the evenings they were taught reading, writing and counting, they would keep quiet and enjoy it, as they would then be able to become master workmen and not be cheated. So evening education is now in full swing, rather to the relief of the rest of the establishment. After work and lessons are over, they all kneel down in the workshop and chant their night prayers, pagans of their own free will joining in with the Christians."

She continues:

" Chinese children are most winning, warm-hearted, truthful and honest by nature. If they grow up liars and thieves, it is because they are taught to tell lies and be sharp. This kind of work among the outside poor, to preserve our own Christian youth and assist the pagans, has not yet been tried. If we succeed, it will doubtless extend elsewhere and be the means of saving numberless souls, besides forming happier and more prosperous families. These apprentices are paid as soon as they can earn; thus, when their apprenticeship is over, they have a little sum in the bank to start life with, unless the poverty of their families requires it before."

Sister Xavier carried on a large correspondence with the benefactors of the House and especially with English, Irish and American children, always hoping and praying that interest in the Missions would bring vocations. She had great faith in the prayers of the children and always turned to them in times of difficulty and danger. In one of her annual letters to them she writes:

" I have actually started a ' Boys' Brigade '; the little fellows learn their drill and already march very well. I little thought when I was taught to march as a child, that one day I should be teaching it to little Chinese lads as a Sister of Charity. We have been given two bugles on which they begin to practise at four o'clock in the morning."

Later she writes again, saying:

" I have good news for you, and that is, the Sisters in this House have baptized over 4,000 little dying babies in the last twelve months. One day, last summer, we visited some large villages in which there was a great deal of sickness and in that one day we baptized 199 babies. It is quite a common thing to baptize sixty or seventy in a day during epidemics, but 199 was a grand harvest.

" It is wonderful how Our Lord allows these poor little creatures to live just long enough to be baptized. One day I was leaving a village when a woman rushed up to me, holding a dying baby in her arms, and exclaiming, ' Can anything be done for this child ? ' I saw that there was not a moment to be lost and five minutes after I had poured the waters of Baptism on its head, it gave a little gasp and the soul took its flight to Heaven.

" I wish you could be here on the first day of the month when all the foster mothers from the country arrive with our babies to be paid and inspected. It is a very noisy assembly and you would laugh to see them holding up the tiny tots to be admired and to show their fat legs.

" Now I beg of you to be very generous to us this year in sending help, for there is a rice famine and food is so dear we do not know how to find the money to buy it. Perhaps you would not care to have rice for breakfast, dinner and supper, but the poor Chinese children are grateful to get it. We have to have three big sacks of rice every day to feed our large family. I know you will try to help as much as you can and our Dear Lord will bless you for your generous sacrifices."

VII

TROUBLED TIMES

Cholera in Shanghai—The Ningpo Pagan Nursery—The Boxer Rebellion

IN November 1895 the Ningpo Sisters suffered the loss of their much loved Superior, Sister Solomniac, by an apoplectic stroke. Sister Xavier writes:

" She was over twenty years here and only fifty-six years of age, full of life, most energetic in visiting the poor and making Baptism expeditions. In fact, it was going out on a bitterly cold day that gave her violent bronchitis and probably hastened the attack. She dropped quite suddenly when dressing, without there being a symptom before. Her work seemed accomplished, her *Nunc Dimittis* sung; but it is so sad to see her lying there, not knowing anyone. We are so short of hands, but God knows what He is doing; everywhere people and Missionaries are calling out for Sisters.

" This autumn there has been a cholera panic, a great many cases, but not as bad an epidemic as at Shanghai, where 1,700 natives died in a few days. Many Europeans also fell victims and among the Helpers of the Holy Souls, five Mothers died within twenty-four hours! Providence has watched well over the Sisters of Charity; surrounded as they are by the dead and dying, not one has taken it.

" Here there have been disturbances, through soldiers passing through the town, and they wanted to break into the Sisters' Houses and search them, saying that European soldiers were hidden inside. The authorities, however, behaved very well and with great energy scattered the mob and placed guards in front of our Houses. Since then we have heard of fresh disturbances, so it was thought wiser to send to the North six of our young Sisters, not long arrived in China. We are anxiously waiting to hear of their arrival at Tientsin, for a six days' journey in carts and small boats through a country overrun by wild and undisciplined soldiers is rather dangerous."

Sister Xavier's letters later give news of fresh chapel-burning by pagan monks at Chusan, speedily checked by the appearance of a man-of-war. She tells also of the death of another zealous and hard-worked priest and of the ordination of some young Chinese priests after a training of fourteen years. She says:

" They are promising and full of zeal but not very healthy; the long years of study are hard on them, though many are very clever."

She adds regretfully :

" They do but replace the six Missionaries who have died since I came here. Another is dying now from overwork; in his huge district it was killing work as the catechumens have increased so rapidly, whole villages are asking for instruction. In one place they have given over the pagan temple to make a chapel and will, in time, become excellent Christians. But God must send priests to the rescue and no doubt He will in His own good time."

There are many letters of this kind written to Ireland, for Sister Xavier was always hoping and praying that Irish priests would come to China. Her hopes were realized by the founding of the " Maynooth Mission to China " and her letters aroused great interest in Ireland.

She writes again on the subject:

" Here the great tide of conversions is going on in the most extra-ordinary way, ever on the increase, even in money-worshipping Ningpo. A catechist was telling me that everyone in the country, rich and poor, is enquiring about Christianity. Oh! if we only had priests at the present moment, they would need simply to speak and all would believe.

" Among our day scholars, a girl who has lately come proves a little of what I told you about women. Her father, a pagan, was taken ill about three months ago. Tchingvong, the girl, instructed him in the principal articles of Faith, taught her mother (a new and not very bright Christian) how to baptize, and made her administer the Sacrament when she saw there was no more hope. They are the only Christians in their village. The mother then caught the same illness, whereupon Tchingvong instructed her for confession, Communion and Confirmation and then brought her here, where she received all before she died."

Tchingvong became one of Sister Xavier's most valued helpers, not only visiting and instructing the sick outside, but later she became head nurse in the nursery. Sister Xavier said: " For ten years I prayed for a good nurse, then Tchingvong came." Over forty years later, this good woman was still caring for the crowded nursery of babies at Ningpo and helping the Sisters to save souls.

The outside visiting continued and in addition to all her other work, Sister Xavier got in touch with the pagan nursery near the North Gate in Ningpo. Here even larger numbers of little abandoned babies were received than at the Sisters', but very little care was taken of them, so that many died of neglect and suffering. Sister Xavier made friends with the directress of this nursery and obtained permission to come and treat the sick babies. She brought presents of much needed clothing for babies and nurses, so she was always welcome.

The directress soon understood that a special remedy was given to dying babies, and she was most faithful in sending for Sister Xavier at that moment. Many hundreds of babies went to Heaven from this pagan nursery in those days. It is interesting to know that over twenty years later the Sisters in Ningpo (Sister Xavier was then at Chusan) were called to see a sick woman near the North Gate. When they arrived they found an old lady who was very near the end, but when they began to instruct her they found she knew and understood a great deal about the Christian religion. Further questioning revealed that she was the old directress of the pagan nursery in Sister Xavier's days, and she was quite ready for Baptism, which she received with joy and then died peacefully. Surely the many hundreds of little angels in Heaven gained this grace for her, as she had been the instrument used by God to obtain Baptism and Heaven for them.

. . . .

In 1900 the Boxer rebellion filled the whole world with anxiety and dismay. Sister Xavier writes:

" The suspense is intense. All fear that the silence will be broken by the account of some fearful catastrophe. Our largest House in Pekin is next to the Cathedral and has over 1,000 inmates, now including large numbers of refugees. It is a great comfort to feel that all is in God's Hands and nothing will happen except what He permits. May all turn out to His Glory and the conversion of this unfortunate people. For over a month our Sisters in the North have been fully expecting and preparing for a violent death."

The heroic defence by a mere handful of French and Italian sailors of the Catholic Mission in Pekin is a matter of history. Sister Xavier writes:

" Only on September 2nd came the first authoritative account of the Missionaries and Sisters in Pekin. Eight Missionaries dead— two massacred and several burned in their Churches—two Marist Brothers and Sister Jaurias (the Superior of the Pekin Sisters). During the siege, she was the heart and soul of the establishment, going about cheering and encouraging everyone, in spite of her being close on eighty years of age—forty-five years in China. Everything was done to destroy the Orphanage—arrows of fire, bombardment and then mines. These last at one explosion killed seventy people, among them all the little ones in the nursery. The day the Allies entered, Sister Jaurias broke down and expired peacefully on August 22nd: a beautiful end to a beautiful life.

"It is really miraculous that during the two months' siege not a Sister was wounded or killed. At the Hospital, which is near the Legations, the Sisters were still there on July 16th, having refused to leave their House crowded with refugees. At two o'clock the next morning some foreign men from the Legations rushed in and compelled them by force to leave. An hour later, the Boxers invaded the House, bringing nine carts to carry off the nine 'European devils' (the Sisters). Like wild beasts they rushed all over the place yelling for the Europeans; they fell on their knees, offering incense to their idols, imploring that they should be delivered into their hands to be taken to the pagoda for execution.

"Certainly God has a glorious band of martyrs this year. 'Between fifteen and twenty thousand was the number of them', wrote Mgr. Favier in his first letter from Pekin after the siege, 'scarcely one apostatized. We are 27,000 Christians instead of 40,000, but I venture to predict that within five years we shall number 50,000.'"

His words have come true.

Sister Xavier writes, July 1901:

"We are sending you a souvenir of the siege of the 'Peitang', in the shape of small cannon balls, two of the thousands that were fired into the Orphanage. They must remind you of the special Providence that watched over and guarded the Sisters in China. Last year six Houses were in imminent peril, three were burned to the ground, the Pekin Orphanage battered to pieces; but not a single Sister met a violent death, though, during the siege, the sight of a white cornette produced a volley of bullets from the Boxers. An altar was promised to the Sacred Heart if no Sister was killed; it has just been erected at the Central House, Shanghai. The columns on each side of the statue and those supporting it are made of cannon balls fired into the Pekin Orphanage."

The disturbed conditions in China, the Boxer rebellion and, later on, civil war, made it very difficult for the Sisters to carry on their works of charity. Commerce was seriously interrupted and that affected the workrooms of the technical schools for a time. However, the London Committee was very faithful to the obligations that had been undertaken, and generous gifts arrived to help the schools to carry on, not only in Ningpo but also in the Kiangsi.

The idea of the founders of this work was to entrust the schools later on to the care of Brothers, especially the sons of Don Bosco, who would develop the resources of the districts, thus making the propagation of religion march hand in hand with the cultivation of industries. By carefully training each child in the trade to which he or she was best adapted, it was hoped to lay the foundations of a rising generation of honest, thrifty, hard-working men and women, practical Christians, whose example would finally dispose of the deep-seated prejudices against which Missionaries and Sisters have often to struggle.

It is relevant to quote here from an article written at that time by an English Consul-General in China, Mr. J. M. H. Playfair:

" THE NINGPO SCHOOL OF EMBROIDERY.

" . . . To teach the poverty-stricken working class of China how to earn two dollars where before they could but earn one, this is the climax of benevolence, the truest philanthropy. It is Missionary hands which have begun the task; it is the hands of Missionaries which must carry it on.

" That European Missionaries of all denominations and sects are doing excellent work in this direction among the Chinese, I am aware by report, but of the results in general I have no personal knowledge except in one small corner of the vineyard. My opinion is that Europeans who desire to show themselves to be friends of the Chinese in the highest sense must begin by casting away every thought of self; they must come to China to benefit the Chinese and the Chinese alone. Utter unselfishness is essential.

" This spirit I have met with in one small corner of the vineyard with which I am intimately acquainted. Two Catholic Institutions at Ningpo form the corner to which I allude, viz., the Convent ' Maison Jésu Enfant ', in the city and St. Joseph's Hospital in the Foreign Settlement. Both Institutions are under the control of the Sisters of Charity of St. Vincent de Paul; one is for women and girls, the other for men and boys. Words fail me to express the admiration I feel for the beautiful lives led by these Sisters, or to give an adequate idea of the immense good their administrations do for the natives among whom and for whom they labour.

" I repeat once more that in order to work with success among the inhabitants of the East, their would-be benefactors from the West must leave all thoughts of self-seeking behind. Here you have unselfishness in its purest and most convincing form. The Sisters have left their homes in Europe to spend their lives in China and to dedicate their labours to the Chinese. And what are these labours ?

" The Convent of ' Maison Jésu Enfant ' is, to begin with, a Foundling Hospital. The Sisters receive, clothe and feed 700 girl children every year, of whom 400 are inmates of the Convent and about 300 are put out to nurse. As these children grow up, they are taught useful handicrafts and when of sufficient age are married to suitable husbands. Every one of these girls, if she had not been rescued by the Sisters, would probably have died in infancy. In addition to the Foundling children, the Convent is an asylum for the very old, for cripples, for imbeciles, in a word for all the flotsam and jetsam of humanity. There is also under the same roof a Hospital and Dispensary; in the one the suffering poor are received and nursed back to health, in the other medicines are distributed to out-patients, all free.

" Even now I have not told all, though it seems incredible that more should remain to be told. This Institution has attempted to find a solution of the problem to which I have already made allusion, viz., how to teach the people of China to earn two dollars where before they could earn but one.

" It is now a dozen years since the Ningpo Convent established a School of Embroidery in which the art is taught to women and girls. Many of these, who were penniless, by their skill and industry now earn a livelihood and keep the wolf from the door for themselves and their families. Starting from a modest beginning, when but few workers were employed, it has gradually and surely increased its scope and is now flourishing exceedingly well.

" To mention but one direction in which it has developed, the Sisters were wont to buy the satin, on which the embroidery is worked, in the native shops, but several years ago they set up looms of their own on which the material is woven, and this home-made satin is admitted to be superior in quality to any bought outside.

" One difficulty they had to contend with for many a long day. It was not sufficient to produce the embroidery, it was also necessary to find a market for its sale. A certain amount could be disposed of by kind friends in the ports of China and in England. Queen Alexandra and the Princess of Wales have bought several pieces and have expressed their great admiration of its artistic beauty and execution. A bedspread had been sent by the Convent as a souvenir of the Diamond Jubilee to Queen Victoria and had been graciously accepted. There was no question about the excellence of the work, but its existence was known to very few. What was wanted was that some London tradesmen with reputations should become agents for the sale of the Convent's productions.

" There are two specially noteworthy points about this School of Embroidery. It is almost Utopian in its co-operative constitution. Here Capital is associated with Labour in unique terms. The Convent supplies the Capital, the workers constitute the Labour and ALL THE PROFITS GO TO THE WORKERS. Never did the most generous employer divide his entire profits among those he employed. It is unselfishness *in excelsis*. Secondly, this School of Embroidery is strictly undenominational. Pagans and Christians are welcomed alike, which is the apotheosis of tolerance.

" This School is so flourishing and is proving such a success, thanks to the unflagging exertions of the Sisters and their friends,

that the Ningpo Sisters have felt encouraged to extend their useful-
ness further and are trying to establish various such technical schools
in other places.

"My heartiest good wishes go with them. I think they have every
reason to hope for success, if only because their efforts are of the
nature of the truest philanthropy. 'Charity', in the popular sense
of the word, it is not, that is to say, it is not almsgiving. But
'Charity' it is in the original and noblest signification of the term.
All honour to the Sisters of Charity; they have come from their
homes in the West to lead the sweet waters of love to the thirsty
people of the East.

"Kipling said, 'East is East and West is West and never the
twain shall meet.' He meant that, owing to the difference between
the modes of thought of the European and the Asiatic, due in its
essence to divergence of races, it makes it impossible for us to climb
into that 'Fourth Dimension', where the soul of the Chinese is like
a star and dwells apart.

"But, maybe, the Sisters of Charity have found the true road to
the as-yet-undiscovered 'Fourth Dimension' of the Chinese mind.

(Signed) J. M. H. PLAYFAIR,
Consul General."

In May 1911 Sister Xavier Berkeley received her marching
orders to leave Ningpo and proceed to Chusan Island, where she
was named Superior of the House.

Before following her to Chusan a few words can be said on
Sister Xavier's relations with her Community in Ningpo. We
have spoken of her receiving much criticism from those around
her of different nationality, but it was often good-humouredly
given and she took it so. She was, like her cousin, Sister Feilding,
an ardent, enthusiastic person, full of ideas and wanting to go
ahead and develop her works. Such characters always suffer,
and in this case the difference in nationality sometimes brought
opposition and misunderstanding. But, as we have seen in Sister
Xavier's spiritual notes, she made light of these and if she really
suffered she took it before the Blessed Sacrament in the chapel.

One sees by her notes that she very early understood in her
Chinese Mission that "the Cross is a sure sign the work is God's
work", and she writes:

"Receive trials, sufferings, humiliations with the same dauntless,
fearless simplicity and spirit of Faith. God has allowed them to
happen and it is therefore His Holy Will that you should bear them.

"You must become a Saint by the faithful accomplishment of
the Will of God in a spirt of love and sacrifice, doing little things
and big with equal fidelity.

"All the little miseries in Community life, sharp remarks, etc., seen in their real light, are like mosquito bites, not worth thinking about."

Though sometimes misunderstood, there is no doubt that Sister Xavier was much loved and appreciated by her Sisters at Ningpo. She was always ready to do a kind service, to share her gifts with others for the improvement of their works, and it was her special joy to nurse her sick Sisters. Many have spoken of the kind treatment they received from her when they were suffering. In her later years at Ningpo, the Superior was very delicate and often ill; we are told that Sister Xavier nursed her with loving devotion, often rising two or three times in the night at her call.

She was the heart and soul of the "Baptism Expeditions," preparing the medicine baskets herself with the greatest care, so that the sick poor outside should be really benefited. She was very anxious that the Sisters should buy their own boat for the river journeys, but this project was never realized in Ningpo. A companion of those days related that often in the stifling, hot summer days, Sister Xavier would sit down at the bottom of the boat, resting against the seat, and fall fast asleep. The older Sisters used to say, "Let her be; she has so little sleep at night in this weather." But when the boat grated against the landing place, she would spring up and be the first to land and spend a long afternoon walking from village to village, caring for the sick people.

In her old age Sister Xavier spoke with great affection of her Ningpo Sisters, their strong missionary spirit, and willing sacrifice of comfort, convenience, everything for the saving of souls. She remembered them personally: "That dear good Sister Noguet, who always mended my clothes for me, I was never any good at sewing"; and of her devoted companion, Sister Germaine Doverschaun, she said: "We always told each other our ideas, and discussed them, and worked together in perfect union." Sister Doverschaun went to God in 1903, much to Sister Xavier's grief, and in a letter to Irish children she tells them of this good Sister's devoted labours among the Chinese and especially her loving care of the nursery babies.

In Sister Xavier's Retreat notes, we read:

"My Community life: Love your Community, pray for it daily and consider it one of the greatest privileges of your life to have been received into its midst. Love and be loyal to your Superiors, Sisters, and the Missionaries, as a family most dear to you in Jesus

Christ. Not only never make disadvantageous remarks but on the contrary let your words be full of sisterly affection and respect, interpreting shortcomings in the most charitable manner. Above all, be most loyal and full of spirit of Faith with regard to your Superiors; never act without permission. All may not have the same views; everyone is free to have an opinion which must be respected, though it cannot always be followed. For you, consider God, the poor and the necessary permission; then act with all peace and fearlessness; you are doing the Will of God.

" Especially see God's Will in each Rule which you have chosen and bound yourself to keep; one little infraction leads to another. Be most exact to be at Community exercises, try never to be late more than once a week "! (Punctuality was not her strong point and required great efforts on her part.)

" Towards your Sisters, be full of gracious cordiality; show that you are pleased to be with them, pleased to do them any little service, in fact, they are your Sisters. Pass quietly over any sharp word, show that it is forgotten. Towards your Superior, be full of gentle respect, deference and consideration to her slightest wish; do nothing without her permission and always take her part when others criticize her conduct.

" Towards the Poor, burning, indefatigable zeal and tender loving charity, seeing Our Lord in each one. Nevertheless, preserve with all persons and at all times the calm gentle dignity of a Spouse of Christ. With your servants, show a calm inflexible firmness without impatience or sharpness.

" In all things, at all times keep yourself interiorly and closely united to God, having but one aim—the accomplishment of His Divine Will and in the way He wills. You will thus draw down the grace necessary to accomplish the work you have been brought out here to do or rather He will do the work through you."

VIII

FIRST YEARS AT CHUSAN—THE ANGELIC WORK

EVERY ship that sails the China seas has to pass the Archipelago of Chusan, which lies to the south of Shanghai, off the Chekiang coast, on the route to Hongkong. It guards the entrance to the big " Blue River ", the Yangtse Kiang, and is a strategic position; before the war, gunboats of many nations often cruised among the Chusan Islands.

The Archipelago consists of over eighty islands and islets and the principal one is Chusan Island, with its chief port of Tinghai, which is the seat of the Government authorities. The population of all the islands is estimated roughly as a little over two millions; rice fields and the cultivation of vegetable plots occupy the islanders, also fishing and salt drying. The big sweet potato is largely grown on the mountain-sides, together with other vegetables, and it is strange to our foreign eyes to see peas, beans, wheat and barley growing in terraces on the mountain slopes and even on the summits. The sweet potato forms a large part of the food of the islanders; it is often grated, dried on bamboo trays and stored away for the winter to mix with the rice for food.

The peasants also raise pigs, fowls, geese and the famous Chusan turkey, which is a speciality of the Shanghai market in peace times. The islanders are quiet, hard-working and simple, though intensely pagan, and in every inhabited valley one sees the red roofs of pagodas and temples, and pagan shrines on the mountain tops and at the sides of bridges. It must be confessed, however, that there is a strong breed of brigands and pirates.

It was in 1842 that the first Catholic Missionary put his foot on the islands and established himself at the port of Tinghai. This was Fr. Danicourt, a Vincentian Father, who afterwards became Vicar Apostolic of the Chekiang Vicariate, later of the Kiangsi. But there is a tradition that St. Francis Xavier, on his last journey, was obliged to land for some days, during a storm, on the island of Kindong in the Chusan Archipelago.

When Fr. Danicourt arrived on Chusan Island he found no native Christians, only the Catholic soldiers and sailors of the English occupation after the Opium War. There are many interesting stories of this good priest's devoted work among these poor men, many of whom had brought their young wives and children with them. Owing to the poor food, change of climate and bad housing, they died like flies and the little British cemetery at Tinghai is full of their tombs, on which we read the names of young men in their twenties with wives and children. Fr. Danicourt also nursed and helped them through a terrible epidemic of cholera.

He and his Bishop, Mgr. Rameaux, did much to break this very pagan ground, and gradually had a small number of fervent native Christians. The succeeding Bishop, Mgr. Lavaissière, was even more zealous, making his second residence at Tinghai in a tiny native house, and his work was much blessed. The number of Christians increased so rapidly that the pagans began to be uneasy; if a premature death had not carried off Mgr. Lavaissière it is said that the whole island of Chusan would have been converted. This zealous Missionary Bishop died in 1849 and, according to his own wish, he was buried in the islands. His tomb is seen to-day close to the Sacred Heart chapel at Hamen, a village about ten miles to the north-west of Tinghai. At that time the Catholics possessed eleven chapels in the island of Chusan, most of them old pagan temples which had been offered to them.

Alas, a terrible persecution broke out, owing to the imprudence of some of the new Christians and bad faith of others. Large bands of pagans, supported by the governing powers, attacked and demolished these chapels, among them that of the Sacred Heart at Hamen. They profaned the tomb of Mgr. Lavaissière and one can see to-day the marks of their blows on the stone, but the crucifix at the head is untouched, although they tried, without success, to smash it.

When the new Vicar Apostolic, Mgr. Delaplace, arrived in 1854, he found ruins and desolation awaiting him. Hardly a dozen good Christians remained. The new Bishop settled in a tiny native house in Tinghai and surveyed the situation. On all sides he was hated and despised, the chapels had been given back to the bonzes (pagan monks), and no one would sell land to the Christians. The holy Bishop was not discouraged; he awaited God's hour in prayer and patience. His decision was to go gently and use humble means. " Do a little, if you cannot do more, but do it always and do it well " was his motto. God rewarded the humble means he employed.

Among the few fervent remaining Christians was a zealous young convert, a blacksmith by trade. The Bishop named him his first *Médecin Baptiseur*, put a basket of simple remedies under his arm, and sent him to ply his trade at the forge, and at the same time visit and treat the sick people in a neighbouring island. He soon returned with an empty basket and a little harvest of five Baptisms of dying babies. From a second excursion came eleven Baptisms, from a third, seven.

The Bishop thanked God for a good beginning, and prepared to attack all the inhabited islands and the villages on Chusan in the same way. " Give me," he said, " five *Médecins Baptiseurs* and two Missionaries and the Chusan Archipelago shall be on fire! " Thus was the Medical Mission work and the Holy Childhood established in the islands. In less than three years there was a flourishing little orphanage in the charge of an old widow woman, and in 1868 the Sisters of Charity were brought to Chusan by a French gunboat to take on the work.

The first Sisters lived in a small native house near the North Gate of the city in a narrow, crowded street. They began at once to visit and treat the sick poor in the town and neighbouring villages, and little by little became known and much appreciated. It is interesting to know that amongst those first Sisters at Chusan was Sister Perboyre, the sister of the martyr. She was so successful in her ministrations to the sick that she soon became known among the poor Chinese outside as the " Old Doctor ".

The Sisters lived in great poverty during those early days, eating native food. The mother of Mgr. Ou, Bishop of Haimen (he is of a Chusan family), who died lately at the age of ninety years, related that she was the next-door neighbour of the Sisters in their first house. Knowing their poverty, she often used to pass to them, over the fence at the back, some fresh meat or vegetables.

Afterwards they moved to the present site near the West Gate opposite the fine church of St. Michael (which was built there);

but their works were arranged in the poorest and humblest manner. Indeed, when tired Sisters from the General Hospital, Shanghai, were sent to rest and have change of air at Chusan, they described the House as a " horrible hole ".

.   .   .   .

Before Sister Berkeley was nominated, the Sisters at Chusan had been left some weeks without a Superior. During this period Mgr. Reynaud, their Bishop from Ningpo, visited them, and naturally the conversation turned on the expected new Superior. Who would she be and from where would she come ? One of the Sisters, Sister C., a rather outspoken person, said to the Bishop, " We should like to have the big English Sister who is at Maison Jésu Enfant, Ningpo." " Oh, ho! " replied the Bishop. " You would like to steal our best Sister from Ningpo. Thank you! That would never do."

However, a few days later the new Superior was announced to be arriving with Sister Visitatrix.[1] Two Sisters went to meet the boat at the port, and as the little Ningpo steamer drew close to land Sister C. gave an exclamation of delight. " It is the big English Sister. Look! She is standing by Sister Visitatrix."

It was on May 3rd, the Feast of The Finding of the Cross, that Sister Berkeley arrived at Chusan, and she had a very warm welcome from the Sisters and children. She found a household of about 200—orphans, old people, sick and infirm—living in dilapidated houses, overcrowded and in great poverty. The House cash-box was empty and the rice granary had only one week's store left in it! The new Superior was obliged to begin life in Chusan by getting into debt, of which she had always a horror.

There is a letter written to her by her cousin, Sister Feilding, at that time, in which she sympathized with her over her debts and, with her usual generosity, managed to send her 100 dollars. When Sister Berkeley was named to go to Chusan, Sister Feilding was much disturbed, and wrote respectfully to expostulate with Sister Visitatrix, saying, " She will die of hunger at Chusan! " " Oh no, my dear Sister," replied the Visitatrix, " no one is hungry at Chusan; there are so many sweet potatoes."

In her old age one drew some memories from Sister Berkeley about those early days. She said:

[1] The Head Superior of a Province is called the Visitatrix.

When I came to Chusan, God showed me that He wanted me to gain souls for Him by the practice of great poverty. I found a House without foundation, with no annual income, living on gifts from day to day. All my life in Chusan has been spent in poverty, looking twice at every dollar, making sacrifices, but Divine Providence has never failed me. The House has been much blessed. God has worked miracles and many souls have been gained for Heaven."

For thirty-three years she laboured among the poor and suffering of the Chusan Islands and her charity and open door won all hearts.

Finding only 200 inmates in the House, Sister Berkeley promptly asked Our Lord to give her 500. Twenty years later, for her Golden Jubilee of vocation, the 500 were in the House and indeed more, and all were housed in good, strong, airy buildings with simple, homely comfort, and many new works had been organized. But in the first years she had to go very slowly and humbly; this was not easy for her energetic nature. One is reminded of another saying of the holy Bishop, Mgr. Delaplace: " At Chusan one must always go *la tête sous l'herbe.*"

One thinks of Sister Berkeley leaving her many works in Ningpo, her busy, full life, and then the sudden change to the quiet country place, in a small house, which had the reputation of being " impossible to develop ". It needed the " live wire " whom God now sent to Chusan. Among the Sisters she found in her new House was Sister Pauline Souen, the devoted Chinese Sister, who lived to the age of ninety years and died three months after Sister Berkeley.

In her old age, a companion asked her, " What did Sister Berkeley do during her first days in Chusan ? " Sister Pauline thought awhile, then said simply, " She dug new wells." " Ah," she continued, " you who are here to-day little know the poverty of this House when Sister Berkeley came to it. We had very little land, were overcrowded, with houses badly fitted up, poor food and insufficient fresh water. Often in the summer droughts, I had to go out at two o'clock in the afternoon with a man swinging two big water buckets from his bamboo pole, and we went to the houses of rich men to beg a little fresh water from them to cook the House of Mercy supper rice."

It was like Sister Berkeley to begin by making wells. She had heard of the terrible epidemics of cholera which swept over

Chusan and the islands, due to an insufficient supply of good drinking water. How often she was heard to lament, " With those lovely mountains, the people of Tinghai could have the best drinking water, if only someone would take the trouble to bring it into the town." She often spoke to the notables of this need. In later years splendid waterworks were made at Sinkomen, the fishing port on the other side of Chusan Island, and it was her grief that the same good work had not been done for Tinghai. However, on her land, more wells were dug, and big cisterns made into which all the rain water was drained and filtered; and in later years rarely did the House of Mercy suffer from want of good drinking water in the summer.

Another Sister, when asked the same question, said: " Sister Berkeley at once began to go every morning to the Chinese kitchen to arrange the dinner for the children and poor. At the hour of service she was always there in her white apron, to superintend the serving of the rice from the big cauldrons. She also visited the houses at the hour of dinner to see that all was cleanly arranged and served and everyone satisfied." This custom she continued until her eighty-second year.

When rice was bought or fish and vegetables arrived, she was always on the scene, watching the weighing, noting all and asking questions as to the quantities needed. She was much distressed to find that only one dish was served to the children and poor to eat with their rice; one day vegetables, another day fish.

In her first letters to her mother from Chusan she spoke of the poverty of the food, and the devoted mother gave a sum of money which, when invested, would provide a second dish each day for the Chusan family. Sister Berkeley took much care in arranging these dishes, and after her death a small notebook was found in which was written the suitable food to be eaten each month, e.g. fish when it was fresh and cheap, and the different vegetables and the way they must be prepared with sauce, etc., also the quantities required for drying and salting.

. . . .

The work of the *Médecins Baptiseurs* begun with such zeal by Mgr. Delaplace in the islands was carried on with great energy by the new Superior, who had devoted so much time to it in Ningpo. Over the big island of Chusan, through the long valleys into all the mountain villages she went with the Sisters, visiting and

G

treating the sick people and baptizing dying babies. She insisted
that all the Sisters in the House should take their turn in this
blessed and privileged work, the first given to them by St. Vincent.
The Chinese Sisters, who with their small feet could not walk
long distances, visited the streets and courts of the city.

Sister Berkeley wished each Sister to have some personal contact with the suffering poor and to care for them. She expected
all to take the trouble to arrange this and to be generous in replacing one another and lending their women servants to accompany the Sisters on their excursions. She also trained them to give
intelligent, beneficial service to the sick. Sometimes Superiors of
other Houses asked her how she managed to do so much outside
visiting at Chusan with so few Sisters. When she explained to
them how it was done, some thought that this would make great
disorder in the intern works, but Sister Berkeley used to say:
" One must sacrifice a little order and personal convenience and
think only of the welfare of the poor and the great work of saving
souls."

These " Baptism Expeditions ", as they are called in China, have
been much misunderstood and criticized, some people having the
idea that the Sisters roam about the countryside merely looking
for dying babies to baptize and doing nothing effective to cure
sick babies. This is not true. They go to nurse the sick poor in
their houses; the contents of one of their medicine baskets proves
this. These have to be arranged with great care to be as light as
possible, yet to have everything necessary to treat the sick people.

The medicines are arranged carefully in little packets which
can be handed out quickly: aspirin and quinine for fevers,
purges, iodine, sulphur-powder packets for itch, semen-contra
and bicarbonate of soda, boric ointment, bismuth, and a little
compartment for eye and ear remedies, heart tonics, a syringe
and injections. A neatly arranged pocket attached to the lid holds
forceps, scissors, and scalpel for opening abscesses. At the bottom
of the basket are bandages, compresses, also permanganate of
potash for making an antiseptic solution in which to wash and
dress ulcers and wounds.

Lastly we see the tiny pot of water and the little box of round
red plasters, one of which is stuck on the forehead of each baby
baptized. The parents never forget this red plaster, so that if a
baby recovered for a time one would know on the next visit that

it had already been baptized, but this is rare. The Sisters baptize
only when they feel sure that the baby will not recover, or is too
frail and delicate to be reared. Behind the pocket in the lid of the
basket are packed small gaily coloured bibs or bonnets for babies,
which are distributed here and there and give great joy to poor
mothers.

When her Sisters returned from these excursions, Sister
Berkeley not only wanted to know how many babies they had
baptized but also what sick people they had treated. Many sick
and dying men and women come in to the hospitals through these
visits; sometimes they return with the Sisters, or a sedan chair is
sent to carry them in the next day, if they cannot walk. It is a
great charity to nurse and restore to health a sick mother or father
with a big family; children too can often be cured of very serious
diseases, if brought into the comfort and efficiency of the hospital.
The gratitude of the country people is touching. They greet the
Sisters with: " Oh, what a long time it is since you came; we are
always looking for you."

In her first years at Chusan Sister Berkeley tried opening small
dispensaries at certain places to which the Sisters would come
once a month on a specific day. She organized one of them at
Hamen in the Residence of the Sacred Heart chapel, two Sisters
going there every first Friday of the month (an eight-mile walk).
Another place she tried was Tchusain, the nearest spot on the
continent, a district with thickly populated villages where the
little steamer from Ningpo stopped each morning and again in
the afternoon on its return trip.

But it was found that this work did not succeed very well, for
the country people did not remember the days on which the Sisters
were expected. They are very primitive and few leave their own
villages. Nothing succeeds so well as the house-to-house visiting;
a little dispensary is opened for a quarter of an hour in a courtyard and the sick people are seen more easily in their own houses.
Sister C., who was in charge of the workroom, says:

" Sister Berkeley said that I must also go out sometimes to visit
the poor. I remember her zeal for this work and how quickly she
walked; we could hardly keep up with her. I was frightened of the
Chinese dogs, which were sometimes very fierce in the country, and
she used to spread out her apron to shield me from them. If we

made all-day excursions, each one took in her pocket a rough sandwich, a native fruit and a bar of chocolate; she always gave us chocolate if she had any, saying that it was very strengthening on our long walks. This meal would be taken in a small room in the house of a Christian or pagan, and the people were delighted to give us some hot tea and rice. We soon realized what a good Mother God had sent us; she took such care of the Sisters and spared nothing to keep them well."

Sometimes excursions were made by boat to the islands; these always started with an *Ave Maris Stella* and the Rosary for the souls of the pagans around. Many years later, on a journey to Shanghai, Sister Berkeley showed a companion an island with a big fishing village on it. She related that once in her early days, having failed to land on two other islands because the tide was against them, they pulled into this one. To their surprise they were received by crowds of people in their best clothes, and they learned that it was a special day of sacrifice at the big pagan temple there, so all from the neighbouring islands were flocking in to take part in the ceremonies, bringing their sick children to place before the idols in the temple.

Truly the Hand of God led the Sisters there, for in other islands they would have found empty houses. A harvest of seventy baptisms of dying babies was gathered from that day's excursion. Ordinarily in Chusan the day's harvest was between fifteen and twenty, or even less, for the children are more healthy and the villages scattered, not like Ningpo, teeming with people crowded together.

In 1914 a good Missionary wrote a beautiful article in the *Ningpo Herald* on this work of the *Médecins Baptiseurs*. We quote some of it as it is very apropos at this moment when this work is much criticized and misunderstood.

" How many little pagan children around us seem born only to die quickly. If we cannot gather them into our Christian orphanages, at least we can try and procure for them a better and happier refuge in the glory of Heaven. The Baptism of these little pagan dying children, before the age of reason, is the most beautiful and fruitful work of the Holy Childhood. It is often called the ' Angelic Work ', the work which makes Angels, for thousands of little souls are gathered into Heaven every year with so little trouble or cost and such a sure result.

" Many of these little pagan children are the most miserable of beings, weak, sick, neglected, knowing only the bitterness and

suffering of life. Yet it was for them that Our Lord said, ' Suffer
the little children to come unto Me, for theirs is the Kingdom of
Heaven.' He calls them, but how many obstacles surround them!
Far away from Christian influence, ignorance and the hatred of the
devil combine to deprive them of the grace of Baptism. Yet Our Lord
says to His missionaries, ' *Sinite* . . . help these little children to come
to Me; bring them to My arms for I have prepared a place for them
in Heaven.'

" So we have the privilege of opening Heaven to these poor little
dying pagan children. We pour the waters of Baptism on their heads,
saying, in the name of God, ' To-day I have given you life, I have
saved your soul for Heaven.' And Our Divine Lord, smiling at
them, says, as to the Good Thief, ' To-day you shall be with Me in
Paradise. Yes, to-day, perhaps in a hour or in a few minutes, you
will be with Me for ever in happiness.' When a little child dies
after Baptism there is no doubt of its salvation; every Baptism saves
a soul.

" We are not astonished to see in the history of the Missions in
China such constant persevering efforts to develop and carry on
this work by most of the greatest Missionaries, who knew its value.
It was the ' oasis in the desert ' of their hard and lonely labour for
souls. When they baptized even one little dying pagan baby, they
thanked God for having called them to China, and they forgot their
sufferings in the joy of this Baptism. They passed on this work to
their zealous Christians, training them to seek for these little dying
pagan children, and the work is still flourishing, sending thousands
of little angels to Heaven every year."

During these excursions Sister Berkeley sought out all the
Christian families in the villages and islands. She made friends
with them and invited them into the House of Mercy for the
big Feasts of the Church. Since 1868 there have been at least
four generations of married Holy Childhood girls. With the
valuable aid of Sister Pauline Souen, notes were made of the
families, the children who had already been admitted to the
Sacraments, and those who should be called in to learn their
prayers. Sister Berkeley soon knew them all and she became a
good mother to all. During her thirty-three years in Chusan,
grandmothers, mothers, children and sons-in-law, all came to her
in sorrow and in joy, sure of welcome and help.

During her second year in the islands Sister Berkeley had her
first experience of a typhoon. She describes it in a letter to
English children in 1912, from which we quote:

" A terrible typhoon has swept over this poor stricken part of
China. It would make your hearts ache to see the distress and

misery it has caused. Howling gales of wind and storms of thunder and lightning, such as you never experience at home, caused the rivers to break their banks and to plunge the whole country into one vast sea of rushing water. Towns and villages were carried away. The poor inhabitants clung in vain to the wrecks of their houses; they were washed away by thousands.

" In one case, a poor little girl, who had floated down on a beam, was saved; she was the only survivor of her family and was calling piteously for her parents. Now these little orphans are brought to us in large numbers and must be fed and brought up. I know you will help us in this blessed work, and you will share the privilege that we have of bringing up these little souls to the knowledge of God and the True Faith."

She continues in the same letter:

" Not long ago we had quite a festive day, opening a chapel far away in the mountains and blessing a statue of Our Lady that had been given to us for it. The Christians on that side of the island are very scattered and it is too far for them to come often into the town; so one of the Missionary Fathers will go to say Mass sometimes in this little mountain chapel. Our Holy Childhood children walked in procession for the opening and sang the Mass so well. They had a very happy day.

" It is interesting to know that this was the chapel of the Sacred Heart, built at Hamen to replace the converted pagan temple there, which had been taken back by the bonzes. The new chapel, with a little residence for the visiting priest, is quite near to the tomb of Mgr. Lavaissière and the pagan temple is still there. When one visits Hamen, it is strange to go into it, again full of its pagan idols and superstitions and to think that the Holy Sacrifice was offered there on the same altar that the pagans now use for their sacrifices to the devil. Quite lately a visiting priest, examining the temple closely, found a stone near the altar marked I.H.S. He reverently removed it."

IX

NEW RESPONSIBILITIES

Visitors from Ningpo—The First Cholera Epidemic—The Holy Childhood Children

IT has been said that if one spirit more than another is supposed to characterize the Community of the Sisters of Charity, it is the spirit of sacrifice. They must be ready to go here, there, according as the duty of obedience or needs of souls calls them. It doubtless cost Sister Berkeley much, humanly speaking, to leave her Ningpo works, especially that of the *Jeunesse Ouvrière*, which she had helped to found and develop. To her grief, this work declined for a time after her departure, due partly to misunderstandings and also to the disturbed times of the country. For women and girls the workrooms were continued, but the boy weavers and designers were dismissed.

Sister Berkeley related that many of these poor lads followed her to Chusan and begged her to install the weaving school there, but it was not possible. Chusan is not a silk-producing district; there are no mulberry trees or silkworms, and Sister Berkeley was not in a position, when she first arrived, to undertake new works. She was crippled with debt and had to feel her way slowly.

She had great pity for these poor boys, received them with kindness, gave them a night's lodging, meals and their fare back to Ningpo, but even in her old age she spoke of them sitting disconsolately on the city ramparts opposite the Sisters' House. In later years, grown-up men often came to visit her, bringing their families, saying, " Don't you remember me ? I was one of your weaving boys at Ningpo."

Not only the Ningpo boys flocked to Chusan, but women and children also, who were inconsolable at Sister Xavier's departure. The famous Tchingvong, of whom we have spoken, brought her children and baggage and announced her intention of staying with Sister Xavier in Chusan. Others wished to do the same. They said, " She belongs to us, ' Xavier Momo '. She is a Ningpo *Ninn* [person]; she was so many years with us, we cannot live without her." But Sister Berkeley firmly and gently sent them all back to their own work in the Ningpo House, though they never forgot her, and when she visited Ningpo numbers of her old friends always flocked to see her.

The work for the boy weavers was later installed at St. Joseph's Hospice, Malou, where it was successfully carried on. It was not really a Sisters' work and the founders always prayed (and hoped) that it would be confided to Congregations of Brothers. Later they welcomed warmly the coming of St. John Bosco's sons, the Salesians, to China.

.   .   .   .

In her spiritual notes we see that at Chusan Sister Berkeley set before herself firmly the work for which she believed God had brought her to China. The means to be used were: humble prayer and self-abasement which would draw her to interior close union with God, with but one aim—the accomplishment of His Divine Will and in the way He wills. The Chusan Islands, teeming with paganism, stirred her missionary soul and she set to work with zeal and energy.

The natural beauty of her new surroundings gave her great joy. She loved the mountains and the islands in the sea and we see in her notes that she takes herself to task seriously to purify this love.

" A Sister of Charity lives a supernatural, not a natural, life; her pleasures are supernatural, her wishes are supernatural and above the comprehension of externs. Natural pleasures have been spurned; it would be folly to return in the least to them. What natural pleasures come your way ?—Fine views, etc. They are a present from God, enjoy them, but preserve moderation. Do not let nature get the upper hand, or let externs think that you are repining for other pleasures outside the supernatural ones of your vocation."

On one occasion, many years later, she was standing on a first-floor veranda of the Sisters' House, the eastern side, and she pointed to a big ugly Chinese house and said, " We used to have a glorious view of the mountains on this side, until a wretched man built his house there and blocked it." A few minutes later she walked to the western side of the veranda and her companion said to her, with a twinkle in her eye, " We used to have a glorious view here of the mountains on the west, until a wretched woman built a big house for her orphans and blocked it!" She laughed and took the joke against herself; but when one saw her enjoying natural beauty one always felt that she was seeing God's work in it and thanking Him.

Another fierce typhoon brought a rickety old building containing a nursery dormitory crashing to the ground; beams, bricks and tiles all fell on the little beds, which, thanks to an ever-watchful Providence, had been vacated just twenty minutes before. Sister Berkeley had not delayed in laying the needs of her new Mission before her good friends in America, though she begged them not to diminish the alms for Ningpo houses as their needs were also great.

Fr. Walsh, of the Boston Office of the Propagation of the Faith (later Bishop Walsh, founder of Maryknoll), sent her generous help, and the Rev. John Dunn (later Bishop Dunn of New York) was also a valuable friend of those days. They found new godmothers for the Chusan babies and gathered gifts for the rebuilding of the ruined dormitories. Sister Xavier built a strong new block, with a new dispensary on the ground floor, and above, two big airy rooms which she really intended for schoolrooms but which for the time being had to be used as dormitories.

Another of her first works at Chusan was to make a school for the younger children. She related: " I found them having no schooling, only just sitting round their refectory, roaring the catechism and prayers." With the arrival of a new Chinese Sister to help her, the children had real primary education, and Sister Berkeley insisted that the girls in the workroom should also study for a certain part of the day.

In 1912 came a terrible epidemic of cholera. A letter to England describes its horrors:

" We had about sixty cases in our own House and over forty died, generally in a few hours. It was most heart rending; each night, we never knew who, and how many, would be dead in the morning! Children quite well at breakfast suddenly fell ill, walked of their own accord into the cholera room, received Extreme Unction and were in their coffins before midday. We could not get enough coffins, and two little ones were frequently nailed down and carried out in the same one."

This was only the first of three devastating epidemics of cholera which Sister Berkeley experienced at Chusan. Though she had arranged for a good supply of pure drinking water for her household, there were still other problems to be solved for safety against this terrible scourge. The House of Mercy was situated close to the city walls, inside the town. About eighty yards between it and the walls was a straggling village where huts were crowded together and teeming with the lowest class of people. It is said in China that respectable people never live close up to the city walls; you find only beggars and rascals there.

Cholera broke out in this big village of Lokodio, and, according to the pagan superstitions and customs, no dead bodies were put into the coffins until the hour and day fixed by the diviners. The result was that the corpses were lying two or three days exposed in the heat of August, and this only a few yards from the Sisters' orphanage! The infected odours were unbearable, night and day; the priest saying Mass in the chapel could hardly continue to the end, and naturally the children succumbed one after the other, dying like flies.

Sister Berkeley was almost desperate, for not only was infection gaining new victims but also fear, which in cholera is a strong agent for its spreading. The children were terrified and the strength of the Sisters, under the strain night and day, was giving way.

A sudden idea came to her; she must get them away and as soon as possible. She sent word to the priest in charge of St. Vincent's Mission, Podong, outside the North Gate, in the mountains, and begged him to receive her children and pack them into empty barns. The good priest at once invited them, and Sister C. relates: " We packed up everything and rushed the living children out of the House to the mountain village of Podong; as soon as they got outside the city gates and on the rice paths they were different, and began to laugh and enjoy the outing, and there were no more cases of cholera."

The priest in charge of the Podong Mission at that time was Fr. A. Defebvre, C.M. (now Mgr. Defebvre, Bishop of Ningpo), and he gave them a warm welcome, putting a big farmhouse at their disposal. Bishop Reynaud of Ningpo sent special messengers to enquire for them and huge packets of biscuits which the children were delighted to receive. A big barn was used for dormitory, refectory and even workroom, for the embroidery frames were brought and the big girls set to work, though often out in the fresh air. Sister Berkeley came to see them every second day and Sister C. did the shopping and cooking.

Though the cholera for that year was finished, the danger for coming years remained, and Sister Berkeley set before her the accomplishment of the only efficacious remedy—to buy up the land between the House of Mercy and the city walls, to demolish the village and build a big healthy house for her children on the site.

We read in a letter to England at that time:

" We have been praying our hardest to be able to buy the tract of land over our boundary wall, where hovels are crowded together, full of people, filthy and foul, physically and morally. The proprietors formerly were opposed to selling but are now offering a portion of the land, so we are storming Heaven for the wherewithal to buy it. It is a terrible price, about £250 for the whole tract. They are now offering one third of the land, for £85; if we accept, they will gradually sell the rest. To secure this land is a most important matter for this House.

" I am sending you a photograph of our children playing on the hillside; it was taken last Sunday. See how strong and healthy they are. Well, just before the cholera, numbers more of our little ones were just as healthy, jumping and dancing about the garden one August evening, and before morning a number of them were lying dead or dying, felled by the foul odours that came from our unfortunate neighbours. If we can get possession of this land, we can purify our surroundings, enlarge our works, and have a clear, healthy space up to the city walls, beyond which is open country. We are imploring Heaven to hear our prayers."

It took Sister Berkeley ten years to gather sufficient alms to buy this land and build a good children's house.

One often heard that she was rich, had rich relatives and friends and could get all she needed without difficulty. This was far from true; her own personal inheritance was long ago exhausted, and in her native country those who possessed land and property were in very low water in those years. Sister Berkeley's devoted mother and sisters helped her in every way possible, gathering in gifts from those interested in Foreign Mission work in China, but the first need at Chusan was the daily rice and the upkeep of the works, with gradual improvement in equipment for simple comfort and health.

There were some who complained that Sister Berkeley was too

careful over little things, always hesitating at a new expense. When she heard this complaint she would smile and say quietly, " They do not know how poor we are. We are always waiting for something to arrive, but knowing that it *will* arrive; Divine Providence never fails us."

With *la tête sous l'herbe*, she slowly arranged the houses with the strict necessaries and developed the works. They were hard years through which she passed, but in her old age she said that the worst were those of the cholera days. They sapped her strength and courage, for she was no longer young but in her fiftieth year when she came to Chusan. In her spiritual notes we read:

" The greater part of my life is passed; during the short time that remains let every act, every minute, be for God."

The Sisters with her were most of them with delicate health and feeble strength, sent to the good air of Chusan for those reasons. Sister Berkeley said: " The human loneliness sometimes was intense; no one to turn to for advice, no doctor, no nurses. All treatment seemed useless; one was almost in despair." She appealed to Shanghai for help, but none could be sent. Before the Blessed Sacrament in the chapel she drew her strength and renewed her confidence. We read in her notes:

" Receive trials, sufferings, humiliations with the same fearless simplicity and spirit of Faith. God has allowed them to happen; it is therefore His Will you should bear them.

" His Will and only His Will and in the way He wishes. Let this submission make you indifferent to success or failure, you work entirely for Him.

" Look on the Cross and then you will not shrink from any suffering or sacrifice.

" Hunger and thirst for Our Lord in Holy Communion, prepare for His coming with humility, confidence and love."

In the later years at Chusan Sister Berkeley received every summer generous gifts of anti-cholera vaccine, first from the Pasteur Institute and afterwards from the Shanghai Public Health Office. Not only the inmates of the House of Mercy received this injection but it was given to all in the town who wished for it. Sister Berkeley sent her Sisters to establish centres here and there in shops to which the people round about could come. So near was it to her heart to prevent this terrible disease, for she had suffered so much from its ravages during her early years in Chusan.

In all their expeditions to the country and islands through the summer months the Sisters took syringes and anti-cholera vaccine. At first it was sometimes refused by the country people with fear and suspicion, but hostility rapidly disappeared, and for ten years or more, until the Japanese occupation, the Sisters gave thousands of anti-cholera injections throughout the islands and the people were saved from epidemics. This great charity was made possible by the generous aid of the Shanghai Public Health Office of the International Settlement.

. . . .

As a missionary Sister in China, Sister Berkeley put her hand to every kind of charitable work, yet the one nearest to her heart was that of the Holy Childhood children. She had already served her apprenticeship in the crowded nursery of babies at Ningpo, and at Chusan her love and devotion for the children was outstanding. She saw the Divine Infant in each one of them, and spared nothing for the salvation and well-being of these little chosen souls, who help to form the foundation of the Church in their native land.

At Chusan fewer babies and children are received than at Ningpo, where sometimes over 2,000 a year are brought to the Sisters, many of them in a dying condition. In the Chusan House of Mercy the yearly numbers average 150 to 200. They are, however, more healthy children and larger numbers in proportion are reared. Most of them come of respectable though very poor parents, and the death of the mother is generally the cause of the baby being given to the Sisters, or it may be that there are already too many girls in a very poor family.

Sometimes the bell rings in the night and a kind steamer-man hands in a basket, which the catechist of a port farther down the coast has confided to him. Inside two or three little black heads show themselves among the rags. It may be from an inland mountain village that a kind-hearted neighbour brings an unwanted third or fourth girl from a poor family. Perhaps he picked up the bundle on the mountain side, and he offers it to the Sisters, saying, " I know you do good works."

A rich mother brings her babe or little girl, terrified because the bonzes tell her that it was born on an unlucky day and will bring misfortune on her family; so the little one must be destroyed or hidden. On one occasion such a mother consulted the " Devil's Advocate ". Should she kill the child, or give her to the bonzesses, or send her to the Sisters ? The answer from the devil was, " If you wish your child to be the least unhappy possible, give her to the Sisters." Here we see the devil forced to give in to the Will of God, who wanted that little soul.

Again, a party of starving children from a famine district are put off a boat at the port, whence friendly rickshaw men bring them with confidence to the House of Mercy. The Guardian Angels are busy day after day, bringing in these little souls who have been specially chosen by Our Lord for Heaven. Sometimes a quick glance at a newcomer shows that there is no time to be lost and the babe is baptized by the Sister on the spot; perhaps in less than half an hour the little one flies away, having just looked in for a " ticket to Heaven ". In the Missions the Sisters often call them the " Little Thieves of Heaven ". But the greater number, having been comforted and fed, receive Baptism in the big church with all ceremony and then become members of this happy family of Catholic children.

An amusing story called *The Brown Paper Parcel* was sent by Sister Berkeley to her friends, the children at home:

" It was not the postman who brought this ' brown paper parcel ' to the Sisters on Chusan Island, but a big schoolboy of about fifteen. And such a parcel! dirty, torn paper and bits of old string! Where did it come from and what was inside ? When the boy offered it to the Sister, she wonderingly turned back a corner of the paper— behold, a little baby! Sister carried it carefully away to the nursery, where it was unpacked, the dirty paper thrown away, and the little blackheaded baby cleanly dressed, tucked into a warm crib and fed with a bottle of good milk.

" After a sleep, she was wrapped in the gaily coloured Baptism cloak and taken to the church to be made a Child of God. She was named ' Madeleine Sophie ', for she was to be the godchild of a zealous band of Child Missionaries in a Sacred Heart Convent. Their first adopted baby went to Heaven after a bad attack of measles, so a new one had to be given. These little godmothers now have the ' brown paper parcel ' baby, as well as a little angel in Heaven to pray for them.

" Back from Baptism there must be a snapshot taken of the transformed parcel. Nurse Martha takes Madeleine Sophie in her arms, dressed in her padded red coat, clean bib and knitted bonnet of red, blue and gold. There is plenty of colour in the Chusan nursery. Madeleine Sophie comes before the camera and she looks contented until the moment arrives to snap. Suddenly her mouth begins to open and shut like a tiny baby bird in a nest. Impossible to take the photograph!—evidently a sudden attack of ' dobie-gnaw-se-lai ' (hunger) has come upon her. There is nothing for it but to bring a bottle of warm milk. She drinks, smiles, and the camera snaps. Presently a good nurse from the country comes and takes her away; she will be brought in on the first of the Moon every month to be inspected and the nurse paid.

" Now a word about the boy who brought the parcel. He is the son of ' Pingsang Siesang ' (Mr. Pingsang), a very good Christian who keeps a general shop at Tsadio, a big village on the nearest point of the continent to Chusan. More than thirty years ago Pingsang Siesang was the only Christian at Tsadio; behind his shop lived a poor crippled woman. She heard of the ' White hat Sisters ' at Ningpo who cured many sick people, so Pingsang sent her there for treatment. Nothing could be done for her crippled legs, but she became a Christian and stayed with the Sisters to help them in whatever way she could.

" Pingsang Siesang often came to visit her, for he was a kind man. When she was converted, she used to reproach him with his want of zeal. ' You have been a Christian such a long time,' she said, ' and you have done nothing to convert the people of Tsadio.' So Pingsang went to the Bishop and asked him to send a catechist and build a chapel there. ' When you have seventy Christians ', said the Bishop, ' I will build a chapel.' Poor Pingsang thought this was a very big number, but he set to work and very soon there were over 100 Christians at Tsadio and the neighbourhood around and now there are over 300. The chapel was built, the catechist sent and it became a flourishing Christian district.

" Pingsang had one precious son and he carried abandoned babies regularly to the Sisters at Chusan. People know that if there is a motherless or unwanted baby or a little blind, infirm child that no one wants, they only have to take them to Pingsang, and he will undertake to send them on to Chusan. It is nearly always his school-boy son who says, ' Father, let me take it ', and he puts some ground rice biscuit in his pocket to feed it on the journey. He first takes a boat along the canal to Tchusain and then the little steamboat to Tinghai, carrying the dirty little bundle so carefully and paying no attention to the laughs and jeering remarks he receives from those around.

" Sometimes he says to the Sisters, ' How many babies have I brought this year ? ' or he asks after special babies. ' How is the pretty one I carried last time ? ' or ' Is the one with the sore legs better ? ' He wants no reward, and if offered his boat fare he says, ' Oh no, my father would not like that.' He will not even stop to ' eat rice ', but the Sisters bring him a big slice of English bread, thickly spread with jam, and this he takes with a schoolboy's delight, like the famous Irish ' Patch.' Say a little prayer for this zealous apostle of the babies."

As at Ningpo, foster-mothers are sought for to bring up the tiny babies and this work is very successful at Chusan. Nurses in the mountain villages and islands are numerous and the babies thrive in the good air. On the first of the Moon, when they are brought in to be inspected and the nurses paid, it is indeed a noisy day, for everyone shouts. Being a mountainous country, the normal speaking voice at Chusan is as if you were calling your neighbour on the next mountain!

Sister Berkeley watched very closely over her babies in the country; only good nurses were given babies and they were frequently visited. She liked to bring the children in from their nurses at two years of age, though this was a great grief to the poor women. The reason was that when weaned they do not receive enough nourishing food in the poor country families— too much sweet potato! Also, at Ningpo, where they leave the children with the outside nurses up to four or five years, being a very crowded House, it was Sister Berkeley's experience that these little Christian children were often taken to adore idols in the pagan temples with their foster-parents, and many had already learnt pagan superstitions and prayers.

It was the dream of her last years to build a large house for these " toddlers " from two to four years old on the mountain outside the North Gate, where they would get a good start in health and strength before being exposed to infectious diseases in the city, such as the terrible Chinese measles, which kills so many little children, especially when numbers are living together.

This dream was partially realized in later years by the little convalescent house of " Lorette " on the North Gate mountain, where at least a dozen babies could be tucked in with the bigger, delicate children. Many lives were saved there, not only of the children but also of tired and convalescent Sisters from the city houses in China, another good work to which Sister Berkeley gave herself with great enthusiasm and devotion.

The real " Toddlers' House " is still waiting to be built. The site of it is there behind Lorette and the first foundation gift arrived for it, with its name: " The Elizabeth Ann Seton Babies' Home ". The Japanese war prevented further developments, but it will surely come some day.

The little ones of seven had the joy of making their First Communion, when His Holiness Pius X gave them this

RESCUED BABIES,
CHUSAN

THE BABIES
GROW UP

ON THE MOUNTAIN
AT LORETTE

AIMEY, KONEYPAO, HONGSI, FOUDGHING

VEH-CHE-KO-MAH?   HAVE YOU EATEN YOUR RICE?
LAIKE-CHE   WE ARE EATING IT NOW

wonderful privilege. Those early Communions gave intense joy to Sister Berkeley and she fostered them in every possible way. She often spoke of the great change in the children's characters through this privilege of early Communion. " They are quite different," she said, " and their pagan instincts less strong."

A Sister who arrived in Chusan in 1923 relates:

" I was immensely struck by the fervour and joy of these little Chinese children in their Communions, and their confidence that their prayers would be answered. They had at that time a devoted parish priest, who loved and reverenced the Holy Childhood children. One day I heard him say to Sister Berkeley, ' I must speak to that little girl [he named one]; she is always laughing when I give her Holy Communion.' The child was called and he said to her rather reprovingly, ' Why do you laugh when I give you Holy Communion ? ' The little one answered simply, ' Because I'm so pleased, Father.' The priest smiled and said no more."

These little children were Sister Berkeley's *Orantes*; she sent them to the chapel or confided to their Communions all the difficult affairs to be settled and there were many miracles of grace. Once one of their little companions was suffering from a terrible disease, *cancrum oris*; all her face, nose, etc., had fallen away but she could still swallow, so life dragged on in this horrible state. Sister Berkeley said to a band of First Communion children, " To-morrow morning, when you thank Our Lord for coming to you, ask Him to take little Ipao to Heaven quickly." The children nodded their heads; they understood. At half-past five in the morning Ipao took her breakfast and showed no signs of dying, but at ten minutes past six she slipped away to Heaven, just the hour of the Communion thanksgivings. The children were delighted but not surprised, for they were sure their prayers would be heard and answered.

H

X

THE GIRLS OF CHUSAN

The Workrooms—Preparations for Marriage—Married Life

THE bigger girls in the workrooms received the same love and care from their Good Mother as the babies, and under her inspiration the work produced by them improved greatly in quality and quantity. The London Committee for Technical Schools in China sent gifts regularly, but for some time Sister Berkeley shared these with Ningpo and Kuikiang. She made a workroom for outside pagan women and girls in Chusan, which was much appreciated by the Chinese of the town. Many interesting stories could be told of conversions which come in later life among these pagans, long after they have left the Sisters' workrooms.

We give one. One day a Catholic lady, with friends, was visiting a Protestant hospital in Shanghai. As they passed through the wards a woman was pointed out to them as being very strange. " Look," said the nurse, " she insists on that cup of water being placed at her bedside, but she never drinks." As the Catholic lady passed this bed, the woman called her and said, " You are a Catholic." " How do you know I am ? " asked the lady. " Because I see part of your Rosary hanging out of your pocket," answered the woman. " Quick, quick ! I want you to baptize me. I am going to die and I am waiting and praying for Baptism. The water is there in that cup. I know all the doctrine necessary; I believe in God and want to go to Heaven. I was a workroom girl in the Sisters' House at Ningpo many years ago, but being engaged in babyhood to a pagan man I could not be baptized. I have never forgotten what I learnt and I want to be baptized before I die." The lady baptized her and shortly afterwards the woman died peacefully.

In the Holy Childhood girls' workroom beautiful church vestments are made and Chusan is especially renowned for delicate gold embroidery. Sister Berkeley much regretted that the lovely coloured satin embroidery, China's native work, was no longer in fashion. As there was no sale for it, work had to be done which would buy the ' daily rice '—hand-made laces, Venise point lace, Filet and the beautiful white linen embroidery. It seemed strange to have to import Irish linen into a Chinese workroom.

The girls were also taught to cook, wash and make their own clothes and shoes. In later years, when the little sanatorium of Lorette was built, Sister Berkeley liked to send older girls there for a time to learn to be housekeepers in preparation for their married life. It was not all work and no play for them, and the Sister in the workroom complained sometimes that too many holidays were given, but Sister Berkeley used to say, " Their health is the only heritage we can give them."

Nothing pleased her more than to send her children to scramble on the mountains, for they have no bound feet in the Chusan orphanage and skipping and jumping are their joy. Even the blind and infirm went on these excursions, for it is the custom in Chusan to rear the infirm children among the others, if possible. Sister Berkeley said it gave them a happier life, and she would tell you with delight that the blind children found wild flowers like the others, in a marvellous way. Each infirm child had an " Angel Guardian " among her companions, who always looked out for her, and it was beautiful to see the children leading their blind friends up to Communion in the chapel.

There were also excursions to the opening of new chapels in country districts or on special Feast Days. The Holy Childhood children were much in demand because their choir was well trained and could sing the Mass on these occasions. Then when the business of the day and the picnic meal were over, there was always time for rest and recreation before starting back. That was the moment for the Sisters and their medicine baskets; if it was at a country chapel festivity crowds would have flocked in and the Sisters would be besieged on all sides for remedies and treatment. There were always some little " Thieves of Heaven " among their clients, which added to the joys of the day.

Those were indeed happy days, and the happiest person was the " Good Mother ", sitting among her beloved children with her beautiful smile. With her, they were always welcome, and the door of her room was always open to them. The Sisters'

House at Chusan is a low two-storied building of single rooms, side by side, each with a door in front and one at the back; to pass from room to room you must go outside.

Being in the centre of the compound, the covered way before the Superior's room was used by all, going and coming. From the children, as they passed to school or the dispensary, one would hear " Ta Momo ", and at once they received a smile and a nod. The tiny tots, with kindergarten manners, would sometimes make gracious bows, bobbing their heads with such jerks that Sister Berkeley would say, " I hope those heads won't drop off one day! " After this performance, they would shriek with laughter and race away to their nursery, but some would stay awhile, sitting on the step of the door or by their Mother's side, chatting. The photograph taken of her like that was not a posed one; it was snapped as one often saw her, with little ones by her side.

Married girls from the town or country villages, bringing in some lace or embroidery to be paid for, passed the door: " Ta Momo, I have brought my work." They got a smiling welcome and went on their way. A quarter of an hour later they returned: " Ta Momo, I have been paid and I am going home." Again a smile and perhaps a few words and invitation to dine if they were from the country.

A beggar would slip in by a side door, knowing that at the front entrance he would be told to sit down until someone came to attend to his wants. He preferred to look in at the window or the open door and present himself before " Ta Momo ", who would probably get up herself to fetch his dinner. New babies and children arriving, sick people and aged for the hospital and hospice, all were sure not to be refused at that door; there was always the same gracious welcome.

A newly arrived Sister from Europe said: " But this is terrible. How can you write letters or do your accounts? You should shut your door when you have important writing to do." " Oh no," said Sister Berkeley, smiling, " I could never do that; they would be so pained. Besides, if I shut my door, they would all go round to the back, and look in at the window to see what I could be doing to shut my door against them! "

.   .   .   .

When settlement in married life had to be arranged for her children, Sister Berkeley was not easy to satisfy. The Chusan

Holy Childhood girls are much sought for as brides, and
there is rarely a lack of Christian boys wanting a wife from
amongst them. Sometimes their importunity is rather trying when
there are no children old enough for marriage. Pagan girls are
married at fifteen, or even younger, but Sister Berkeley kept her
children until their eighteenth year, or later. Even then they
were often loth to go, and sometimes said with tears, " Let me
stay and ' eat good rice ' a little longer in my home here." To
' eat good rice ' means to be happy and prosperous in China.

The " Good Mother " made many enquiries about her prospective sons-in-law and had to be perfectly satisfied that they
belonged to good, practising Christian families, where there was
enough to eat, and proper arrangements made to receive a
daughter-in-law, before she would allow an engagement. If the
would-be husband lived in a village near by, she sent Sisters to
inspect his home; if farther off, a respectable Christian woman
who could be trusted. On one occasion the Sisters went to a village
where the family was pressing for a hasty marriage. They found
the new room for the daughter-in-law only half built and nothing
arranged. " Why did you say all was ready ? " they asked.
" Momo, the *pig* is ready to be killed! " was the answer. It was
the most important part of the wedding festivities.

The girls are always free to accept or refuse, and as far as
possible make their personal choice; one often saw Sister Berkeley
having long earnest conversations with them. Every child in
Chusan knows her native place and her surname (if she had none,
then one was given to her on arrival). You hear them saying,
" I am a Chepoo Ninn, Wenchow or Haimen Ninn, Chusan,
Sinkomen or Dgiansain Ninn." Sister Berkeley liked to marry
them into families in their native places if possible. Sometimes a
girl would say to her when a marriage was proposed, " I don't
mind about the man, but I have heard that he has a kind mother,
so I would like to go there." The mother-in-law is a big factor
in the lives of the daughters-in-law in China.

Sister Berkeley gave generous trousseaux to her girls and
industrious workers had an extra box of clothes. They were
married in state in the scarlet satin bride's clothes (hired), and
carried away in the big red ' marriage chair ' just like outside
girls. She always sent a good woman with them to the wedding
ceremonies in the house, so that they should not be frightened or

lonely at first. After a month or so of married life it is the custom
for the little bride to come back and visit her family. The Holy
Childhood girls come with joy, delighted to be children again in
their old home, though it is amusing to see them with the dignity
of little married women.

There were always many confidences to give to their Good
Mother; one saw them at her side, telling her all. One little
bride said dolefully, with tears in her eyes, " Oh, Ta Momo, it
is so dull being married. Here everyone is always laughing and
talking, but in my new home no one laughs, and *he* does not
talk to me! " One smiles at the young countryman, rather
taciturn, and tired when he comes in from work, not accustomed
to making conversation, but the little wife missed the gaiety of
the House of Mercy.

Another confided to Sister Berkeley, " Ta Momo, they say
that the mosquito curtain on my bed was only lent for the wedding
and must be returned. What shall I do, Ta Momo ? I shall have
no mosquito curtain on my bed and I shall lose face! " The Good
Mother at once sent a woman to buy a mosquito curtain and the
little bride went back happily with her package; she knew Ta
Momo would help her and not let her lose face. They were always
loaded with presents from the cupboards in Sister Berkeley's
room which her Sisters loved to keep filled for her—gaily coloured
stockings, handkerchiefs, scarves, etc.—and when the babies
arrived little outfits were sent to each one with a gift of money,
a Miraculous Medal and a packet of fine vermicelli.

On big Feast Days of the Church, many of these married
couples come in for two or three days, go to the Sacraments and
show their children to Ta Momo and the Sisters and receive words
of advice and encouragement. If some failed to come in for a
long time, Sister Berkeley sent a woman to call and find out the
reason. If there were disputes or unkind treatment she never
rested until things were put right.

The first years of the daughter-in-law are always hard until
the son arrives, but the responsibilities and duties of married life
are well explained to them, and the parish priest sends forth
these Holy Childhood girls as little apostles to their new homes.
" Remember," he says to them, " we look to you to keep the
Faith alive in your villages." Most of them do their best, helping

the priest by teaching catechism to the Christian children and leading the prayers in the chapels.

Some time ago, near the village of Hamen, a pagan man was possessed by the devil and in great suffering. The pagan monks were called in to help him and received large sums of money for their prayers and superstitions, but the man grew steadily worse. At last he called in the Christian catechist of that district; the young man gathered together several married Holy Childhood girls and brought them to pray at the man's side. He was cured, and he and his family all became catechumens, were baptized and around them have built up a new fervent Christian centre.

The young catechist spoken of was the grandson of a Holy Childhood girl. His grandmother was carried, many years ago, a little unwanted baby, to the Sisters' House and was brought up to be a good Christian wife and mother. In later life she accompanied the Sisters on their outside excursions, visiting the poor, and she herself baptized thousands of dying pagan babies. In her old age she was totally blind and lived for the joy of her daily Communion. The young wife of the catechist also belonged to a Holy Childhood family.

It was a great joy to Sister Berkeley when, in a Holy Childhood family, the priest discovered the dawning of a vocation in a much loved little son. She helped to send many, first to the Apostolic School, then to the Seminary, and it was a great day when she welcomed the young priest who came to say a Mass of thanksgiving in the Sisters' chapel. Sometimes she had several grandsons in the Seminary and she was a good Mother to all, following them in later years with her prayers and generous gifts.

Priests, European and Chinese, looked on her as a fairy godmother to supply their many wants. She kept in touch with friends at home and Altar Societies who would send vestments to the poor Foreign Missions. Big parcels of these arrived, especially from her good friend, Mrs. Begge, in London, and a visiting priest would not only receive a warm welcome from her but would take his choice of what he needed. She also wanted to know all about his Mission; she had such a wide outlook and was interested in any work for souls. The native priests, especially, who visited Chusan went away with fresh courage and zeal to their hard lonely lives. She nursed them when they were ill, and found benefactors who would send them gifts and Mass stipends.

In Ningpo we remember how she sympathized with the hard-worked, sick priests and said that the Sisters' House was a kind of " mother's home " for them. It was the same at Chusan. How many of them she received and nursed back to health and strength! Poor as she was, the best of everything must be got for them. They turned to her in their troubles; when famine seized their districts she received large bands of starving children at their request, from Haimen continually and from Wenchow in the great famine of 1930.

Fr. Marquet, C.M., of Wenchow, was heard once to say, " That good Superior, Sister Berkeley, never refuses me, no matter what I ask of her." Orphan children, poor women who must be got away from danger to their souls—he always turned to Chusan and got the same answer, " Send them along." We read in a letter, " In any work for souls, we are always ready to help you."

Once, the Superior of the pagan nursery at Wenchow, which is under the care of the Sisters, had three big girls sent to her by the municipal authorities. They had been stolen by brigands from their homes in Shanghai, and when the brigands were caught the girls were sent to the Sisters at the pagan nursery. The Superior had no place or means for bringing up big girls; what could she do ? She said, " I will send them to Sister Berkeley at Chusan; she will not refuse me." At once they were received into the Chusan family, were soon baptized and later married happily into Christian families. Bedridden and infirm people, those attacked with revolting skin diseases, etc., who were refused everywhere, always found a welcome and home with Sister Berkeley.

" The Open House " it was called by a new Visitatrix on her first visit. " It is a real House of St. Vincent, always open to the poor, and living by miracles of Divine Providence from day to day." Although she trusted entirely in Divine Providence, Sister Berkeley did not neglect human means to put her House on a good foundation. She bought small pieces of land, here and there, which were offered at cheap prices, and gradually, outside the West Gate, running along by the city walls, she had a big vegetable garden planted, and a small farm for pigs, cows and poultry. She bought a small island mountain in the sea which brought in good harvests of sweet potatoes, and on its rocky slopes she planted fir trees, the branches of which are cut for firewood in the autumn. One heard her say, " My successor will have good supplies of wood for cooking," and every year in the spring she insisted on hundreds of tiny new saplings being planted.

It must be said that Sister Berkeley had a very great affection for trees; in her old age she admitted that this love came from her childhood days, passed in a beautiful park full of noble trees. At Chusan she planted trees everywhere, much to the dismay of some who wanted more clear vegetable land, for trees are always growing and it was very difficult to persuade her to have even the branches cut. To her it was a mortal sin to cut down a tree! She said: " You pull down a wall; you can build it up again to-morrow if you have made a mistake. But a tree, oh no! How many years it will take to grow again! " God permitted that it was not until after her death in 1944 that the Japanese stripped her mountain lands of all the big trees to build their aerodrome; it would have been a great grief to her.

.   .   .   .

During Sister Berkeley's earlier years in Chusan, gunboats of many nationalities often cruised among the islands and their crews paid visits to the Sisters at Tinghai. Admiral Seymour of the English China Squadron was a Catholic and family friend of the Berkeleys. He often visited the Mission House on Chusan Island and he was much distressed on his first visit to find the little British cemetery at Tinghai in a very neglected condition. Sister Berkeley undertook to have it cleaned up, and she planted several good trees and made flower beds, with rose bushes, daffodils, jonquils, etc. Ever since, the Easter altars are always decorated with spring flowers from the British cemetery.

Later, Admiral Seymour was delighted to find it so well cared for. We have spoken of this little cemetery. It is a tiny plot of ground lying in a hollow behind the cliff at the eastern side of the port, on the slope of the mountain on which stands the big pagan temple called " Tsong-Ou-Kong ", which dominates the port of Tinghai. In this little cemetery are tombs of the officers, soldiers and sailors of the English occupation forces after the Opium War; there also are the names of many of their young wives and children.

Sister Berkeley took great interest in keeping this cemetery in good condition, though it was not easy with all the daily work to be done. In the hot months of the summer it had to be left for a while, as the mountain alongside is always covered with unburied coffins and this makes it an unhealthy spot and not safe in cholera months.

After the Japanese surrender in 1945, when the foreign Sisters returned to Chusan they found the cemetery in a sad state, its iron gates removed, tombs broken, and big holes in the walls, but the rose bushes that Sister Berkeley had planted were still blooming.

XI

THE WORK EXPANDS

St. Joseph's Hospital—A Permanent Doctor—Sister Vincent McCarthy

IN the early years at Chusan the *ko* (unthrashed rice) was always beaten and sifted by hand. Sister Berkeley wished to make one of the Chinese mills, worked by a cow or buffalo walking round and round in a circle, and she began to build one on her land, close to the Chinese kitchens. A deputation of notables arrived and implored her not to do this as they had the superstition that these rice mills must only be built outside the city walls, in the country; if placed inside they would bring great misfortune on the people of the city.

Though the building was nearly finished, Sister Berkeley, with her usual gracious friendliness, at once stopped it and gave up the project. We find among her papers a letter of grateful thanks from these Chinese gentlemen, who offered to pay the expenses. On another occasion she changed the arrangement of a new building, which they said " would give offence to the serpent which governed the road facing it, and also interfere with the wind and water spirits' influence "!

Sister Berkeley was much esteemed by the pagan Chinese of the town and had many good friends amongst them. Two of these, Mr. Ou and Mr. Li, helped her to buy land, that of the cholera villages and also that on which she built the men's hospital. For the latter, it was a very difficult business, because a rich merchant wanted it to build a big Chinese house for himself, and he offered a higher price than the Sisters could pay. As this land lay alongside the House of Mercy, it would have been very disagreeable for the Sisters to have a big pagan house there.

After several attempts Mr. Ou and Mr. Li said that it was impossible, and the idea must be given up, as they could not win the merchant over to help the Sisters. Sister Berkeley was

not discouraged; she lit candles before the Sacred Heart and set
her children to pray. Sister C., who spoke Chinese very well and
did all the business, went back to the two gentlemen and said,
"We must try again. My Superior is an Englishwoman and a
very tall one; when the tall English say they must have something, it has to be done!"

The two Chinese gentlemen smiled and bowed and the three
set off again to discuss the affair with the merchant and the owner;
but alas, these would only make one concession: that the matter
should be placed before the devil's advocate and his decision be
accepted. Knowing that they would probably bribe the devil, it
was rather a forlorn hope, but to the joy of all the devil's answer
was, "Sell it to the Sisters." The owner at once accepted,
though he received a lower price than the merchant had offered.

. . . .

In Chusan Sister Berkeley gave to the Medical Mission work
the same zeal and devotion that she had given to it in Ningpo.
We have told of her organization of the visiting of the sick poor
outside and the harvests of Baptisms that this work brought; it
is no exaggeration to say that she herself must have baptized tens
of thousands of dying pagan babies during her missionary life in
China. In the Chusan House of Mercy, from the earliest years,
the Sisters had opened a small hospital for the poor, in a few small
rooms. This was always full; good work had been done and many
souls saved, but it was carried on under very poor conditions.

Sister Berkeley wished to build a real hospital, but it was an
unrealized dream for many years until the arrival of an invalid
Irish Sister, Sister Gertrude Hanley, who was sent to Chusan
for rest and a change of air. Sister Hanley had many good friends
and relatives in America and she appealed to them for this good
work. There was a generous response and it is interesting to note
that most of the gifts came from Boston. Indeed Sister Berkeley
always said, "The men's hospital was built by Boston friends."
Later she said the same of the new Holy Childhood house.

On the famous piece of land which was sold to her by the devil's
decision, she built a nice little hospital, dedicated to St. Joseph.
He indeed watched over it, for there was no foundation or regular
income; it depended, like all the works at Chusan, on Divine
Providence, gifts from day to day. Rarely a patient entered who
could pay even the cost of his rice, though many showed their

gratitude for cures by bringing fowls, eggs, fish (from the fishermen) and sometimes a goat. These gifts were very welcome, for it was always a struggle to carry on from day to day.

In 1925, through the help of the New York Catholic Medical Board, the services of a trained doctor were secured. For many years at Chusan the nearest doctor to be called was at Ningpo, 100 miles away by sea; this often meant great anxiety in nursing the sick. Fortunately the doctor now secured worked also at a Protestant hospital in the town, so he was only engaged to visit the Catholic hospital when needed, which made it possible for the Sisters' limited means. Little by little the hospital equipment was improved and a small operation room fitted up in which minor operations could be performed. Later a laboratory was arranged, with the gift of a microscope.

This development in the medical work and the appointment of the doctor were made possible by the help of Sister Berkeley's devoted cousin, Lady Winefride Elwes. On a visit to the States, at this time, Lady Winefride appealed to her friends and addressed meetings to gather alms for the Chusan House of Mercy. The generous response made it possible to carry out many improvements, not only in the medical work but also for the comfort and health of the orphan children.

Many souls are saved among the patients in the hospitals, who, after their cure, go away with some knowledge of the One God and the True Faith which leads to eternal happiness; and there are conversions even of pagan monks (bonzes). One could tell many interesting stories, not forgetting cases of possession by the devil.

An old bonze over seventy years of age arrived exhausted with fatigue and illness. He was making a pagan pilgrimage, during which one of his vows was never to cut his toe nails! These were a sight to behold, like long curling feathers! He was instructed and baptized before his death. The bonzes, strange to say, are not difficult to convert on their death-beds; many of them are men who have studied deeply and done great penance in their lives. The mercy and forgiveness of Almighty God strikes home to them and they become like little children in their faith and simplicity. Some are tormented by the devil, and frankly say that he refuses to free them from his power, but prayer, the

Miraculous Medal and the Green Scapular are instruments which draw miracles of grace.

One pagan man, a warder in the prison, came to the hospital suffering from an internal cancer. Seeing all means for the cure of his body exhausted, he listened courteously to Christian instruction for the soul, but it seemed to make no impression on him. Suddenly he decided to go to the home of a friend to die, and sent for a sedan chair to carry him there. When the chair arrived he was too weak to sit in it, so an invalid chair was ordered for the next day.

The Sisters made last efforts that night to gain this soul; a Green Scapular was put under his pillow, a Miraculous Medal inside it, another at the foot of his bed, and all besieged Heaven with their prayers. The morning saw a wonderful change; this man, formerly so cold and reserved, was a different being. His first request was for the priest to come and talk to him again, and he told him that for many days and nights he had seen a black devil sitting at the foot of his bed, threatening him. That night it had disappeared and great peace had come to him, with a longing to save his soul for eternity in Heaven.

The priest found him quite ready to believe in the One, True God and very soon afterwards he was baptized and died peacefully.

A very touching side of the medical work in Chusan is the reception of the homeless dying, and there are many such cases. In one month alone, six poor consumptive fellows came in to die, being far away from their native provinces and with no means. After weeks of care and comfort, such poor men pass away peacefully, having received the grace of Baptism and sometimes other Sacraments also. They die thanking God for the charity which cares for the soul as well as the body. Some who have been cured come back, years later, to " die with the Sisters ", as they say.

Sister Berkeley also arranged better medical care for sick women and children. When she arrived at Chusan these were nursed in the Old Women's Home with scant comfort. She soon arranged a separate room, to which others were gradually added, until a well-equipped and comfortable Hospital for Women and Children was organized. Here she made a beautiful airy, sunny infirmary for her Holy Childhood children, and it was her joy to see it arranged with gay-flowered bedcovers and every comfort possible.

How often she mounted the stairs, even in her old age, to visit her sick children, always bringing some delicacy for them! She built up their strength with good nourishing food, fresh eggs, liver, etc., and if they expressed any want at once she fulfilled it, if possible. She was indeed a loving, tender mother, always wishing to be with them at the last moment if God called them to Heaven. She also visited the other patients, men and women, regularly, keeping *au courant* with their sicknesses, treatment, etc., and sympathizing with their sufferings. She would sometimes say to the hospital Sister, " That man wants to have a little packet of sugar by his bedside, for himself; get it for him," or mention some other wish of a patient.

The hospital Sisters in charge often spoke of the help she gave them, especially her practical advice, in the days when there was no doctor to appeal to. How often she pulled out her big Ningpo notebooks and remarked, " I had a case like that many years ago and Dr. Molyneux treated it with a very good prescription." She had her finger on the page in a few minutes. She particularly insisted on the convalescent patients being given very nourishing food to build up their strength.

Many young men with a tendency to consumption came in for a while to the hospital and with the help of homely remedies, good food, eggs, milk, cod-liver oil, etc., gained enough health and strength to go home and work again for many years. Sister Berkeley often said, " That ' boy ' must be cured " (they were all ' boys ' to her, and many of them were her sons-in-law and grandsons); " he has a wife and family. What should we do with another widow and five children on our hands ? " Sometimes it meant keeping the wife and children for some weeks while the father was undergoing treatment, for he was the " rice-winner ", and there was nothing to eat at home when he was laid up sick.

Bonzesses (pagan nuns) are much more difficult to convert than the bonzes, for they are generally very ignorant and proud, and the pride of ignorance is the most difficult to overcome. The Sisters are often called to treat sick bonzesses in their pagan convents, but unless they come to the hospital and die there it is very difficult to instruct and baptize them.

Sister Berkeley related that once at Ningpo she visited a sick bonzess, quite a child in her teens, who was wasting away from tuberculosis. At first, when spoken to of the Christian Faith, she seemed to want to listen, but always refused Baptism with a look of fear. The day she died a big serpent was seen coiled up under her bed; as soon as she was dead the serpent uncoiled itself and moved away!

For the poor, homeless pagans who came in to die Sister Berkeley could not do enough to make them happy; their faces lighted up when she entered the ward. Sometimes poor outcast women were heard to say, "All my life no one wanted me or loved me, and now the Sisters teach me that God wants me and loves me; they are so good to me that I believe them."

One poor old man over eighty years of age, begging in the streets, fell from exhaustion and was brought to the Sisters' hospital. He was not an ordinary professional beggar but had no longer anyone to care for him. When he was put to bed his personal belongings, clothes, etc., were put away, labelled, as is the rule, but he was very distressed about a little paraffin lamp to which he seemed much attached, and he continually asked for it. As he had not many days to live, the priest gave him the necessary instruction, preparing him for Baptism. One point is always difficult with the pagans: the forgiveness of those who have done them injury. The old man listened carefully, then he said, "Must I forgive the Sister who took away my little lamp?" Sister Berkeley insisted that his lamp should be restored to him, and he died peacefully with it beside him.

Some of the cases she presented to the hospital were those with sick souls. A Sister relates:

"I had not long arrived at Chusan when Sister Berkeley put me in charge of a new room which she wished to be organized as a real hospital for women and children. It had only six beds, six bed-covers and pillows and six chairs; everything else was wanting! At my look of dismay, she said with a smile, 'If you could have seen my hospital at Ningpo when I opened it; there was no glass in the windows and hardly any equipment!'

"Of one of the first patients she brought me, she said, 'Treat this woman for indigestion, but she is really here for her soul. She is from a Christian family but was married many years ago to a pagan without a dispensation, and she has forgotten how to go to the Sacraments. Sister Pauline will come and instruct her every day. Be very kind to her and her soul will be cured.'

"After some time the woman went to the Sacraments and when her pagan husband, a good man, came in to see her, her marriage was put right and she became an exemplary Christian. She converted

A HOLY CHILDHOOD WEDDING COUPLE

BRINGING THE FIRST BABY TO SHOW THE SISTERS

THE FIRST YEAR IN CHUSAN
Sister Berkeley with Sister Boscat and the old men

THE CHILDREN'S INFIRMARY (HOLY CHILDHOOD), CHUSAN

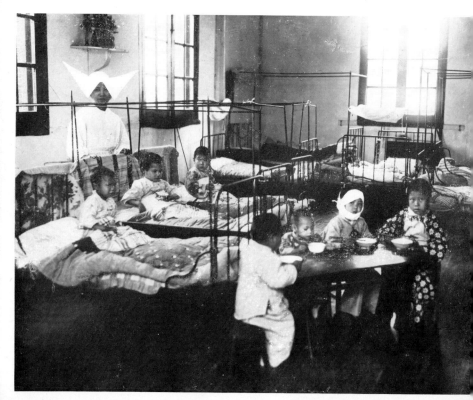

her husband, brought up her children well and formed a little Christian centre around her house."

This woman was one of the " big fishes " of Sister Pauline, the old Chinese Sister.   In the interesting notes of her life we shall see that she always called these souls that she was hunting for " big fishes ".   How many she caught and brought back to God! Sister Berkeley had the greatest veneration for her.

One day a rickshaw arrived at the door; in it was a dying woman with two little boys, aged eleven and six.   They had come in the little steamer from Sinkomen, the fishing port on the other side of Chusan Island.   The elder boy related, with tears in his eyes, that his father had died the year before, and they had been left in great poverty.   His mother became seriously ill and the neighbours advised him to bring her to the Sisters' hospital at Tinghai.

There was no time to be lost; the woman was quickly put to bed, gently washed, and given clean clothes, for she was in a terrible state of dirt and neglect.   Evidently she was of a respectable class, for tears of gratitude rolled down her cheeks.   " I had no one to care for me," she said.   " Oh, how good it is to be clean again."   Quickly the necessary instruction was given to save her soul, for in spite of heart injections and other remedies, the end was very near.   When a Miraculous Medal was shown to her, she gave an exclamation of delight.   " Why, it is the beautiful Lady on the tower of the Sinkomen Church!   They call her ' Sing-Mo-Maleeya ' [Holy Mother Mary]; I often look up at her; she shines in the sun."

When Baptism was offered to her, the little lad of eleven, with tears in his eyes, cried out, " Oh Mother, believe what the Sister tells you and you will go to Heaven and see ' Sing-Mo-Maleeya '." She was baptized, and her soul was with God only three-quarters of an hour after her arrival.   The two boys were sent to the Sisters' orphanage at Ningpo, where they have been baptized, are being educated, and will later learn trades and be established as Christian workmen.

There were many similar cases on both the men's and women's side; with Sister Berkeley, every work a Sister touched was for souls.   How many concessions she made, rules she relaxed in the hospital work, to " save that soul "!   Sometimes she heard that a poor man or woman was dying in a beggars' shelter; at once she sent a nurse with a rickshaw to bring him or her in.

I

Another charity she showed them, which will be hardly understood by foreigners. Some of the dying patients, who had no relations or who were far from their native places, were much distressed at the thought of dying and not having a big Chinese coffin to be buried in. The Chinese think much of their coffins and the hospital could only give rough ones of four planks, made by their carpenter. Sister Berkeley used to send to a rich man in the city, and ask for a coffin for a poor respectable man or woman; she was rarely refused in the good old days before the war. It is a charity much practised by the Chinese. The poor patient would die in peace, thinking that he had not " lost face " even after death.

. . . .

The year 1922 saw the coming to Chusan of Sister Vincent McCarthy, aged eighty years, who asked to spend her last days with Sister Berkeley. This holy old Irish Sister was in the Paris Seminary with Sister Howard in 1868; she worked for some years in the Liverpool Blind Asylum, but in 1877 she came to China and was one of the first band of Sisters to go to Tientsin after the martyrdoms of 1870. These Sisters were taken into the city in closed sedan chairs, without cornettes, and entered their new House with the greatest secrecy. For many months they suffered through having practically nothing to do, but little by little their care of the poor in the dispensary became known and appreciated and they could go out with safety. Their devotion to the victims of a bad cholera epidemic cleared the air and the usual works started again.

Later, Sister McCarthy was Superior for many years at Kuikiang Hospital, then at the General Hospital, Shanghai, where she was much esteemed by the foreigners of that big port. When the Sisters were withdrawn from the General Hospital in 1913 by their Superiors, as their work there was chiefly for the rich foreigners and they could not follow the works of their vocation among the Chinese poor, Sister McCarthy was again sent to Kuikiang for a time, but she spent the last two years of her life at Chusan.

All around her, Sisters and Chinese, were greatly edified at this holy old Sister, who, in spite of her great age, continued caring for the poor, working daily in the dispensary. The pagan gentleman, Mr. Ou, who had so often helped the Sisters to buy land

and do other Chinese business, was immensely struck to see this aged Sister still working for the poor. Every day she went across the road to visit a poor sick woman and to dress her leg, which was covered with foul ulcers. Mr. Ou often watched her from a distance with profound respect.

In the autumn of 1922 cholera broke out again at Chusan in the town but there were very few victims in the Sisters' houses. Amongst them was their compradore, a good Christian man, who had been so imprudent as to eat some small fresh river water fish, which are very dangerous in times of cholera. Sister McCarthy, thinking herself at her age immune, nursed this man and she fell a victim to cholera, dying within twelve hours.

No European priest was in the islands at that moment, for the parish priest was away making his Retreat. Sister Berkeley sent an urgent messenger by the early morning Ningpo steamer, calling for a Ningpo priest to come by return, but it was not until six o'clock in the evening that Fr. Buch, C.M., arrived. Sister McCarthy had died at midday. A Chinese priest was with her and gave her the Last Sacraments.

The Holy Childhood children followed her coffin in procession to the Sisters' cemetery outside the North Gate, singing the *In Paradisum* and chanting the prayers for the dead. They passed the house of Mr. Ou, who accompanied them part of the way, listening to the chants with great interest. The next day he came to ask Sister Berkeley what the children were singing, and she explained to him that they were calling the angels to come and carry the old Sister to Heaven.

A few weeks later Mr. Ou's wife died and he hastened to the Sisters and begged that the children should come and sing at his wife's funeral, so that the angels would carry her to Heaven. It was explained to him that this could not be as his wife was not a Christian, who believed in God and Heaven. Not long afterwards Mr. Ou himself was struck down with serious illness. Knowing that his end was approaching, he sent for the Sisters and begged to be instructed and made a Christian, so that he could go to the " Heaven of the old Sister ".

Sister Pauline visited him with Sister Berkeley and they instructed him very carefully. He received Baptism with great joy, but one thing troubled him. He knew that his sons and their families would offer pagan sacrifices and prayers to the devil for him after his death, and indeed they were already doing so; the beating of the gongs and the prayers of the bonzes could be heard in the rooms below. It was explained to him that these pagan proceedings of his family would not affect his soul, which was ready to go to Heaven. He then called his family around him, and said to his sons, " I am going to the ' Heaven of the Sisters '. I go my way; you go yours." Shortly afterwards he died peacefully.

XII

THE GREAT WAR AND AFTER

*Poverty and Isolation—Father Walsh of Maryknoll at Chusan—
Sister Berkeley's Visit to Europe, 1923*

THE years of the first great war, 1914 to 1918, were hard
ones for the Foreign Missions and for Chusan especially
in its isolated position. Sometimes months went by without news from Europe and naturally very few alms came through
from that side. There is a little notice written by Lady Catharine
Berkeley in 1916, which she sent to the *Tablet*, the leading Catholic
journal in England. In it we read:

> " I have just received a very distressing account from the Convent
> of the Sisters of Charity at Chusan Island, China, of the great
> poverty to which they are reduced and the consequent difficulty
> they have in maintaining their technical schools, orphanage and
> other good works.
> " The stress of the war, which is devastating the West, is also
> felt acutely in the East, and though the Sisters are straining every
> nerve to make ends meet, they are actually in want of the necessaries
> of life for their children and poor people.
> " Although the needs of our valiant soldiers at home have a
> supreme claim on us, I cannot resist making known the vital needs
> of those other soldiers of Christ, who are fighting His battles in the
> pagan East and rescuing His little ones from pain, sorrow and
> infamy."

There is also a letter to children at that time, dated 1916:

" My very dear Children,
" How can I thank you for coming to the help of your little brothers
and sisters in China at a time when this help is much required ?
In England you are all very anxious about this terrible war, probably
your father and brothers are fighting and in danger and yet your
warm little hearts make you still remember poor little children in
China.
" Some of the babies you have helped us to save have reached
the age of seven and, like you, have been allowed, though so young,

to make their First Communion. Now, since the war began, some of these little ones go in turn every day to Holy Communion to pray for our brave soldiers and sailors, so that they may be protected and return home safely. So you see, dear children, your own little ones are trying to pay back, by their prayers for your dear fathers and brothers, what you have done for them all these years.

"These little babies are still brought to the orphanage when their parents do not want them. A fine baby of two days old has just been handed to me. A kind-hearted neighbour had walked fourteen miles across the mountains to bring the tiny mite to us, instead of throwing it out to die. Yesterday, from a distant island, came a little hare-lipped baby, eighteen months old, a real little skeleton, but with two bright black eyes which seemed to take in everything that was going on.

"For each bearer, we give about one shilling, which is not an expensive bargain to save an immortal soul. Still shillings at the present moment are rare and difficult to get and that is why I am so grateful to my little friends in England who, I feel sure, often refuse themselves dainties and pleasures to send help for the Chinese babies. Pray for us, dear children, pray for our Missions that are going through a very difficult time and we will pray that God may protect your dear ones who are fighting and bring them safely home.

"From your affectionate old friend,
"SISTER XAVIER BERKELEY, Sister of Charity,
"Chusan Island, China."

Sister Berkeley had other sufferings which God sent to her in those years, many misunderstandings, even calumnies, of which we speak only to show how God loved this eager generous soul, and how He answered her fervent prayers for closer union with her Divine Lord and Spouse by giving her a deeper sharing of His Cross. We read in her spiritual notes:

"If we are generous with God, God is generous with us.

"It is the holiness and sufferings of a small band of good souls that will draw down God's blessing on the millions of pagans (Curé d'Ars).

"Do not fear mortifications, humiliations, contempt; love will make these easy to bear as it is from an all-loving Hand they come.

"Look on the Cross and then you will not shrink from any sacrifice or suffering.

"Think frequently of the Passion during Meditation and Mass; Our Lord declares it is by far the most useful and efficacious of exercises.

"Hear Mass in a spirit of sacrifice; try and fill yourself with the spirit of sacrifice Our Lord had on Calvary; unite yourself to the priest and follow the circumstances of the Passion."

It was on the Feast of the Finding of the Cross that Our Lord brought Sister Berkeley to Chusan and so it is not surprising that her path was thickly strewn with crosses, but we see by her notes that she prepared for them.

"Do not fear the little crosses which are daily presented to you; do not cast them from you, they are precious treasures, which, if accepted in a spirit of penance, will go far towards purchasing a speedy entrance into eternal life."

Her retreat notes now begin, and end with:

"Union with God and His Will and in the way He wills, seeing God in all things, heedless of what is thought or said of you. This will give you the moral courage you need, will help you to speak fearlessly when necessary.

"Union with Our Lord in the spirit of Humility, Simplicity, Charity and Silence. Raise yourself above all the contradictions and little miseries and sufferings that surround your daily life.

"Keep your eyes fixed on God alone with perfect confidence and calmness, not letting your mind dwell upon thoughts likely to disturb its peace. Let to please Our Lord be a kind of passion in your soul."

"Advice of Fr. Meugniot:

"Practise this union with God, first by uniting yourself, your intention, closely to Him in morning prayer and meditation and Mass. Frequently renew this intention during the day, when the clock strikes. Secondly, in moments when this union with God is threatened to be disturbed, you are crossed, you are contradicted, etc., brace yourself up with the thought that all comes from His Hand, is His Will and keep yourself perfectly calm.

"Don't make a martyr of yourself for little worries, trials or unkind sayings, heard or reported. Keep the eyes of your soul fixed on God alone. Offer Him these very small troubles and be sorry you have nothing greater. What are they compared to Calvary?"

The appeal for help during the years of war was also sent to America and there was a generous response. Indeed Sister Berkeley was often heard to say, "America fed Chusan during the war."

In 1911, the same year that she came to Chusan, the American Foreign Missionary Society was formed and the Seminary at Maryknoll, Ossining, New York, opened to the first students under the guidance of Fr. Walsh and Fr. Price. Both of the founders often said that this work owed much to the inspiration and encouragement of Sister Xavier Berkeley, whom they called "Maryknoll's big Sister". Starting from a humble foundation

in great poverty, it developed with amazing rapidity, and in 1917
Fr. Walsh came to China to look for a field for his young Society.

One of the first Missions he wished to visit was Sister Berkeley's
at Chusan, and he speaks of it in his book, *Observations in the
Orient*. We quote from it:

> " I came to Chusan that I might have the privilege of meeting
> Sister Xavier Berkeley, a Sister of Charity, with whom I had been
> in correspondence for more than a dozen years and whose work for
> God I had followed at a distance. We recognized each other readily
> enough, and after a talk that revealed the depths of this noble woman's
> interest in Maryknoll I accompanied her through the several houses,
> which, to the little ones she mothers, the helpless, the deaf mutes,
> the aged, the blind and even the idiots is *home*. Home it is for them
> and Home for her, who, for the love of God and for the unloved of
> men in a foreign land, gave up much that this world considers worth
> having.
>
> " As we arrived at one building, I noticed a stagnant canal along
> which was stretched a row of Chinese huts, and I remarked that it
> must be an unhealthy spot. Sister Xavier then told me how, five
> years before, cholera had broken out and she knew it had reached
> her precious charges through these huts. ' I stood it ', she said,
> with tears in her eyes, ' until more than forty of the children caught
> the dreadful malady and died the next day. Then we bundled all
> that were left off to the hillside and they slept anywhere and every-
> where until the plague was over.'
>
> " Since then, Sister Xavier has been trying to buy and burn these
> huts and fill the canal; she has faith that little by little the means
> will come. The cholera recurs every six years and Sister Xavier is
> pleading hard with St. Joseph."

As his boat is leaving Chusan, Fr. Walsh writes :

> " I confess to a feeling of sadness as I looked over towards the
> Mission and contrasted Sister Xavier and her needs with others and
> their affluence. May God forgive those who do not realize that they
> are stewards rather than masters."

During his visit, Fr. Walsh told Sister Berkeley that his intention
was to go to Rome again and he hoped then to make another visit
to England. She gave him many introductions to English friends
and, amongst them, one to her aged mother, who, since the death
of her father, had left Spetchley Park and was living at Malvern.
Fr. Walsh went to England and he visited Lady Catharine Berkeley
and said Mass for her in her private chapel. He had many conversations with this noble Catholic lady, who was then over ninety

years of age. He told her of all he had seen at Chusan, and she confided to him her craving to see once more the child she had given to God so many years ago.

Fr. Walsh returned to Paris, where he visited the Central House of the Vincentian Fathers at St. Lazare, and he had a long interview with the Very Reverend Fr. Verdier, the Superior General of the Vincentians and the Sisters of Charity. He told him about his English daughter in her Chinese island Mission, and he also spoke of his visit to the aged mother in England and her great desire to see once more her child. The kind face of Fr. Verdier smiled, and he nodded his head understandingly, but said nothing.

In the autumn of 1922 Sister Berkeley received a call from Paris to go to England to represent the Holy Childhood of China at a big Missionary Exhibition to be held in Birmingham in 1923. Like all Missionary Sisters she had a horror of leaving her post even for a few months, and she wished to refuse this invitation, but the call from Paris named her specially and she had to obey.

When she arrived in Paris, she went to present herself to the Father General at St. Lazare. He received her very kindly, took great interest in her Mission, finally saying to her with a smile, " And now, you will go to England to see your mother. How old is she ? " Sister Berkeley, much surprised, replied that she would be ninety-three that year. " Well," said Fr. Verdier, " when you see her, give her this picture from me, and tell her how pleased I am to send you to see her."

Sister Berkeley was much touched at these gracious words and later on she visited her mother and spent long hours with her. There was a family reunion before she returned to China, but the year following death claimed four members, among them the saintly mother.

Lady Catharine Berkeley always called herself the " Chusan grandmother ", and she sent her last gifts to her Chusan grandchildren in 1923. These were big rolls of blue serge to make coats for the children, dark blue for the big girls, a lighter blue for the younger ones, and rolls of pink flannelette for the babies.

Rarely a year had passed without some generous gifts from the " Grandmother and Aunts " at home; most of them simple, homely ones, showing kind thought; new utensils for the Sisters' kitchen; knitted scarves and jerseys for the children; notebooks and pencils for their schools; hot-water bottles for the hospital and infirmary; tonics and warm clothing for delicate Sisters. These came with hosts of small treasures which they put aside with the remark, "That might come in useful at Chusan."

The little operation room in the hospital was furnished by them with an unexpected windfall that came their way: the beautiful miscroscope was a gift that came through their influence; swings in the children's garden, a magic lantern, seeds for the land, all came from the same source, and it meant constant self-denial on their part, for they were no longer rich, and lived in modest circumstances. But their hearts were overflowing with kindness, zeal and ingenious thought for relieving the struggling poverty of Chusan. True "Home Missionaries" they were, partners, sharing in the works and merits from the harvest of souls gained for the Kingdom of Heaven.

Sister Berkeley left for Europe in January 1923, and when she was in Paris the Father General asked her to accompany some of the American Sisters to Rome. This was a privilege which she greatly enjoyed. She had also the pleasure of making a pilgrimage to Lourdes, and the consolation of visiting the "Battlefield Cemeteries" in France, where she found the grave of her brother, Captain Mowbray Berkeley, who fell at Mailly in 1916.

Sister Berkeley was in England only for a few months, and during this time was much occupied with preparations for the Missionary Exhibition in Birmingham, at which she and Sister Gilbert from Ningpo represented the Sisters of Charity in China. She made her headquarters in Carlisle Place Convent, London, where her lifelong friend, Sister Petre, was Superior, and she gave her a warm welcome and much valuable help.

She visited very few of the Sisters' houses, did little of what is called "propaganda work" for Foreign Missions; yet a wave of enthusiasm passed through the English Province during those months and over seventy Sisters wrote to offer themselves to China.

Very few Sisters met Sister Berkeley personally, yet the mere news of her presence seemed an inspiration, and it showed clearly that among English-speaking Sisters there are seeds of strong vocations for China. Many of these do not ripen; it is not God's Will, or perhaps they become vocations of prayer, sanctified by the obedience which calls them to work for souls in the homeland.

There is a charming letter written during those months in Europe to English and Irish children, with whom she kept up a big correspondence, as we have already remarked. These letters were often sent through the Holy Childhood Society, and others were personal letters to children in convents and private families. The alms they brought were small, children's offerings, but Sister Berkeley's thoughts were for the future. She often said, " Make good Missionaries of the children and later there will be zealous priests and Sisters to fill the ranks in the Missions."

" April 1923.

" My dear Children,

" You have always shown so much love and zeal for my babies on Chusan Island, that now I am in Europe for a few months I must come first to thank you from my heart for all you have done for my little ones, and then tell you a little about them and their surroundings. The orphanage on that lonely island in the Pacific is the only one in the Archipelago of two million inhabitants. From far along the coast of China, and also from the interior of the Province of Chekiang, abandoned babies are brought to us, especially during famine.

" Eighteen months ago a little old pagan gentleman from Chepoo, a place over 100 miles away on the coast, arrived at our door and asked to see me. He told me how distressed he was at the number of babies that were thrown out to die in his district; one had even been found dead on his doorstep. He then heard of the House of Mercy out in the islands, where Europeans received abandoned children, and though he had never spoken to a European in his life he came over to find out if we could help him. There was but one answer to give, his babies would be most welcome and he was to send them over. ' There are about 100 every year ,' explained the old gentleman. ' Send them along, the 100 or more, if there are any. We shall be delighted to receive them all', was the answer.

" Immensely pleased, the old gentleman was then shown over the House. First the nursery, where the newly brought babies in their little cribs slept quietly, except for a couple of lusty mites who wanted to be carried. Most of these babies are for Heaven; they have suffered too much to revive. Those that are well and strong are out in the villages with their nurses, who bring them in regularly to be inspected. The nurses, as a rule, love our babies very much and are delighted to show how fat and healthy they are. When, at two years old, we take them into the nursery, the poor women are quite broken-hearted and often come to see their former charges and bring them cakes.

" Then we took the old gentleman to the second nursery, where the babies up to six and seven years old were romping and making a great noise. They all ran to the Sister as she came in, wanting a caress or a biscuit, or anxious to give a piece of news. Upstairs in big airy schoolrooms he found about 120 children at their lessons. This pleased him very much as, up to a few years ago, little girls in China were not allowed to study. He was very pleased to see our little people reading, writing, counting and even doing physical exercises.

" Well, leaving the schoolroom, the old gentleman proceeded to the workrooms where the older children were doing lovely embroidery and lace work; others were learning how to make and mend their own clothes and shoes. These last will soon be eighteen years old, when they will be married to good Christian boys and start new Christian families.

" Turning to the right, we looked into the day boarders' workroom, where about sixty little pagan girls were learning net work and embroidery. Then on to the Women's Hospital and the Hospice for Old Women, who, being homeless and friendless, come to us to spend their last days peacefully and prepare for Baptism and death. Among them are poor infirm girls and idiots, thrown out of their pagan homes. One was brought in whom her relatives had tried to drown, but she was rescued by a passing Christian.

" Then the old gentleman passed to the day school, where our little Christian girls from the different villages and islands were studying, also to the Catechumenate, where a band of women were preparing for Baptism. Finally he crossed over to the men's department where, in the hospital, he found many poor sick men, among them a dying prisoner. The Sisters, when visiting the prison, found the poor fellow very ill and got permission from the governor to transfer him to our hospital. He is preparing for Baptism, for he has not long to live.

" On to the Home for Aged Men, who, broken in health, friendless, penniless, are passing their last years under the Sisters' roof. Our visitor was leaving the House very delighted, when he noticed a crowd of sick people, seated in the dispensary, their ailments and wounds being cared for by one of the Sisters. ' Why ', he exclaimed, ' do you come such a long way from your distant country to look after these poor creatures, whom we in our own country despise and do not want ? '

" Dear Children, you and I can answer that question, can we not ? We know how very dear to Our Lord are the souls of all these poor children and people for whom He shed His precious blood. Every day say a ' Hail Mary ' for the babies and poor pagans in the Chusan Islands, that many, a great many, may be brought to Baptism. You will then be real Missionaries, helping to save souls, and perhaps

later on when you grow big, Our Lord will whisper to you His wish
that you also should come out and help in this great work.

" God bless you, my dear Children,
          " Your affectionate old friend,
     " SISTER XAVIER BERKELEY, Sister of Charity.

" P.S.—I forgot to tell you that the old gentleman keeps his word
and his servant arrives regularly with two basket loads of babies."

The fortunate four Sisters from the English Home Province who
were chosen from among the seventy to accompany Sister Berkeley
back to China in 1923 had the privilege of making a wonderful
journey with her through the United States. The Sisters from
the Eastern and Western Provinces in America were sending
Sisters to the China Mission; indeed in 1923 the first group had
already arrived from St. Joseph's, Emmitsburg. The Father
General thought that an old, seasoned Missionary like Sister
Berkeley, speaking their own tongue, would help the American
Superiors to understand the nature of the new Mission to which
they were sending their Sisters, and to smooth away some of the
initial difficulties.

A warm invitation was given by the Sisters of Emmitsburg and
Marillac to Sister Berkeley to pass through America on her way
back to China. It was a delightful journey and the most striking
part was the warm welcome and generous kindness received by
the visitors all the way from New York to San Francisco. It
was not really surprising, for all belonged to the same great family
of St. Vincent, and the visiting Sisters passed from one " home "
to another as they were received in all the Houses of the Community on the route. They found their own simple charitable
spirit, the same regularity of rule and custom, the same spiritual
exercises.

At New York there is no House of the Community, therefore
they were met by Sisters from Emmitsburg and taken to Bridge-
port, an hour's journey away, for the first night. Having important
business to arrange in New York, Sister Berkeley and her companions received for some days the kind hospitality of the Mothers
of the Sacred Heart at Manhattanville, among whom Sister
Berkeley had many friends, especially Reverend Mother Burnett,
who overwhelmed her visitors with kindness.

One of the objects of the New York visit was Maryknoll, which
the Sisters had special permission to visit. Fr. Walsh, the founder,

had met them at the wharf, and he could not do enough to show his appreciation of this visit from the missionary Sister whom he had followed so many years in her zealous work. A special visit was arranged to Maryknoll, where the Sisters had the privilege of being present at an Ordination in the Seminary chapel. They were also warmly welcomed by the Maryknoll Sisters, and this visit was a red-letter day in the journey.

At St. Joseph's, Emmitsburg, the Central House of the Eastern Province, the visitors had the privilege of seeing, and hearing many memories of, the Venerable Mother Seton, whose Cause for Beatification is advancing so rapidly in America. They were loaded with kindness by the Emmitsburg Superiors and Sisters during their stay in this beautiful Maryland valley. Visits were also paid to the fine hospitals at Baltimore and Philadelphia, and there was a day's excursion to Princeton, the Vincentian Apostolic School, and the Seminary at Germantown, where they received warm welcomes. The students begged Sister Berkeley to speak to them about China and some vocations were born for that far-off Mission.

Fr. Skelly, C.M., of the Miraculous Medal House at Germantown, showered medals and gifts on the missionary Sisters, telling them they " might take anything they liked that was not nailed down " !

At the Marillac Seminary, the Central House of the Western Province, St. Louis, much kindness was also received by the Sisters and they had the pleasure of meeting the aged Father Director, Fr. O'Sullivan, who left a never-to-be-forgotten memory in their hearts. They were all struck by his physical resemblance to St. Vincent, and he showed great fatherly kindness to the visitors.

On the last day of their visit he called the four young companions of Sister Berkeley and said to them, " I am going to treat you as I do my own Seminary Sisters," and he presented each one with an envelope containing a five-dollar gold piece and a picture of St. Vincent, with many kind words of advice. This holy, much esteemed and loved Father Director of the American Sisters, first in the Eastern and then in the newly-formed Western Province, died soon afterwards. His life was written and is read and appreciated by the English-speaking Sisters in Britain and China.

The long journey to San Francisco through the beautiful State of California was much enjoyed and another warm welcome awaited the Sisters in the big Pacific coast city, where they made their headquarters at the Catholic Orphanage and were mothered by the good Superior, Sister Helen. After visiting the interesting works of the Sisters there, and receiving every possible kindness, Sister Helen and another Sister accompanied the visitors up to Vancouver, and saw them safely on the big C.P.R. steamer.

On the long train journey through California a friendly lady passenger made an amusing remark to the Sisters. She said, " I do admire you ladies and your works of charity, but what bothers me is how, on a long journey like this, you manage to get clean hats! " She did not realize the happiness and privileges of Community life even in such temporal matters. The needs of the Sisters were generously provided for, from one " home " to another, on their long journey through the United States.

Sister Berkeley had not neglected to visit her friends in the Propagation of the Faith Offices in the different American cities, and she was warmly welcomed by them. At Maryknoll she had the pleasure of meeting Bishop Dunn, of New York, an old and valued friend. He always remembered with great pleasure that, during a very grave illness, the children of Chusan had prayed daily for " John Kong-kong " (Father John)! The venerable Mgr. Freri and Mgr. McDonnell (now Bishop McDonnell) in New York gave the missionary Sisters a warm welcome, but to Sister Berkeley's great regret it was not possible to fit in a visit to Boston, where Chusan Mission had so many good friends.

From the four companions, new missionaries to China, some memories were drawn in later years of this American journey. One said:

" I first met Sister Berkeley when she visited my House in North William Street, Dublin, in 1923, but I had heard much of her from my Superior, Sister Barraud, who was a great friend of hers. From that first meeting, Sister Berkeley was one great inspiration to me. Her wonderful zeal for souls was perhaps what struck me most ; she never let an opportunity pass when she thought a word might do good.

" I remarked especially, during our long journey, whether on land or sea, she seemed to be always on the look-out for souls ; God alone knows the secret of how many she helped to save for Him. Hers was indeed a beautiful soul, and one is almost tempted to say that it is a pity such souls must leave us, but we feel that our dear one will not forget the work she loved so well, now that she is in Heaven."

Another said:

" I first met Sister Berkeley and passed some days with her at the Birmingham Missionary Exhibition in 1923 and I was greatly struck with her patience and generosity. Nearly all the cases of Mission Exhibits for the Chusan stall were held up by the dock strike, and arrived too late, but Sister Berkeley took this calamity good-humouredly, and with the greatest generosity helped Sister Gilbert at the Ningpo stall, bringing up all her friends to buy the famous Ningpo bath towels.

" I remember meeting Fr. Nugent for the first time and Lady Winefride Elwes, Sister Berkeley's cousin, who rushed to stop the band in the big hall so that Fr. Nugent's lantern lecture could be heard clearly! In those days in Birmingham, I particularly noticed Sister Berkeley's spirit of poverty. We made many purchases together for China, and she was so careful of every shilling, always pulling out her little notebook to write her accounts.

" The first day of our journey showed us her strong faith and piety. At Cherbourg on the Saturday evening we went on board the big Cunard steamer *Berengaria*, very tired after many hours' waiting on the tender. Sister Berkeley's first thought was for Mass the next morning, and she hunted up the officer in charge of making arrangements for it. There was only one priest on board and he decided that the Sunday Mass should be at twelve o'clock midday. The Catholic officer said with a smile, ' So, Sisters, you must content yourselves to-morrow with a Spiritual Communion '. ' Oh no,' replied Sister Berkeley in a surprised tone, ' we shall certainly go to Communion at the twelve o'clock Mass.'

" Her companions said to each other afterwards, ' She did not ask us if we could do that long fast; she took it for granted that we were like herself, willing to make any sacrifice in order not to lose our Communion.' A Sister who lived with her later at Chusan said, ' It was always like that with her, often on our journeys between Shanghai and Chusan the boats were delayed by fog, etc., but never until late in the afternoon would she reluctantly break her fast and give up hope of receiving Communion that day. She suffered physically for it, having a weak heart, but she took no notice of that.

" Sister Berkeley was sixty-three years old when she made that last journey to China, but we, her companions, found her so youthful in spirit and indeed in physical energy that we could not think of her as someone old. She was one of ourselves and was delighted with our exuberant spirits; we were overflowing with happiness, making a delightful journey at the end of which was China, our long hoped-for Mission.

" Sister Berkeley wished us not only to enjoy the natural pleasures of the day but to learn all that we could. She herself was our

TWO BASKET LOADS FROM CHEPOO

TWO LITTLE SCHOOLGIRLS

BABY WITH COUNTRY NURSE

example; she wanted to see everything and deputed one of us to take notes for her. She often said, ' That might come in useful in China, note it.' She was especially interested in all that is done in America by electricity and she studied closely the children's works and the rearing of tiny babies in our Sisters' nursery houses.

" On the journey she won friends all along the line. We often saw passengers on boat or train, ladies and even gentlemen, talking to her like children to a mother, telling her their family troubles and difficulties. She gave them kindly sympathy and some spiritual advice, for she always saw a soul, and some work to do for Our Lord. One heard people say, ' I have gained a friend,' and many corresponded with her later.

" With all our natural enjoyment, Sister Berkeley never let us forget we were Sisters of Charity. Every possible Community custom and all spiritual exercises were followed with great regularity, even to the ringing of a tiny bell for the Angelus in our cabin. We often said the Rosary together in a quiet corner of the deck, regardless of onlookers. She was absolutely without human respect in her duty to God and the Community.

" We all remarked her great spirit of poverty, her old patched mended habit. Indeed, when she arrived in Paris in 1923 Fr. McHale, the American Assistant at the Mother House of the Lazarists, said to Sister Reeves, the English-speaking Secretary at the Rue du Bac, ' Can't you get anyone to give that poor Sister Berkeley a new habit ? ' Sister Reeves set the affair going, and when Sister Berkeley returned to Paris in September the new habit was waiting for her and she was profusely grateful, but—she did not wear it!

" On the Atlantic steamer we all tried to brush ourselves up to be respectable representatives of the French and British Provinces. With the greatest difficulty, for she hated new clothes, we persuaded Sister Berkeley to put on her new habit. In New York all our luggage was sent on to Emmitsburg, but when we arrived there some days later, Sister Berkeley called one of us and said in her most commanding tone, ' You will find the luggage, open my trunk, and bring me my old habit! ' There was nothing for it but to reluctantly obey, and the old habit appeared again, not improved after a hasty packing.

" We laughingly told her that we consoled ourselves by telling the American Sisters, when they remarked the old patched habit, that it was a sign of her holiness. She looked annoyed and said seriously, ' How very naughty of you to say such ridiculous things.'

" It was the same with shoes. Sister Berkeley always wore Chinese shoes, made of cloth with rag soles. She came off badly in Rome where it rained all the time, and she had to buy some leather shoes. One pair of Chinese shoes completely gave out when she was in England, staying at the Central House, Mill Hill, and had to be abandoned. It is amusing to relate that they were seized upon by the Sister in charge of the Mill Hill kitchen, Sister Bridget Coleman, who had a strong vocation for China but was not one of the chosen four that year.

K

" She venerated Sister Berkeley's old dilapidated Chinese shoes and, to the amusement of her companions at Mill Hill, wore them every night for recreation, hoping and praying that they would take her to China. They did so, for she was called two years later, and gave many years of loving, devoted service in the Holy Childhood Infirmary at the Pekin Orphanage. She won her crown early, for she died of consumption in 1934.

" On the long American train journey another Chinese shoe gave out, and Sister Berkeley brought it to one of her companions and said simply, ' Sister dear, would you patch my shoe ? ' The Sister consulted with another saying, ' Will you tell me where, on this train, I shall find a piece of black cloth to mend Sister Berkeley's shoe ? ' It was a problem and not likely that the negro porters could help us. A sudden idea came. The Sister lifted up a corner of her habit and cut out a neat square from the black serge lining of the big hem, and the shoe was patched.

" We all naturally talked a great deal about China on that journey, asking many questions of Sister Berkeley. She had nothing but good to say of the Chinese, their fine qualities, their lovableness, what good Christians they made, etc., etc. At San Francisco we had to obtain ' visas ' from the Chinese Consul. An appointment was made with him by telephone and some of us were rather anxious as to whether he would be punctual, as we had an important engagement directly afterwards. Sister Berkeley said in a surprised tone, ' Why yes! he said, three o'clock, so of course he will be there. A Chinaman always keeps his word.'

" We laughed sometimes and said, ' With you, Sister, everyone and everything is beautiful in China and the Chinese.' She smiled, and then said seriously, ' Oh no, not everything. There is great poverty and suffering in China and you will have your share; be prepared. To win souls for God, one must suffer. Before, God asked blood for souls from the martyrs, now He asks suffering. But if you are generous you will be very happy in China in spite of suffering. One must have generosity and a great spirit of faith. Take all from God's Hands and do His Will in the way He wishes and you will have great happiness.'

" She also often told us, ' In China you must be patient, or you will go mad! ' We never forget her words; they were those of a great missionary Sister."

On November 2nd, 1923, the travellers landed in Shanghai, having made a day's visit to Kobe in Japan, where they had a warm welcome from the Mothers of the Sacred Heart Convent there. A few days later, all were dispersed to their new Missions and Sister Berkeley, with one of the new companions, went back to Chusan Island.

XIII

RETURN TO CHUSAN, 1923

WHEN Sister Berkeley returned to her Mission on Chusan Island in 1923 she received a great welcome. Her new European companion wrote an account of it to children at home, telling them of the fireworks which greeted the arrival of the boat, the Chinese brass band and procession of extern school children which preceded the Sisters through the town. All the streets were crowded with Sister Berkeley's Chinese friends, delighted to see her home again.

The House of Mercy was beautifully decorated with coloured lanterns and banners, and in the corridors were all the Holy Childhood children dressed in their new clothes, the gift of their English grandmothers. They were shouting, " Konshi, Konshi, Ta Momo " (" Welcome to our Good Mother "), and many little pagans came running in to share in the rejoicings.

The new Sister was amused to hear Sister Berkeley telling the Sister in charge of the kitchens that " everyone must eat rice " and " che-pao ", which means " full up ". There was a fine feast ready, and afterwards presentations, songs of welcome and visits to all the inmates of the House of Mercy, children, old men and women and the sick and infirm.

Alas, the rejoicings were soon turned to tears, for Sister Berkeley had to break the sad news to her much-loved family at Chusan that she must leave them again. The Superiors at Shanghai had asked her to go to Yaochow in the Kiangsi Province, and spend some months with the Western Province American Sisters, who had lately taken over that Mission.

Only one week did she stay at Chusan before taking a mournful departure. It was a heavy cross and sacrifice for her, but she accepted it with the strong faith and blind obedience which is a hall-mark of the spirit of the Sisters of Charity. She knew herself that it probably meant she would never return to the islands, and

this opinion was shared by many, but the Chusan children and
poor used the mighty weapon of their prayers.

Paganism may be overwhelmingly strong in the Chusan Islands,
but in such places fervent prayer seems to have stronger power
than anywhere else. Day by day Heaven was besieged for the
return of their beloved " Ta Momo ", and on the Feast of the
Holy Innocents that year God brought her back to them, and
she settled down to the last twenty-one years of life in her
island home.

The first months after this second return found her battered
in health and spirits, with failing courage to take up the heavy
burdens which awaited her. A year's absence of the Superior
from a House brings many disorders and troubles which have to
be put right. Much of the luggage she had brought from Europe
had gone astray and took months to trace, while correspondence
with benefactors and others was in heavy arrears.

Strength and courage were needed, and she was now sixty-three
years old. Many years later she confided to a companion that on
her return from the Kiangsi she had felt so weak and unfit to take
up her heavy burden that she wondered if it was her " breaking
up ". We see in her notes that again she turned to the Holy
Eucharist with her strong faith and piety and tried to empty
herself of all that would hinder her close union with God.

"Each morning, dive deeply into the abyss of your own nothingness. Then, and repeatedly during the day, turn with boundless
confidence to the Blessed Sacrament to seek help, strength and
guidance. On these foundations, build up great zeal for your own
sanctification and for the salvation of souls.

"Beware of useless talk and reading; let every moment be for
God, His poor and souls, with all calmness, and self-forgetting
gentleness and kindness.

"Accept all in a great spirit of faith; see the Will of God in every
duty, under every circumstance, perform it with great simplicity,
showing *charité sans borne, bienveillante et devouée.*

"Love God, O my soul, love Him only and then with a light
heart go your way.

"In every duty, sacrifice and suffering, see the Divine Will of
Our Lord in the Holy Eucharist, then speak, act or keep silence as
He inspires you to do, as He Himself would have done; He is your
model.

"In meditation, tell Him all your difficulties, sufferings, hopes
and aspirations. He is your light and your counsellor, your strength

and joy. He will arrange all for His greater Glory, the good of souls, the greater good of the works. Watchword: ' God and my Duty '."

The new companion who came to Chusan with Sister Berkeley in 1923 writes:

" When Sister Berkeley returned from the Kiangsi I found her much changed and looking older; for some months she suffered physically and could no longer go on the expeditions through the mountain villages; she even walked with a stick sometimes in the house. This cost her much, one could see, and she said one day with tears in her eyes, ' I wonder, are my days for visiting the poor finished ? ' But she set to work to train me as a real Missionary, and I had much to learn in my first years.

" She at once launched me into the visiting of the poor in the country and town, telling me that this must always be my first work. I was enchanted to be at once in contact with the poor, and enjoyed the long walks and mountain climbing on which I studied my Chinese notebook. Best of all was the arrival in the villages, where the people came out to greet us with smiling faces, bringing the sick to be treated.

" Suddenly, in the middle of our work, the old woman who accompanied us, ' Sofy Bo ' (Grandma Sofy), would call us aside, and we would find a little dying baby in a corner. ' Baptize,' she would say in a low voice. The next minute she would bring us a little white-faced rickety child of two or three years. The healing waters would flow on their heads, and the little red plasters be stuck on the foreheads. On the homeward walk, we said Rosaries of thanksgiving for the harvest of little souls gained for Heaven.

" One could not live long by the side of Sister Berkeley without being infected by her love of souls and her purity of intention in all she did: to gain souls for Our Lord was always before her. ' How privileged we Sisters in Foreign Missions are,' she would say, ' we live and work so near to souls.' When I was in Europe, it seemed to me that there was so much talk about the importance of this and that committee and the organization of the administrators, etc., etc., and the souls for which they were working seemed so far away. In the Foreign Missions, it is much easier; every day we should thank God for the great grace and privilege we have to be so near to souls in all that we do."

Although she could no longer go on the long daily walks to the country, Sister Berkeley was always ready for the special visits, and indeed the presence of " Ta Momo " was always called for on those occasions. Not long after her return to Chusan, there was an interesting excursion to a far-off village to visit a new chapel, and make contact with the people. An account was sent to England, entitled " How the Faith came to Poseur ".

"A Chinese carpenter was very ill in the Sisters' Hospital at Chusan; as he seemed to be dying, he was instructed in the Christian Faith and received Baptism. But with good care he recovered from his illness, and asked to enter the Catechumenate, where he remained for some months, learnt the catechism and prayers, made his First Communion and became a very fervent Christian.

"Before he went home he came several times to Sister Berkeley and begged her to ask the priest to send someone to teach the people of his native village, called Poseur, three mountains away from Tinghai. "They are such good people, Ta Momo,' he pleaded, 'and would make good Christians if they only knew about the One True God in Heaven.'

"Alas, at that time there was no one to send, but later on the priest sent a good young catechist and his wife. They settled in a little house in Poseur and had so many visitors that the poor fellow complained they gave him no time to have his meals. After a while he brought in some of the men from this village to see the priest and stay some days in the Catechumenate, but no woman would venture in for a long time.

"The catechist told them about the Sisters and the good works they do for the poor and sick people. They asked all kinds of funny questions: 'What do the Sisters do with all the children who are brought to them? We heard that they take out their eyes and boil them to make medicine.' The catechist had a good answer to that, for his young wife was a Sisters' girl and had a dear little baby.

"He promised to ask the Sisters to come and visit Poseur one day and bring medicines to treat the sick people. In the month of May the priest went for the first time and said Mass in the little house where a chapel had been arranged. He was delighted to find several families of catechumens who were able to say some of the prayers at Mass, and the village gave him a great reception.

"At last the Sisters managed to go, Sister Berkeley and two others, although it was not easy to get out for such a long day. Poseur was fifteen miles away and they had to be carried in sedan chairs, which was rather a trial for them. However they walked some of the way and insisted on climbing the mountains on foot. It is a very painful experience to be carried up a mountain side in a sedan chair; they swing you from side to side, which gives a feeling of sea-sickness. Halfway there, the Sisters were received in a big Christian's home for dinner. They had brought their own provisions with them, but were obliged to hide them for all kinds of 'Chinese Chow' were provided!

"The arrival at Poseur was welcomed by fireworks, crackers going off in all directions as the Sisters stepped out of their chairs, and there were crowds of people from all the villages around. After saying some prayers in the little chapel, a beautiful statue of Our Lady and the Divine Infant was placed on the altar. This statue had been given to Sister Berkeley by the representative of Messrs. Burns & Oates at the Birmingham Exhibition.

" The Sisters then went outside and established a little dispensary for the sick people, numbers of whom had been brought to Poseur. The baskets were full of every kind of remedy, for fevers, sore eyes and ears, wounds, and the eternal ' dobie tong ' (tummy ache). Later Sister Berkeley and another Sister went round the big valley, visiting the villages. The people were rather afraid of them at first, for they had never seen ' Nakko Ninn ' (foreigners) before, but after a little talk and lots of smiles they grew very friendly.

" On that day the Sisters had the joy of baptizing many dying babies and little sickly children under six years old, who could not be reared. The babies and children die by millions in China. Even if the Sisters go out in the town for a few minutes' shopping, they will probably see a little wasted face in the corner of a shop, just waiting for a ' ticket to Heaven '. Sometimes it is a baby being carried, wrapped carefully in a red satin cloak, which means it is very ill and has been placed under the protection of the devil! With what joy the Sisters steal his prey from him!"

The new Sister from Europe continues:

" Sister Berkeley also put me in charge of the pharmacy, which had been much neglected in her absence. When I exclaimed in dismay that I was not trained or certificated to work in a pharmacy, she smiled and said, ' In China, my dear, one has often to do without training. One must just pick up what one can, trusting to God to do the rest. There are plenty of books [waving to the bookshelves] ; always consult them and study when you have a few minutes free. I did it like that in Ningpo.' Having a fair knowledge of Latin and some medical training, I struggled along with her help and was just getting on my feet in the pharmacy when she launched another bomb on me. ' You will also have charge of the tiny babies' nursery and you will have plenty to do to pull it up to a higher standard.' It had fallen very low in her absence through careless nurses and want of supervision.

" I wondered how and where to begin. There was always a number of tiny, suffering mites struggling to Heaven, full of disease when they were brought to us; nothing could be done for them but to keep them warm and clean and alleviate their sufferings if possible. But the healthy babies all went out to nurses in the country and this work appalled me at first. I thought it would be so much better to bring them up with bottles under clean, healthy conditions in our house nursery than to give them to these coarse, rough and often dirty women in the country.

" Sister Berkeley sent me to visit them in the villages and I came home shocked. I found some of the babies dirty, but I could not deny that they were fat and healthy. I had to learn, what a Maryknoll Missioner once said, ' to shut my eyes to a little careless dirt in China '! My experience soon taught me that Sister Berkeley was right, that Chinese tiny babies cannot thrive under artificial feeding; also, to rear them well, it must be ' One mother, one baby ', which is impossible in a house nursery.   After a time I found myself praying fervently for a good supply of country nurses, when our nursery was over-full.

" While they were with us, I began by making them prettier and cleaner; in some big bundles given by the American Red Cross after the war, I found delightful ' layettes ' and I put little white and pale blue bonnets on my babies. The staff of ' amahs ' (nurses) arrived before Sister Berkeley in a state of horror! ' The new European Sister has dressed the babies in mourning clothes; we Chinese use white and pale blue to mourn the dead; the babies will all die! '

" I compromised by changing the bonnets to pale pink, but they shook their heads at my extravagance: 'How often they will need washing ', they cried, ' and soap—dark blue and grey are much cleaner, for they don't show the dirt! '   However, my tastes soon became thoroughly Chinese, and not only rose pink, but scarlet and all bright colours with big flowered patterns were used for the babies. The smaller the baby, the bigger the flower or pattern is the custom in China.

" In the same building at that time were the babies brought in from their nurses, two and three years old to six and seven, a merry band who became the joy of my heart. For them also I insisted on pretty clothes and Sister Berkeley supported me, though it was not Chusan custom to be pretty every day. You kept all your gay clothes in cupboards for great occasions and feasts, while any old dark rags did for every day.

" However, my babies donned pink and flowered pinafores, and there were red pockets on them, which roused great excitement in the house. One heard, ' The new " Nakko Momo " has given the babies red pockets on their everyday pinafores! '   Heads were shaken again at my wild extravagance, but the babies were delirious with joy over their red pockets, into which all sorts of treasures were packed. A three-year-old baby, who was isolated in the Old Women's Home with smallpox, heard the excited talk about ' red pockets in the babies nursery '. She was heard wailing, ' Hong deydi yao ' (I want a red pocket).   Needless to say, she got one.

" Those were the days of long pantaloons to the ankles, padded in the winter, which made the babies almost square in form, and they waddled about like ducks. In the summer I put them into short knickers to the knees, and little short-sleeved slips. I chose a scarlet and white check, and of course there were red pockets.

" Sister Berkeley rarely gave a word of praise or approbation to a Sister, for her own intentions were so pure, so thoroughly for God alone. But sometimes an exclamation of almost childish pleasure escaped her, such as, ' I passed the nursery, the door was open and I saw your babies playing in the garden. They looked such ducks! I like your new clothes, especially the red pockets!'

"That year, 1924, there was famine in Haimen, a port farther down the coast, and the parish priest there, Fr. Pêche, C.M., often sent bands of starving babies, children and women to Tinghai, where he knew they would receive a warm welcome from Sister Berkeley. The babies and children came to me and it was a great joy to receive them, though I shall never forget their faces on arrival; some were green and shrivelled up with hunger! It was beautiful to see, after a few days, wan smiles coming on those poor little faces, when they realized that there was good rice to eat three, or rather four, times a day in the nursery, with the lunch of rice gruel between meals. They could hardly believe it, but loving care soon developed them into merry little children.

"Sister Berkeley liked to give her European Sisters ' hard nuts to crack ', especially in their first years. I shall never forget the first St. Joseph's Feast I passed in China. During her absence in Europe three babies out at nurse in the country had been stolen. The nurses grow very fond of their little foster-children, and would often like to keep them to become future daughters-in-law. Very close supervision is needed to prevent them from being stolen or changed, and during Sister Berkeley's absence the nurses had not often been visited.

"In all three cases the children had been reported as dead of cholera, so the little corpses had not been brought in to be identified. On her return, Sister Berkeley doubted the deaths of these children, but she went slowly to work, sending responsible men and women to visit casually in the villages and listen to talk. Gradually she learnt that all three children were living, so she prepared for action. With some trouble the two in the country were found and brought in, but the third was on an island.

"On the eve of St. Joseph's Feast she called me and said, ' The stolen child on that island, I hear, is to be taken to Shanghai the day after to-morrow; it will then be very difficult to trace her. To-morrow you will go to the island, Si-Hadgee, with the compradore and a woman, and you will find her and bring her back.' Barely five months in China, I wondered why I, the poor European, was chosen for this difficult task, but she added, ' It is a very bad crossing to that island and no one but you could stand the sea.'

"I put the affair in St. Joseph's hands and early the next morning we started out. At the port there was heavy rain and strong winds and I saw that my companions did not like the task at all. After some consultation apart, they came to me and said, ' We cannot go, Momo; there is no boat.' I replied, ' We must go. Ta Momo said the child is to be found to-day and she must be obeyed; to-morrow will be too late.' At last a boat, a small sailing junk, was found, and we passed to the island of Si-Hadgee in very heavy seas. On arrival at the nurse's house there was no child; she was hidden and there was a very violent scene lasting some hours. The nurse had hysterics, the foster-father broke furniture, and tore out his wife's hair; they both did all they could to frighten us away!

"I took a chair and sat in the little courtyard outside, reading *Spiritual Combat*, but keeping an eye on them. The man found a big rusty knife and he walked round me, brandishing it, but I knew he would not dare to touch me, for, sad to say, he was a son-in-law; his wife was an old Holy Childhood girl. I told them we should have to spend the night there and perhaps many nights until the child was produced, for Ta Momo must be obeyed.

"All of a sudden, the game was up; they knew it was useless to continue. The little girl, aged two and a half years, was brought from a neighbour's house, and everyone became friends, saying that we must all 'eat rice' together, and they began to prepare a feast. I wanted to get home quickly, but we had to wait for the tide, so in a small room apart I had my share of the feast.

"We then walked through mud to our knees, embarked in a small boat to go out to our junk in the sea, were caught in two whirlpools, but at last got on board safely. The passage home was even worse than that in the morning; the sail was up and several times the junk was nearly submerged. I clung to the big mast on deck, having a horror of the black hole below where passengers were stored. Good St. Joseph brought us safely home, and I think Sister Berkeley was rather pleased with me, though she did not tell me so."

After slowly gathering in alms for over ten years, at last the land of the cholera villages was bought; what a business it had been! The tiny piece of land had several owners and one never knew if the one selling it had really the right to do so. It required infinite patience and the help of two very shrewd Chinese friends. Even when the land was bought, there came the difficulty of turning out those dwelling in the huts, but at last all was in the hands of the Sisters. With what joy Sister Berkeley called all willing hands in the House to help in pulling down these dilapidated houses. Then came the erection of a large children's house, with lofty airy rooms, wide verandas, and gardens back and front, with an open view of the sea and mountains on the south.

Into this good building Sister Berkeley put all her nursery babies from three to seven years on one side, and on the other, the school-children's division, from seven to twelve years old, about 200 altogether. There was a wonderful improvement in their health, at which she rejoiced. They were indeed happy children, and photographs showing them playing in their new gardens went to England and America to thank the benefactors who had helped in this good work.

The new Director of the Boston P.O.F. offices, who had succeeded Fr. Walsh of Maryknoll, was Mgr. McGlinchey, another valued friend; rarely a month went by without a gift from Boston for Chusan. Knowing the desperate efforts which were being made to buy the cholera villages, Mgr. McGlinchey at last sent out a special appeal to Boston friends of the Missions, which was liberally answered, bringing enough to finish buying the land and to erect the house.

There is a letter in which Mgr. McGlinchey thanks Sister Berkeley for a photograph of the children sitting on the foundations of the new house. He says: " Your photograph gives me much pleasure; the faces of your little children are so happy. In some mission photographs the children look so subdued that one fears the treatment of them is too repressive, but yours are always full of joy and confidence. One feels they are loved."

They certainly were. We remember Sister Berkeley's notes in her early twenties, how she set herself to make each child know she was loved. A Shanghai visiting Sister once said, " I would ask for nothing better than to be a child at Chusan with Sister Berkeley." This same Sister said that she would like to give a present to the children and suggested sending some pretty handkerchiefs and stockings. Sister Berkeley smiled at her and said, " If you want to give them real pleasure, send some trumpets and skipping ropes, for they love to jump and make a noise."

To give her children pleasure was always her aim, and love and welcome they always received from her. " Well, babies," you would hear her say as she entered the nursery and opened her arms to them, and they clamoured around her, " Ta Momo, Ta Momo." " Well, little girls," to the school children, where she received the same welcome, while happy faces surrounded her and gave her news of their daily lives.

The girl who had the proud privilege of helping to clean Ta Momo's room would lift her head from the broom and get a smile and " That's right, little girl." The broom would sweep more vigorously, the cupboards would be dusted and rubbed until they shone. In her heart the child was saying, " Ta Momo said, ' Thatser right-er,' which means she is pleased with me and thinks I can do something well." At once the superiority complex mounted; how often in orphanages it is the inferiority complex which has the ascendancy, so little individuality developed or personal encouragement given; no opportunities to do something oneself alone and well.

Once a companion said to Sister Berkeley, " Why does that girl hang her head and look furtively at you ? " It was a child who had arrived late in years and was not long in the house. She replied, " She does not yet know and understand that she is welcome and loved, poor child." With her, as we have said, they were always welcome, her beloved children, and she could not do enough to mother them and make them happy.

In one of her much-used prayer books was found, after her death, a faded card with a picture of Our Lord welcoming the children and the words of St. Madeleine Sophie Barat, another lover of children: " There are but two things in the world which find place in my heart, Our Dear Lord and the children."

It was Sister Howard who gave Sister Berkeley this picture in the very early days of her Community life.

XIV

FRESH DEVELOPMENTS

Hospices for the Aged—Communist Troubles, 1927—Chusan Meng

THE building fever now seized Sister Berkeley and she went slowly and steadily forward during the next ten years, pulling down old buildings, putting up new ones, using as far as possible the old materials, for her resources were very limited. It was a miracle of Divine Providence that she managed to do so much, for the works of the House were always growing and numbers increasing. But in Chusan life was still very primitive and prices were low at that time. Cheap wood and bamboo came from Wenchow, stone from the island of Tsu-ko-tsien, and workmen's wages were very low, as living was cheap; in those good old days rice was sold at 10 lbs. for a dollar! In 1947 it was 420,000 dollars for a sack of 100 lbs.!

Another piece of land was miraculously obtained through the help of a good friend who visited her at this time, Sister Mary Barbara Regan, the Assistant of the Western Province of American Sisters. She and Sister Berkeley were kindred souls, full of missionary spirit. A delightful Old Men's Hospice was erected on this land, a one-storied building with big dormer windows in the high roof, wide verandas back and front, and a row of dependent buildings at the side of the big garden. Amongst them was a little workshop for the old men, where they made straw rope, sandals, etc. The House rabbit hutches were here under their care; rabbits are very useful in Mission life for the fresh meat they give.

The geese, turkeys and ducks of the farm were taken out daily by some of the old men, wandering along the canal banks and through the rice-fields. Sister Berkeley liked all the members of her big family to do some work, according to their capacity and strength. " It keeps them happy," she said, " and they don't quarrel." The old men gained small wages to buy tobacco, biscuits and little extra portions.

She certainly had a genius for building; she knew what she wanted and went ahead and got it done, in spite of many difficulties caused by country workmanship and materials. She gave as much care to the farm buildings as to others; one saw her with a pile of books on chicken rearing and housing, drawing her plans, and she said, " The chickens must be arranged better; I must read it up." It was the same with the cows; she said laughingly, " My education has been much neglected, for I know nothing about the care of cows."

She not only read it up but visited other people's cowsheds, then drew her plans and carried them through, though simply in the rough country manner. For many years the Sisters at Chusan got milk only from a few goats; Sister Berkeley, very soon after her arrival, bought a cow, and she was always trying to work up a good herd, a most difficult task in Chusan, where people look upon cows only as land animals to pull the plough or turn the rice mill. The point of view of giving milk for nursery and hospital use was not understood, and it was very difficult to find capable men to care for them.

There was one devoted old man who loved the cows like his own children; he had arrived with wife and family, starving, from Haimen during a famine, and somehow all had found shelter and work with Sister Berkeley at Chusan, and they all became good practical Christians. The father, who minded the cows, was too old to learn much doctrine; he barely got through his examination for Baptism, but he certainly had faith in the One True God and a great devotion to Our Lady. He used to say: " When I take the cows out I pray to ' Sing-Mo-Maleeya ' [Holy Mother Mary] for them to be kept from accidents." " What prayers do you say, Lao-kong-kong [old man] ? " he was asked. " You don't know any; you just follow the others." " Oh," he replied, " I just say ' Maleeya ' [Mary] when the cows are passing along the canal bank, and when they climb the tombs to eat grass, I say ' Maleeya ' and they don't fall and break their legs! " There are many tombs on the mountain sides, some covered with pyramids of earth on which grass grows, and it is easy to slip when climbing them.

Another devoted old cowman called ' Tamao Lao-kong-kong ' (the old man from Tamao, an island close to Chusan) said simply to Sister Berkeley: " Ta Momo, the two European cows [Nakko Ninn] don't like eating off the tombs, so I cut grass for them and

take it into the stable; they are rather difficult to please, like all
' Nakko Ninn '!"

Sister Berkeley and her old men were on very friendly terms
and she was always most anxious for them to be instructed, baptized and become good practising Christians. On certain big
Feast Days one saw some of them coming to her door, saying,
" Ta Momo, to-day is St. Peter's Feast and I am baptized Peter,
so it is my Feast "; or it would be St. James's or St. Paul's or St.
John's. Sister Berkeley would wish them a happy feast and
find a picture for them and some nickel coins to buy extras for
dinner.

The old women, too, were cherished and loved by this good
Mother, and she excused them affectionately when others complained that they were quarrelsome and not so easy to manage
as the old men. " Poor old ladies! " she would say, " how can
you expect them to obey at their age ? They have always done
things their own way." Amongst them were many blind and
infirm, some paralyzed, always in their beds. Most of them
became good Christians, which brought joy to their lives, and the
able ones had their hour for the Rosary in the chapel, as well as
the old men. It was nice to hear their old voices singing the
chanted prayers with great vigour, and Sister Berkeley often told
them that they gained many blessings for the House.

Some of them were old bonzesses (pagan nuns) who, as I have
already said, were always difficult to convert. If they had been
" che-tsay-ninn " (vegetarians), who had fasted for the devil
many years, they were sometimes held back for a long time
from the Christian faith by the thought that all their fasts and
sacrifices would be counted as useless. They also had great
fear of the devil, and often said he would not release them from
his service.

In the Old Women's Home were many idiots, most of them
harmless, who did their share of the work with the others, but
some had to be shut up or allowed to go out from time to time
when they had wild fits. A European Sister relates:

" In my first years at Chusan, Sister Berkeley gave me the charge
of the big entrance door. This meant getting up in the night sometimes to receive babies brought on the night steamers. But once I
remember hearing a great battering on the door at midnight, and
my Chinese companion said to me, ' Oh, that is the mad woman

from the Old Women's Home. She has been out for some days, very wild, but she wants to come in now. You must go down and open the door for her.' I must confess I went down rather nervously, thinking to myself, ' In my country they shut up mad people in asylums '. However, the woman came in quietly, thanking me; the madness was over for a time."

Another old lady was a very fervent Christian, but when her madness seized her she went out and broke idols in the pagan temples and wayside shrines! This was very awkward, as Sister Berkeley had to pay for the mending of the idols. The Bishop asked her once with a smile: " How do you explain that expenditure ' mending of idols ' in your yearly accounts, Sister ? "

Another young woman always jumped into a well when she had a mad fit. The poor Sisters used to say, " She always does it in the evening, just when we are sitting down for a little quiet time after the day's work." One would hear a great noise and shouting, " Tatchee is in the well! " That meant all must run to the scene, the gardeners must be called from the farm, and with ropes and great excitement Tatchee would be hauled up, dripping wet. Then she must be given a hot drink and dry clothes, and there was no more quiet for the Sisters that evening.

One of the saddest cases was Eelan Tongtia, a beloved child of the House, who, when married, suffered so much from her mother-in-law that she lost her reason and eventually came back in that state to her old home. Sister Berkeley tried all possible means to cure her, for her husband and little boy needed her care, temporally and spiritually. Eventually she was sent to the newly-opened Mercy Hospital for the Insane, outside Shanghai, at that time in charge of the Maryknoll Sisters. They were delighted to help their Father General's old friend, but all treatment proved useless.

However, after Sister Berkeley's death in 1944 Eelan Tongtia one day pronounced herself cured, saying that Ta Momo in Heaven had done it. She was never again violent, but rather childish, and not long afterwards she died, saying that Ta Momo was calling her to Heaven. She was one of her specially loved children because she had suffered so much.

The Communist risings in 1926 to 1931 brought serious trouble in China, as is well known, but the majority of the Houses of the Sisters of Charity came through these difficult days protected in

A HAPPY NURSERY GROUP

A NEW CHILDREN'S HOUSE, 1924

SOME OF THE OLD WOMEN CARED FOR BY SISTER VINCENT WANG

SOME OF THE OLD MEN CARED FOR BY SISTER LOUISE LIOU

a remarkable way. The Houses in the Kiangsi Province were in the greatest danger. At Kuikiang all Europeans fled and their houses were pillaged, but after making a round of inspection of the Sisters' hospital and works the Communist leader put a guard at the door and wrote over it in big characters, " Here is Charity ", and they were undisturbed.

At Nanchang the town was completely overrun by the Communists, who pillaged everywhere and turned out all the Missionaries except the Sisters of Charity. They used the Catholic Church as a council hall and lived in the priests' residence. The Sisters nursed their wounded in the Mission Hospital and saved the life of a General who was dying of pneumonia, so, by his orders, the hospital and other works were left undisturbed, though life was not very pleasant for the Sisters as there was continual bombardment all around them and soldiers came and went as they pleased.

At Kingan, farther south in the Kiangsi, five foreign Sisters and four priests were taken prisoners by the Reds, and carried off into the mountains from place to place for eighty days. They suffered great privations and dangers, but were finally rescued by the White Chinese troops on Christmas Eve, 1930, and brought back to Nanchang with military escort.

In Chusan there was occasional trouble in the town of Tinghai and also in the surrounding islands, and there were alarming rumours of further disturbances to come. It was reported that the Communists wanted to seize the big foreign house of the Sisters. They said, " Why should they live in a grand house like that ? We shall take it for our own use."

One day a band of rough-looking men came in and marched around the House of Mercy, inspecting everything, finally entering the big new children's house. Here they were surprised to be greeted by a band of happy, dancing Chinese babies, calling out to them, " Siesang hao-va ? [How do you do, Sir ?] ". " Come and see our house. This is where we play, and in that room we eat rice four times a day. Come upstairs and see where we sleep. Each one has her own little bed."

The men passed on to the other side of the house, where 100 little girls were studying in big airy schoolrooms; they received the same gracious welcome. Their faces softened and they turned to each other, saying, " We can do nothing here. It is not the foreigners who live in this big house, but our own Chinese

L

orphans. We cannot touch them." As they went out, they
were shown the old, low-roofed Chinese building occupied by
the Sisters.

There was no more trouble in Chusan, but in other parts of
China a serious outbreak was expected and foreign consuls began
to call in their nationals from the interior and outports. Sisters
from some of the Kiangsi houses were obliged to come in to
Shanghai, but Sister Berkeley begged the Superiors to allow the
Chusan Sisters to stay at their posts, for all was quiet around them.
The English Admiral is reported to have said to a friend in
Shanghai, " If I sent a gunboat to Chusan for Sister Berkeley and
her foreign Sisters, would they come ? " " Perhaps," was the
answer, " if you brought their Chinese Sisters and 300 orphans
with them ! "

At last the Superiors in Shanghai were obliged to obey the
consul's pressing demand and call the Wenchow and Chusan
Sisters into Shanghai. On May 1st, 1927, early in the morning,
all the Sisters, Europeans and Chinese, with fifty of the biggest
girl orphans, left Chusan. The Bishop sent responsible women
from Ningpo to take charge of the house during their absence.

As Sister Berkeley left her house she said with confidence,
" You will see; we shall be back for June, the month of the Sacred
Heart." The people of Tinghai and the islands were much
surprised at the departure of the Sisters. " For what reason ? "
they asked. " No one here could harm them or their children;
we would not allow it. They are perfectly safe with us."

The air cleared, war with foreign Powers was averted and on
May 31st four of the Sisters left Shanghai and came back
cautiously on a Chusan boat. It was a memorable passage down
the Whangpou between lines of foreign gunboats. Two weeks
later the other Sisters and the children followed, and Sister
Berkeley said with triumph, " I told you we should be back for
the 1st of June, to open the month of the Sacred Heart." She
found means to build a little kiosk in the garden, where she placed
a beautiful statue of the Sacred Heart, a memorial of the protection
over the House and works during the troubles of those years.

The Eastern Province American Sisters, who had been obliged
to leave Kanchow in the Kiangsi, at this time received welcome
and hospitality at Chusan. Their first Superior, Sister Pauline
Strable, was with them and she much enjoyed the country

missionary life with Sister Berkeley, accompanying the Sisters on their excursions, and giving them valuable aid in their hospitals. When the American Sisters at last returned to their Mission in the Kiangsi they found an empty house; everything had been pillaged. They had to begin again, and fifteen years later the same happened after the evacuation during the Japanese war. Sister Berkeley foretold great blessings and development for this Mission later, because of the trials and sufferings of the first years.

Chusan Meng (The Door to Chusan)

Chusan Meng was the mountain island in the sea bought by Sister Berkeley for the cultivation of vegetables for her big family. Practically all good mountain land in Chusan is cultivated, and one sees wheat and all kinds of vegetables, especially the sweet potato, growing on the slopes, while flat land is nearly all used for rice-fields.

The island of Chusan Meng is situated in a narrow strait of water; on one side lies the headland of Chusan, while on the other side there is a wider passage between it and the island of Bougee. Then the sea opens out to the harbour of Tinghai, and to a passage through the many islands to the Continent, as also to Haimen, Wenchow and other ports farther south.

When Sister Berkeley set her heart on buying Chusan Meng everyone laughed at her. " You will never get that," they said. " Look at its important position, the entrance to the harbour." Meng in Chinese means " Gate " or " Door ", so " Chusan Meng " was the door to Chusan, and all steamers passing it give their first whistle of approach. However, she and her children set to work to pray, which meant that the affair would be managed, and she purchased the island at a ridiculously low price. No one seemed to want it: " uncultivated, poor soil, many rocks ", they said. In Chusan mountain land is valued by the quantity of sweet potatoes which can be grown on it.

In the Sisters' hands Chusan Meng became a valuable asset for the big household, as year by year more land was opened up on it and splendid harvests of vegetables of all kinds, not only sweet potatoes, were brought in. The wheat for the making of the Hosts was grown here and supplied to three Missions. For many years it was ground in a hand mill by two blind women, and the Hosts were made by three deaf mutes, fervent Christians to whom this work was a great joy and privilege.

Fir trees, planted on the steep slopes of the mountain and between the rocks, gave firewood for the house, and there was a little hollow on the south side in which an orchard was made, with plum and peach trees; this was a real sun-trap. Below, on the rocky shores, quantities of red and white jelly-fish are washed ashore—a most *recherché* food in China; also wildfowl fly around the island. Sister Berkeley persuaded a friend in Shanghai to give her an old gun, with which the gardeners could shoot them, thus increasing the fresh meat supply, always difficult at certain seasons of the year.

The passage from Chusan Island to Chusan Meng is a most difficult one, full of rushing torrents and whirlpools. To cross over safely one has to make a big curve into quiet water. After the Sisters came into possession of this island a deputation of rich Chinese merchants came to ask them to build a bridge across the narrow strait. Their reason was that the rushing currents were evil spirits which took away all their riches to Shanghai; they said that if a bridge were built it would stop the action of the evil spirits! This request had to be refused, for it would have meant an easy road for robbers.

On the top of Chusan Meng a little house was built for the gardeners; in front of it with great difficulty a broad terrace was made. When this was proposed Sister Berkeley was told that it was impossible, but she said, " One cannot come out of the door of the house and fall straight down the mountain! " As usual she got her way, and it was done by means of a broad sunk fence. This terrace added greatly to the value of the house, and was most useful for the drying of wheat and vegetables.

When all was arranged, early one morning the Sisters and a band of children crossed over to the island with Fr. Michael McKieran, C.M., who was on a visit to Chusan. One of the rooms in the little cottage was arranged as a chapel and Mass was said there; afterwards the house and island were blessed and a white cross erected on the roof. " Now ", said Sister Berkeley with great satisfaction, " Our Lord is in possession of Chusan Meng; the ' Door to Chusan ' belongs to Him."

It was a red-letter day when the Sisters went to visit this island to inspect the crops, and Easter and Whit Mondays were always picnic days there for the children. The big girls of the workroom would leave the house after an early dinner, each one carrying an old tin or pot for the crabs they were going to catch. The crossing had to be made very carefully, in two or three relays, no one moving; but once landed their outside coats would be put aside and they were down on the shores, or scrambling all over the mountain. At other times of the year big bands of the girls would be sent to help to gather in the bean harvest or potato leaves for the cows. Sister Berkeley liked to prepare them for future married life in the country.

The younger children were not forgotten on these picnic days; they were packed into big flat-bottomed boats and brought along by the canal to the Chusan shore opposite the island. Here, also, were rocks and crabs and old fortifications of the Opium War days, rusty cannons, dug-outs, etc., delightful places to play in. Shoes and stockings came off at once, and away they went after crabs, big and little. Even the little infirm children were brought, and sat happily on the rocks, their companions finding crabs for them, which were all taken home to be cooked for supper. The blind children, however, caught their own crabs in an ingenious way, by placing a hand on a rock and waiting until a crab ran over it, then, quick as lightning, seizing it with the other hand.

Very soon it was realized that the air on the top of Chusan Meng was extraordinarily invigorating, for the sea and mountain breezes on four sides swept over it. Sister Berkeley began sending three or four little delicate children up there with a nurse, to be packed into one of the gardeners' rooms, eat on the terrace, and play outside all day long; the results were marvellous.

Sister Visitatrix from Shanghai (Notre Mère Lebrun) arrived on a visit, and of course was taken to see the new possession and to breathe the good mountain air. She saw great possibilities there, and proposed to build a Rest House for tired and con-valescent Sisters from the cities, that they might be built up and refreshed by the " champagne air ", as it was called, of Chusan Meng. It was foreseen that this would prevent many serious break-downs in health. Alas, the project of this Rest House on the top of Chusan Meng could not be realized; the position was too dangerous, as there were so many pirates on the seas around, while the difficult crossing made a daily Mass there impossible.

However, the idea did not fall through, and later another site was chosen on the mountains of Chusan Island.

Meanwhile, tired Sisters from city houses began to arrive from time to time for a few days' rest and change; Chusan was growing famous. Sister Berkeley was delighted to receive them and could not do enough for their benefit and enjoyment. She arranged their daily programme; early in the morning a boat in the canal was waiting for them, and they passed through the rice fields to the sea shore, where they crossed over to Chusan Meng and spent all the day there on the wind-swept terrace, or in the little pine-woods on the slopes. In the evening they returned by the same route, arriving just in time for supper and bed. Three or four days of this regimen worked wonders, and visitors began to arrive regularly, not only Sisters of Charity but also nuns of other Communities whose doctors had heard of Chusan. All received the same gracious welcome and devoted care from Sister Berkeley.

On one occasion when some city Sisters were enjoying the last day of their visit on top of Chusan Meng, Sister Berkeley suddenly arrived. She had received a letter from a lady friend in Shanghai, who begged to be allowed to come with a servant and stay some days on the top of the little island. Sister Berkeley regarded critically the room in the little house which was always reserved for the Sisters' use. " It is not airy enough," she declared. " To-morrow we will ' throw out ' another window in this wall." " But the lady is coming the day after to-morrow; there will be no time." " Oh yes," she replied, " they can easily make a window to-morrow. I will call the mason and the carpenter to-night." " Listen to her," said a visiting Sister from Shanghai; " that is the way they do things in Chusan; now, at Shanghai, we must send for a gentleman who will come and survey, and discuss the affair. After a few days he will send an estimate, and, perhaps in a month or so, we may get our window made; but in Chusan, Sister Berkeley says, ' To-morrow we will throw out a window, and it is done.' " The lady arrived, but on the first evening of her stay a violent thunderstorm drove her in terror from the mountain to seek refuge in the town.

Sister Berkeley certainly had a passion for windows. Her Sisters sometimes laughingly said that she roamed about the house to see where she could ' throw out more windows ', and her new buildings were full of them, high and wide with ventilators on the tops.

She herself could not live without air, being subject to asthma. A European companion relates:

"I used to make my afternoon Meditation at an earlier hour than the others, half-past two, because I was on hospital service later. During my first summer I was amused at Sister Berkeley saying to me quite seriously, 'You had better make your Meditation a little later; there might be a wind'! I suppose she had pity on me, and thought I should fall asleep without air in the great heat, but I always said, 'In China, at meditation in the summer, one prays for a wind!'"

Before leaving Chusan Meng we must speak of the little cemetery on the east side of the mountain. Sister Berkeley arranged it specially for her Holy Childhood children who had made their First Communion and whom God called to Himself while yet in their youth. The Children of Mary had their place in the Sisters' cemetery on the Lykousain mountain outside the North Gate of Chusan.

XV

PRISONERS AND BRIGANDS

" I was sick and in prison and you visited Me "—" This day shalt thou be with Me in Paradise."

"NEVER does our Divine Lord seem so near to us as when we visit Him in prison," say the Sisters of Chusan. When they pass through the narrow streets of the town, their neighbours call out, " Where are you going to, Momo ? " Seeing the medicine baskets and big pot of rice gruel, others answer, " They are going to do good work in the prison."

Care of the sick and suffering prisoners was a work given specially by St. Vincent to the first Sisters of Charity. In his life we read of great devotion to the poor galley slaves of those days in their dungeons. He was named " Head Chaplain of the Galleys ", and he not only cared for them spiritually but dressed their wounds himself, and obtained more human treatment for them.

St. Vincent also arranged houses in which the sick and wounded prisoners could be nursed, and to this work he introduced his daughters, the Sisters of Charity, and there are many tales of their patient and loving devotion to these poor outcast men of the galleys. Their holy Foundress, St. Louise de Marillac, we are told, visited them in their loathsome dungeons, bringing them food and trying to soften their hearts with kind words and sympathy. Her Sisters related that when prisoners obtained their release she would bring them to her house, give them food, wash them, and change their verminous clothes for some of her son's.

During Sister Berkeley's years in Ningpo, the Sisters had not been able to gain an entry into the prisons; but in Chusan permission was freely granted by the officials, and regular visits were made. At first there was only distribution of medicines, passed through the grilled doors of the cells with kind words, but sometimes, for a very sick man, the door of the cell was unlocked and the

Sisters allowed to enter. Kneeling beside him on the floor of the low platform, crowded with men, they could give special care, food and medicine.

After a time permission was granted for very sick men to be carried to the Sisters' hospital, where a special ward was given to them and their guards. Many dying prisoners were brought in, and it was thus easy to prepare them for Baptism, which they always gratefully accepted. The Governor and warders at first found it difficult to understand the interest taken in the dying men. The prison custom was to throw them into an outside court for the last hours of their lives, to die like dogs, alone, but the Sisters would beg to have them brought into their hospital, where, during their last days, they were surrounded with comfort and kindness and the soul as well as the body could be cared for. When this was understood, the prison authorities helped in their way, and would sometimes send an urgent message to the Sisters. " Come quickly! A man is very ill. He is good for nothing but your Heaven! "

When a special gift arrived for prison work, the Sisters would prepare big buckets of soft rice or wheat porridge, mixed with fresh vegetables, which would be served for a lunch to about 400 hungry men in the prison. It might be a good " Yamey " (Chinese strawberry) year in Chusan and then big baskets of the fruit would be distributed to the prisoners. A special visit of a Shanghai Superior would be celebrated by taking her to " serve Our Lord in prison " with a bountiful lunch of pies and cakes.

On the women's side, where, alas, there were always about twenty occupants, some with babies in their arms, the Sisters had a warm welcome. As they were few in numbers, fresh vegetables and fish could more often be sent to them to eke out their scanty prison fare. Rice gruel was provided daily for the babies, and pretty bonnets, bibs and warm clothing would be distributed. Needlework of all kinds was given to the women, for which the Sisters paid, so that they could buy much-needed extras. " When they are working for the Sisters," said the old pagan wardress, " everyone is happy and smiling; but when they have nothing to do, they go to bed and cry." A little instruction was given at every visit and some prayers taught, and these were much appreciated. The old wardress used to say, " Momo, I am too old to learn anything and I am very bad, but when you go up to Heaven, let me hang on to your apron and say you are my friend. Then you will pull me into Heaven."

Gradually the Sisters obtained a firm footing in the Chusan prison and the work developed. Twice a week a dispensary was opened in the covered court, from the three sides of which branched off the lines of cells. In a side room was a cupboard where medicines and necessary equipment were kept; this cupboard was made by a prisoner-carpenter, and painted by a prisoner-painter. Work was much encouraged by the Sisters. Sometimes they would engage the services of a prisoner-barber to cut the hair and shave all those who had no money. For the Golden Jubilee of Sister Berkeley in 1932, all the soles of the Holy Childhood children's shoes were made and sewn by the prisoners.

On dispensary days the inmates would be allowed to come out into the court, where benches were arranged for them. The opportunity to get out for a few minutes produced many little ailments and the Sisters had to make a rule that no man could be treated for more than two. If one patient had sore eyes, an ulcer on his leg, a cough and itch, it was impossible to get through the afternoon's work, so only two ailments per man were allowed! Poor fellows, they were so well behaved that rarely had a complaint to be made; they were full of gratitude to the Sisters, in whom they had immense confidence.

Sometimes epidemics broke out, for the prison was over-crowded, insanitary and badly kept. Once there was an outbreak of scorbute and beri-beri, due to want of fresh vegetables. Over ninety men were attacked by one or both of these dreadful diseases. Besides bringing in eight at a time to their hospital at home, the Sisters arranged several cells as little infirmaries in which they cared for them daily. Forty-five of these poor men died, either of heart failure with the beri-beri, or because their tongues became so swollen that they choked. Forty-two were baptized and the other three were instructed and had asked for Baptism, but thinking there was no immediate danger the Sisters had waited to give further instruction. They died suddenly in the night from heart failure, but they surely had Baptism of desire.

The years 1932 and 1933 were called the " Brigand Years " in Chusan. It was said that there were 300 brigands on the island and 600 pirates on the seas around! The country people suffered terribly, and those who had a little property or riches could not sleep in their own houses at night, but went from place to place for safety.

At last a company of Government soldiers was sent to Chusan and by their efforts large numbers of brigands and pirates were caught and the Tinghai prison was overflowing with them. The confinement and poor food told on them heavily, for they were accustomed to an open-air life and the best of everything; many of them fell ill with bad fevers, anæmia and beri-beri. The Sisters nursed them, bringing food and medicines daily, but several died. They listened to Christian instruction very willingly; sometimes a dying man, when asked " Do you believe in the One True God ? " would reply, " I believe in you, Momo. I know you, I don't know God! " The Sister would patiently tell him of his Heavenly Father and Creator who, in His love and mercy, had sent the Sister to care for him. " I believe," he would say, " I believe anything you tell me, Momo, for you are so good to me. No one has ever treated me with the kindness that you do."

It was difficult to make them understand the sinfulness of their past lives. They would say, " I did not know it was a bad life; all my family have been brigands; it was our profession." " Oh Momo," said a dying brigand chief, " it's a fine life, it's a fine life; plenty of money and good things to eat and no need to work." But when they did understand the sin and shame of such a life, they would resolve to give it up if they were released, and some would say simply, " I never robbed or injured the poor, Momo, only the rich; I often did good works for the poor."

Among these brigands, sad to say, was a young Christian, Li Yung-sung, who, though he was only twenty-three years of age, was one of the minor chiefs of the band. As a boy he had been badly spoilt by his parents, but he had studied in the Christian school. Refusing to work in the country, he was sent to Shanghai, where he fell into bad company, and to pay his gambling debts became a brigand.

He was one of the first to be caught by the soldiers and news came to the Sisters that he was in the special prison reserved for very serious cases. They went to the prison and asked the head judge for permission to see this boy, explaining that he was a Christian, and if he was going to die, as seemed probable, he must be helped to prepare his soul for death. The judge at once gave permission, remarking that he himself had been in a Catholic school and he knew their customs.

Li Yungsung was called into the public Court of Justice where the Sisters awaited him. The judge and officials of the court watched curiously to see how he would be received by them. He came in, closely guarded, dragging heavy chains on his feet and hands, but with a bold look on his face, laughing.

Sister C., who spoke Chinese like a native and knew the Chusan patois well, turned on him with vehemence, " You laugh, Li Yungsung," she said. " My God, for what cause can you laugh ? you, who have disgraced your family and the Catholic Church; you, who have brought misery and ruin on so many poor people, how can you laugh ? When we visit in the country, how many tell us of your thefts and murders ? These pagans around us in this court would not be as guilty as you are, for they do not know the law of God. What is the Seventh Commandment of God ?—' Thou shalt not steal '; and the Fifth Commandment of God ?—' Thou shalt not kill '; and the Fourth Commandment, Li Yungsung ?—' Honour thy father and thy mother '; you, who put a pistol to the head of your old mother when, on her knees, she begged you to give up your life of sin. We have not come here to plead for your life; we know, and all know, that you will be rightly condemned for what you have done. We have come to plead with you to prepare your soul to stand before the Judgement Seat of God."

There was dead silence in the court, and the young man was no longer laughing; his head was hanging low in shame and big tears were falling on his heavy chains. " What must I do, Momo ? ' he murmured in a choking voice; " help me." Then the Sister changed her tone and reminded him gently of God's great love and mercy for repentant sinners, and urged him to beg Almighty God to have mercy on him and help him to prepare his soul for confession. He asked for a catechism and prayer book, saying that he had forgotten so much of what he had learnt as a boy.

With the judge's permission books were brought to him, and his parish priest, Fr. Luke Yao, of Sinkomen, was allowed to see him and help him to prepare for and make his last confession. For a time he was kept in the ordinary prison, heavily chained, and the Sisters brought him books and dressed his wounds; he was always quiet and well behaved.

Suddenly one morning he was called and taken in the little steamboat to a village near Sinkomen. Brigands are always shot in the district where they have done so much harm. Yungsung was asked by the soldiers if he had any last request to make. " Yes," he said, " I would like the priest, Fr. Yao, to be called from the Church of the Holy Rosary over there on the hill at Sinkomen." " There is no time for that," was the answer; " give us your message for him." " Tell him," said the boy, " that Li Yungsung asked for him, and begged him to remember him in his prayers."

A few days later, a broken-hearted woman, with tears falling from her eyes, fell on her knees before Sister Berkeley. " Thank you, thank you, Ta Momo, for what the Sisters did to help my son." It was the mother of Li Yungsung, an old Holy Childhood girl, always known as Dorothy of Djao-ka-oah (her village), for hers was the head family there and the little chapel was in their house.

Not long afterwards the Sisters visited that district, making their headquarters in Dorothy's house for treating the sick people around. The chapel was cleaned and opened again, and old Dorothy said, with humble gratitude, " Now I can hold up my head again, for the Sisters have visited me." In the sad years of war, later on, when Christian children of the villages could no longer come in to study in the Sisters' school and prepare for the Sacraments, we heard that old Dorothy, when the sun shone, would collect the children around her on a grassy bank, and teach them their catechism and prayers to prepare for the next visit of the priest.

.   .   .   .

At last the real heads of the big brigand band were caught. The head chief was a famous man called Tze Paoding, whom for years they had been trying to catch. With two other leaders and many of their men he was imprisoned, and the Sisters, during their visits, had the opportunity of talking to him. They found Tze Paoding very well disposed. He confided to them that he had long hated his life as brigand, but gambling debts had thrown him into it. He asked the Sisters to write out clearly the doctrine and prayers they were teaching him. He stuck them on the wall of his cell, and since he was unable to read himself he made another man read and repeat them to all.

It was not difficult to baptize these three brigand chiefs, for they understood the doctrine and were in good dispositions. One did not dare to delay, as each day the condemnation was expected. On the day they were baptized, a man from another cell called out. " I too want to adore God, the Master of Heaven. I have here some Christian books which I have been reading and the doctrine in them is beautiful. The Christian brigand, Li Yung-sung, gave them to me when he was called to be shot, and he had already taught me much in them and some prayers." Poor Yungsung! Perhaps this last act of charity for another soul will have helped him through his purgatory.

In the Court of Justice Tze Paoding was remarkable. He answered simply and honestly, saying that he admitted all his crimes and was guilty, but he pleaded for the men in his gang. " They were not really brigands like us," he told the Judge; " they are good countrymen whom we forced to join us. Pardon them, for they have wives and children at home and are not bad men. Punish us, the leaders."

Some days later the call came, and they were taken to Tatchee, Tze Paoding's native village, three mountains away from Sinko-men. He thanked the soldiers politely when they helped him with his heavy chains into the sedan chair which was to carry him to the place where he was to be shot. A photograph, taken by a catechist when he fell, shows the Miraculous Medal round his neck.

Tze Paoding was very pleased to know that in Heaven he could help the Sisters do good works and also that he could help those whom he had injured on earth. He said to the Sisters, " You are the only friends I have ever had, the only ones in my life who have helped me and tried to make me good. I will never forget you."

It is rather remarkable that after his death, in the districts terrorized by his brigand band there was a wonderful development of prosperity and the Faith has been planted there, a new chapel opened, and many catechumens are coming in. The country people are rather amused when the Sisters tell them, " It is Tze Paoding who is doing good works for you in Heaven! "

.   .   .   .

The Miraculous Medal is much in demand among the prisoners; they have great faith in it, especially those who may be called to death at any moment. Only in certain cases is it possible to know beforehand the day and the hour, and to baptize them; but they are taught the Baptism of desire and the prayers that they should say at the moment of death. They understand the existence of the One True God, their Creator, the Master of Heaven, and they believe that with faith in Him and contrition for their sins, with desire of amendment, their souls may be saved for eternal life in Heaven. Our Divine Lord did not ask for more, or indeed as much, from the dying thief on the cross beside Him, and they are often told of this incident, which shows God's special affection for repentant brigands.

Once, on All Saints' Day, the Sisters were busy in the early afternoon with the monthly meeting of the Union of Catholic Mothers, when suddenly one of the nurses from the men's hospital came in and said to a Sister in a low tone, " I have just heard that three brigands in the prison are going to be shot this afternoon. The procession is now being formed, and there is no time to be lost."

Two of the Sisters slipped out quickly and hurried along the narrow streets, begging Our Lord to save these souls for Heaven. Suddenly the beating of the big gong was heard and people on all sides began to run. Turning the corner, they found the road cleared and the procession advancing. The Mandarin at its head, knowing the Sisters, bowed graciously to them and allowed them to pass the company of soldiers until they reached the three rickshaws in which the condemned men were tied. The little water-bottle was ready; one Sister turned and walked beside the first rickshaw. The man in it was moaning piteously, but stopped when he saw the Sister. She said clearly, " Beg Almighty God to forgive your sins and have mercy on your soul." He lifted his head for the Baptism.

The other Sister had done the same for the second man, then came the turn of the third. When they were all baptized, the Sisters walked by the side of the rickshaws, saying, " Do you understand what we have done ? " They replied, " We do understand, and we thank you, Momo." It was finished, and the Sisters slipped quietly away into a side street, saying a Rosary of thanksgiving on the way home.

On another occasion they saw the two rickshaws with the men heavily chained in them, but they could not get close to them.

When the brigands saw the Sisters, they stood up in the rickshaws and cried out, " Momo, we are going to die, but we will not forget what you have taught us, and thank you, thank you, Momo." The people in the streets were amazed and cried out, " Even these brigands have good hearts. See, they are thanking the Sisters for their good works."

Another young man was in the prison once for a very small offence. When he reappeared there some years later, the Sisters showed their surprise. He said to them quietly, " Momo, this time it is for a very grave offence. I killed a man in anger and I shall surely be condemned to be shot. I beg of you to prepare my soul for death as I have heard you do for others." Several instructions were given to this man and eventually he was baptized. He was remarkable for his good behaviour in the prison; he was so quiet and patient. On Holy Thursday his death sentence came, and he was taken in a rickshaw to be shot. On the way he said to the people in the street, " I am going to die, I deserve it. You people, don't follow my bad example."

Another big epidemic of typhus fever in the prison was particularly connected with the Miraculous Medal. Nearly 300 men fell victims to this terrible disease, and day after day a band of Sisters spent hours caring for them. As it was in the month of August, the hottest of the year, Dr. Chen, the Sisters' devoted doctor, forbade them to go into the cells, which were full of vermin. So the patients were all carried out on the backs of their friends to the dispensary courtyard, where they sat, supported by them. It was pitiful to see these white-faced, blue-lipped men. When they first came out for treatment, they were burly strong fellows, most of them brigands and pirates. After a week or more of high fever they were reduced to great weakness, and it was sometimes difficult to catch them at the crisis stage.

Their first request was for the Medal, and when it was given to them they said, " This will cure me." It certainly did, for very few died; it seemed a real miracle. The Sisters visited them twice a day, and brought not only medicine and injections but big pots of rice water and gruel, soup, etc. Some would refuse all food and would have died of weakness, but after a Sister had gently swabbed their yellow, leathery tongues they would accept from her hand a bowl of rice water with prune juice in it.

When convalescent they would say pitifully, " Momo, I am so hungry ", for there was nothing in the prison diet that they could eat. The Sister would slip a salt egg into one hand and some biscuits into the other, and they would be served with two lunches of soft rice a day. For breakfast the Sisters used to make a huge egg omelette at home, chop it up, and put it into the bucket of thick rice gruel. Breakfast tickets were served out the night before to those who needed it.

Only sixteen out of the 294 sick men died, and these were elderly men with weak hearts; they were nursed in an isolation ward at the Sisters' hospital and all were baptized before death. This epidemic was always called the " Miraculous Medal " one, because so many were cured and also because the Sisters themselves were protected by Our Lady; not one caught the disease.

Gradually regulations became more strict and in later years no permission could be obtained from the head authorities at Hangchow to transfer sick prisoners to the Sisters' hospital. However, in recognition of their services the Governor obtained funds to erect a small building in the prison court, the room on the ground floor to be used for a dispensary and the one above he offered to the Sisters for a little hospital.

They were delighted and through a special appeal to friends who were interested in prison work the necessary equipment was bought and a clean, comfortable, little hospital fitted up. There was just room for seven beds, with a mat on the floor for the " prisoner nurse ", who was very proud of his clean blue clothes and Red Cross apron.

To Sister Berkeley's satisfaction there were windows all round the four walls and on her first visit she exclaimed, " On this side they can see the mountains, poor fellows. What joy for them! " The little hospital was put under the patronage of St. Vincent de Paul, and the prison authorities painted a big Red Cross on the front wall and under it, in Chinese characters, " Charity ".

They objected at first to dying or incurable men being put into this little hospital, for they said it was " too nice for dirty illness ". But the Sisters would not hear of this restriction and they won their way. Many poor fellows passed their last days there in clean comfort; it was good to see their happiness in the peaceful, fresh atmosphere, with every want supplied.

One day the Sister said to a poor man with gangrenous glands

M

nearly choking him (she knew he could not pass the coming night), "You are not afraid, are you ?   Kiss your medal and ask ' Sing Mo-Maleeya [Holy Mother Mary], to take you up to Heaven. Say, ' My God, I believe, pardon my sins '." He replied, " Why should I be afraid ?   Never have I been so happy in my life as I am here, and I die in peace and confidence that all you have taught me about eternal life in Heaven is true."

Ordinarily the Chinese are frightened at the presence of the dying, but in the little hospital they had no fear and would tell the Sister that they had helped the dying man by saying the prayers she had taught them.   One morning the patients said to her, smiling, " Last night the Angels came and took Bao Tchinkwey to Heaven."   " Oh," said the Sister, " did you see them ? " " No, no," was the rather shocked reply, " there was no need to see them.   You told us they would come, and we had faith and believed ! "

This little hospital gave great pleasure to Sister Berkeley, and sometimes when the prison Sister set out for her daily service there she would accompany her.   The sick prisoners were delighted to see her and she would sit there smiling at them, while they were being cared for by the Sister and the nurse.   Then she would herself serve them with the little lunch; three times a day food was sent to these sick men.   Sister Berkeley would say to them, " Look, you can see the mountains on that side."   " Ah yes, Ta Momo," they would reply, " but if we could only run over them ! "   " Man-man lai, man-man lai [later you will]," she would assure them.

Many good cures were effected in this hospital.   One poor boy, who was fast developing pernicious anæmia from the bad air and poor nourishment, said pitifully, " I had my own boat and a bit of mountain land; then a friend tempted me to lend my boat for fifty dollars to the pirates; it was the first time and I was caught and have well paid for it.   I shall die here."   His puffy, bloodless face and swollen limbs drew pity, but after eight weeks in the little hospital he went down quite cured, and full of gratitude and hope for a new future, as in six months' time he would be free. The Sisters begged the Governor to give him outside work to do, such as carrying water.

When the patients were discharged from hospital, cured, it was a hard moment, but there was rarely any trouble.   With smiling courage they would thank the Sister, put on their own old clothes and go down to the crowded cells. There they were never tired of telling their companions of their happiness in the hospital, even teaching them some of the doctrine and prayers they had learnt there. They used to say, " Now that the Sisters look after us, we are treated like kings when we are sick and not left to die like dogs; they are real mothers to us."

It may be asked, " And what becomes of these prison friends of the Sisters when they are discharged ? " Of that, little can be said. On the day they leave the prison they always come to the Sisters for a meal and a small alms and clothes, if needed, to set them on their way. If they are sick and tired, they are received for a time in the hospital to pick up strength, and some come back in later years to " die with the Sisters ", as they say.

On their country-visiting excursions, the Sisters sometimes meet their prison friends, and receive a warm welcome and invitation to drink tea and eat rice in their houses. It was rather amusing to hear Tze Paoding and the brigand chiefs say, " We know you well, Momo. We have often met you in the country and sat beside you in the little seaside shelters waiting for the steamboat to come ! "

One rich gentleman of good family, who had been thrown into prison by an enemy on a false charge, would have died of grief and shame but for the care and help of the Sisters. When he was released he returned to his native province, far away in the Honan, and went to the Catholic Church there with all his family to be inscribed as catechumens. The priest of that district wrote and told the Sisters about him.

Not long ago one of the Chinese priests of Chusan went to visit a new island for the first time. He was very coldly received and heard queer tales about Christians; that they made electricity out of people's hearts, etc.! Suddenly a big burly man came forward and said indignantly, " What are you saying ? I can tell you that Christians are very good people. I know, for I was in the Chusan prison and the ' white hat Momos ' of the Christians nursed me when I was sick. We ought to adore their God, who is the Master of Heaven." He accompanied the priest everywhere, carrying his luggage, and he entertained him in his own house and promised to preach the True Faith until he came back again.

Among the most faithful and generous benefactors of the prison work in Chusan was a friend of Sister Berkeley's girlhood, Lady Victoria Herbert. In England she specially devoted herself to prisoners' aid work and she followed it also with great interest in this far-away Chinese island, sending constant gifts to carry on the work and help new developments. Once she sent a dozen boxes of rubber gloves to Sister Berkeley, begging that the Sisters should wear them during their work in the prison to avoid infection. Among her many gifts to Chusan was a big white shawl for the Sisters' infirmary which she had knitted herself. It was always called " Lady Victoria's shawl " and was much appreciated and often used.

XVI

LORETTE—THE GOLDEN YEARS

WE have spoken of the project of a rest house for the Sisters and that the idea had not fallen through, although the plan to use Chusan Meng was not feasible. Another site had been bought on a small mountain on Chusan Island, outside the North Gate, a superb position, with sea and islands on the south-east, and breezes from the north and west sweeping over it through big mountain passes.

Unfortunately the years of Communist troubles prevented the building of the rest house; everything stood still for a time, the future was so uncertain. Meanwhile Sister Berkeley cultivated this mountain land, and when she visited it realized more and more its health-giving value. At last she obtained permission to erect temporarily, on the top, a small house to which she could send her delicate babies and convalescent children. An ugly, rather useless house in the city compound was transported there and, when rebuilt, made a nice little country sanatorium, with verandas all round and a big terrace in front. It was given the name of " Lorette " because of its transportation.

The kind friend who helped to build this little house for the children was Admiral Seymour's sister, Miss Fannie Seymour. She was a generous benefactor to Chusan, always saying that as her brother's money came from China it ought to be used to do good in China. Hearing that Sister Berkeley wished to arrange two or three rooms on the east side of the building for Sisters in need of rest, Miss Seymour at once doubled her gift, begging that half the house should be for the children and half for the Sisters. With this help it was enlarged, with better accommodation on both sides, and in one room a little chapel was fitted up.

For the opening Fr. Chang, parish priest of the Church of St. Vincent at the foot of the Lorette mountain, climbed the hill, carrying a beautiful picture of the Holy Family, which he blessed and placed behind the altar in the chapel. The house was blessed and the first Mass said. Some of the Sisters and their children were present, as well as many of the villagers from the Catholic parish below.

Almost the first occupants of Lorette were the Mothers of the Sacred Heart from Shanghai; they spent two summer months there and made its reputation. They would have liked to build their own rest house on a mountain near-by, but many difficulties stopped this project, though Sister Berkeley always spoke of the " Sacred Heart mountain " and prophesied they would be there one day. The last two days of their visit were unforgettable, for the worst typhoon ever known in Chusan swept over the island; but the little house of Lorette stood firm, which said much for its foundations and columns.

After that, Lorette was nearly always full. On one side there were the convalescent children and a dozen or so of toddling babies, who spent their days on the terrace or mountain slopes, and many lives were saved in this good air. On the Sisters' side all was arranged in simple Community fashion for the arrival of Notre Mère Lebrun, who paid a special visit to China after six years of government as Mother General in Paris.

She was taken to Lorette and, after visiting the children's side, passed into the little chapel and through the rooms arranged for the Sisters. Knowing what beautiful plans she had drawn some years ago for a rest house, the Sisters wondered how the modest cottage-like residence would strike her, but when she had finished her tour, she said emphatically, " *C'est très bien, très bien. J'en suis si contente.*" One remembered her words on Chusan Meng, eight years before, " It is not only for convalescents that I want this rest house, but for the prevention of illness; if tired Sisters come from the city houses, three or four at a time all through the hot summer, we shall save many from breaking down in health." A Chusan Sister said doubtfully to her, " *Mais, ma Mère, les Sœurs ne viennent pas beaucoup.*" She replied, " *Tant pis pour elles; vous verrez, vous verrez, elles viendront.*"[1] And her words came true. It must be said that it was such a new idea for the Sisters to rest!

That very year Lorette was filled all through the summer and autumn months; some Sisters were saved from a forced return

[1] " But, Mother, the Sisters do not come ! " " So much the worse for them; you will see, they will come."

to Europe by spending two months or more on the mountain, which built up their health and strength. Many came for a week or two and went back to their heavy work in the cities, braced up physically and morally. An aspirant, too tall for her strength, had her turn, and even a Seminary Sister, in white coiffe and fichu, passed a summer at Lorette and was saved for devoted work in later years. She walked about the terrace, always followed by toddling babies; the children called her " Siau Caterina Momo " (Little Sister Catharine), because of her resemblance to St. Catharine Labouré, in the pictures and banners of the Miraculous Medal visions.

Sister Berkeley gave herself to this new work of charity with unparalleled devotion and enthusiasm. With open arms she received her visitors, " Welcome, welcome, my dear. I am so glad to see you and we will make you strong and well here." Everything possible was done for their benefit and enjoyment; the Blessed Sacrament was reserved in the chapel, and when the house had visitors Mass was said there daily.

On the verandas of Lorette high up, the visitors were never tired of the panorama below; the sea and the island mountains in the distance; the fleets of fishing boats with their brown sails; the arrival and departure of steamers; the canals winding like silver threads through the waving green of the rice fields, and the villages dotted here and there, with their turkeys and geese wandering through the fields, led by little sunburnt children. Sometimes lines of coolies would swing over the mountains, and down through the valley, with their loads of tea and wood or other mountain produce. There was life all around, and yet at Lorette one was above it all, high up, in perfect peace, with the cooling breezes of sea and mountains.

Sometimes in the evening a message would come from the city house, " To-morrow there will be *une occasion*! " This was a well-known joke and brought smiles to everyone's face. It meant that early next morning a boat would be waiting in the canal at the foot of the east side of the mountain. After breakfast, the Sisters would go down the hill, pass through the rice fields, round the city walls by the canal, to the west side, eventually arriving opposite Chusan Meng. Crossing over the sea, they would climb to the terrace and spend a long day on the island, with picnic meals bountifully provided by Sister Berkeley, who surveyed everything very closely for her visitors. These *occasions* were always received with smiling joy, and added greatly to the enjoyment of all at Lorette.

During the spring and summer months the Chusan Sisters took it in turn to be housekeeper and mother at Lorette, a second Sister going out each night to keep her company. In the morning they would both go down the hill to the little village church, and hear Mass, with the villagers chanting their prayers around them. The Sisters would say to each other, " To-day St. Vincent is very pleased with us, for we are real ' Parish Sisters ' as he wished."

A little dispensary was opened at Lorette to which came not only the Christians but many pagan neighbours from all the villages in the valley. Often there were special sick calls, and they would say, " It is good to have the Sisters as our neighbours, for they do good works. Besides, we always know the time now that they are here, ringing their big bell three times a day [Angelus]."

One afternoon a Sister was going out to Lorette to pass the night when, at the crossing of two paths, she saw a woman waiting for her, who told her of a very sad case in her village about a mile away. A young woman was dying, covered with a horrible disease, and she had been left alone in her misery. As it was already late in the evening the Sister promised to go early the next morning to this village of Ni-diao-tung (Two Bridges), which she knew well. She found the poor woman covered with leprosy, arms and legs eaten away, and in a terrible state of dirt and neglect.

Two Sisters went daily to care for her, taking food and soothing medicines, for she was in great suffering. They instructed her and prepared her for Baptism for she had not many days to live. The poor woman said: " I never remember having a home. I was sold as a little girl and went from place to place, unwanted, unloved. Now you come to care for me, and you tell me of God, my Father in Heaven, who loves me and wants me in Heaven with Him. It is too good to be true." She was soon ready for Baptism and received it with joy. The last night that the Sisters saw her (they knew she could not live through it), they said to her, " Don't be afraid; to-morrow you will be in the happiness of Heaven, all your sufferings finished." The woman thanked them, with the tears running down her cheeks, and said, " Momo, you will come there too, won't you ? "

The Sisters walked away from the house, deeply touched, saying, " That poor leper woman has invited us to Heaven! What happiness we have in our vocation! We care for Our Lord in the person of the poor and suffering, and it is they who will welcome us to Heaven."

.   .   .   .

Nestling at the foot of the Lorette mountain on the west side is the little Christian village of Podong, with many small farms. It is interesting to know that this settlement dates from the days of the holy and zealous Bishop, Mgr. Delaplace, C.M. He was much interested in the work of the Holy Childhood, and bought a farm there, to which he sent the Holy Childhood boys from Ningpo to be trained as land workers. Later on, the Bishop brought the Preparatory Seminary to this North Gate mountain of Chusan, and afterwards the Major Seminary followed it for a time, and one can still see their first modest chapel.

A Christian parish was thus formed, and there were many conversions; a church was built and dedicated to St. Vincent de Paul as " Parish Priest ", and high up behind the altar is a huge picture of him in surplice, with a crucifix in his right hand. One remembers his zealous work as " Country Curé " in the parishes of Clichy and Châtillon.

There were many of the Holy Childhood married girls in this little Christian village of Podong, and the establishment of the Sisters on the mountain at their side in Lorette brought them into contact with them. Seeing the married life of her children closely, Sister Berkeley felt that more ought to be done for these young Christian wives and mothers, to keep them fervent and pious and to help them to bring up their children well.

With the permission of the Bishop, she established a branch of the Union of Catholic Mothers. This was a work in which she was particularly interested, for it was her youngest sister, Etheldreda, who, as Mrs. Joseph Chichester, had been the foundress of this work many years ago on her Devonshire property of Calverleigh. Sister Berkeley's mother, Lady Catharine Berkeley, was the first President of the Union of Catholic Mothers in England, which now numbers hundreds of branches and thousands of members. In their journal we read: " With the help of her sister, Miss Berkeley, Mrs. Chichester drew up a scheme for a Union of Catholic Mothers and together they wrote the beautiful prayer used in it, which received an indulgence from Cardinal Bourne and later on from the Holy Father."

At Chusan the Catholic Mothers meet on the first Sunday of the month in the Sisters' city house, and after a social meeting, at which necessary advice is given, finish with an instruction in the chapel from the priest. This branch is under the patronage of the Holy Family and St. Louise de Marillac, the Foundress of the Sisters of Charity, for it was in the year of her Canonization, 1933, that it was started in Chusan.

The special features of its rule are: The saying of family night prayers together, with the Rosary, if possible; the bringing up of their children to be good practising Christians, teaching them their prayers at an early age, sending them to the Catholic school if there is one, and discouraging marriage to pagans. The Christians are so scattered in the islands that there is a great temptation to marry pagans, but the Union of Catholic Mothers has helped to remedy this defect.

Moreover, it encourages its members to practise active charity to their neighbours, pagans as well as Christians. Many of the women baptize dying pagan babies, bring unwanted orphans, especially the blind and infirm, to the Sisters, help the poor sick, visit them and invite them to the hospital if necessary. During a cholera epidemic the Catholic mothers especially distinguished themselves by their devoted charity. One went to care for a poor dying pagan woman, not only instructing and baptizing her, but also combing and arranging her hair and putting her into her best clothes, according to Chinese custom, regardless of the infection.

Another Christian woman offered herself as head nurse in a little cholera hospital arranged by the Sisters outside the city walls in a beggars' shelter. She nursed the patients most devotedly, and saved many souls, before she eventually fell a victim to cholera herself and nearly died of it. This woman also gives invaluable help to the Sisters with the sick prisoners; and when the Sisters, in 1942, were interned by the Japanese in their own House, she carried on all the active work in the prison, under most disagreeable and difficult conditions, and not one sick prisoner died without instruction and Baptism.

Another member, a new Christian, a widow, who now lives at Tinghai, opened up a big village to the Faith in her native district, Dgiansain, farther down the coast. After her conversion she brought many families to the Catechumenate and there is now a Christian centre in their village with a little chapel. This is entirely due to this widow, one of the elderly members of the Union of Catholic Mothers.

One of the most striking fruits of the Union has been the charity and good spirit found among the members; there are practically no quarrels, whereas formerly it was very common to see families who, after disputes, did not speak to one another, and even neglected their religious duties from this cause. At the reunions of the Catholic mothers one now looks round on about eighty members of all ages and classes, chatting cordially together and living on amicable terms. This, with the Chinese, is most wonderful, for their natural indomitable pride, desire of " good face ", difficulty in forgiving, especially among the women, makes quarrels frequent. Moreover, the Union has greatly improved the relations between mothers-in-law and their daughters-in-law, because both are invited. It is amusing to see their joy in leaving the house to the care of their menfolk on that day, and setting out together in their best clothes to ' kai-wey ', as they call their meeting. The daughter-in-law carries the smallest baby, and the mother-in-law leads the two- or three-year-old.

In the month of May they make a pilgrimage to the Church of the Holy Rosary at Sinkomen on the other side of the island. They carry their own banner of the Holy Family and St. Louise in procession up the hill, and pass a happy day of devotion to Our Blessed Lady, gaining many graces and favours.

When the Apostolic Delegate, Mgr. Zanin, made his official visit to Chusan, the members of the Union of Catholic Mothers were presented to him. He was delighted, saying that it was the only branch of this work that he had seen in China.

The Chusan Union of Catholic Mothers has been affiliated to the International Branch and shares in all the privileges and indulgences.

Before leaving Lorette, a sad story must be told. Although the Japanese never occupied this little house, yet Chinese workmen were lodged in it when the munition go-downs were being blasted in the mountains around it. When the Sisters returned from camp in 1945, after peace had been declared, they found a scene of desolation and ruin, though they thanked God the house was still standing. There are heavy repairs to be done before it can again be used, but it is the same in the city houses. The problem first to be solved is the finding of sufficient food for the children and poor; repairs must wait, though some of them are very urgent. The children have to sleep on the ground floor when it rains, for in the dormitories their beds are soaked owing to leaking roofs.

There have been so many signs of Sister Berkeley's continued interest and care of her beloved Mission that one has confidence Lorette will again be built up, and the valuable work for convalescent children and Sisters renewed. She will surely also obtain the Toddlers' Home, to be built on a site behind Lorette, which was the last plan she made for the welfare of her children.

In looking back, one thinks of the years 1931 to 1937 as the golden years of Sister Berkeley's life at Chusan. The House of Mercy, under her inspiration and guidance, had opened its doors in a spirit of faith and charity to all the poor and suffering in the islands, and they were cared for in good airy houses, with everything necessary for comfort and health. All the works were flourishing. You would hear, "There is not another empty bed," yet something had to be arranged for newcomers, some of them little abandoned babies in rags, some Christian children for the extern school, and some old people, worn with age and sickness, who would say pitifully, "If the ' white-hat ' Momos do not receive us, to whom shall we go ? " The House of Mercy numbered over 500 inmates in those years.

There were 150 babies being nursed in the country, treated like princesses by their foster-mothers; this meant that a strong generation of children was being reared, and in the house nurseries, schools and workrooms, it was a joy to see such large numbers of happy healthy children, from two to eighteen years old, not forgetting those at Lorette.

Sister Berkeley's work of predilection, the visiting of the poor sick in the villages and islands, was in full swing; the hospitals, too, were doing good work for the sick people of the islands, and there was rarely an empty bed in them.

This had meant many years of patient striving and economy for the Good Mother at the head, but with her look of confidence she would point to the chapel and say, " Our dear Lord does it all; we just leave it in His Hands." It was a succession of miracles of Divine Providence, for the House had very little income and depended chiefly on gifts from day to day.

Rarely was a large donation received. The House subsisted chiefly on small contributions from the kind Propagation of the Faith and Holy Childhood Offices in England and America, godmothers, and children in schools. Sister Berkeley carried on a very large correspondence with these friends, and this was not easy in the busy life of a Sister of Charity. She confided to a companion that in her earlier years she had obtained permission to write for an hour at night after the others had retired, but she never gave this permission to her Sister secretary.

It gave her great pleasure that so many benefactors of her House were poor people, servants, nurses, clerks in humble station. She spoke of them with real affection; there was the good Emma Jerdo, a children's nurse in New York, who sent a generous yearly offering for her godchild in Chusan, though she had also to support her widowed sister's family, and she told Sister Berkeley all about these and received sympathy and advice.

There was Mrs. Bryant, the farmer's wife, who sometimes wrote apologizing that the offering for her " Mary " was late, but she had to wait until the farm produce was sold; another, Estelle Weigel, who with her two brothers, clerks, even when on half-pay, kept up their offering for their godchild. From this kind girl came every year a delightful Christmas parcel, full of treasures, rosaries and small objects of piety, remnants of gay-coloured cloth, needles, thread and even hard candy. We must not forget " Ada the cook ", who gathered in subscriptions from the butcher, the baker and the grocer for Chusan babies.

There were many others, and they were all Sister Berkeley's personal friends, rich and poor. She insisted that kind, affectionate letters should be sent to them with Mission news and photographs of their godchildren, telling them that they were " partners in the work of saving souls ", and shared in the merits. She asked the Holy Childhood children to pray for them and their intentions regularly, and she liked the Mass of the first Friday of every month to be offered for them. One often heard of answers to prayers which were attributed to the Chusan children.

One good godfather in America, Mr. J. Smith, after supporting a little child at Chusan for many years, wrote to tell Sister Berkeley of his ordination to the priesthood in Rome. She was delighted to think that an act of charity to Chusan had helped to make another good priest for God's service. Good Mrs. Swendeman, another faithful benefactor, was so pleased when she found out that she and Sister Berkeley were the same age, " Now we are both eighty years old! " she wrote in her last letter before the war. She constantly sent gifts for her godchild and also for the baptism of pagan babies. When godparents were unable to continue financial help, Sister Berkeley wrote begging them for their prayers. Chusan had also many " working partners " for the saving of souls in Carmelite Convents; miracles of grace were often attributed to them.

Of the children we have already spoken, for since her early days in Ningpo Sister Berkeley had made friends with them, always hoping to inspire future missionaries. Many convents had their godchildren, and not only money gifts were sent but clothes made, caps and scarves knitted and the children's own treasures sacrificed for Chusan. The Third Division at Roehampton for many years had a " Cecily Madeleine Sophie " for whom they made sacrifices.

The Sacred Heart Convent children of St. Julian's, Malta, ran a most zealous Missionary Society. They regularly sent gifts and accounts of their lectures, concerts and plays for the benefit of the Missions, their own godchildren especially. Not long ago a young girl presented herself at the Central House of the Sisters of Charity, Mill Hill, London, asking to enter the Community. " I know nothing about the Sisters of Charity," she said, " except that at the Sacred Heart School, Malta, we had a Missionary Society, of which I was secretary, and we always wrote to Sister Berkeley on Chusan Island, China, and—I want to be like her! "

Irish friends were not behindhand, and their gifts came specially through the kind and zealous missionary, Fr. Arnold, O.S.B., of Buckfast Abbey. Chusan was much favoured by him; he sent generous gifts regularly for Baptisms and was an old and valued friend of Sister Berkeley.

THE GOLDEN JUBILEE

The chapel at Chusan was on the first floor of the old building used by the Sisters and, with the ever-increasing family, was becoming seriously overcrowded on Sundays and Feast Days. Many times Sister Berkeley had been asked by others, even by Superiors, " When are you going to build a real chapel ? " She would smile and say, " When I think of a new chapel, Our Lord always seems to show me that He wants the poor and the children to be arranged more comfortably before I make a better house for Him."

However, in 1931 the floor of the old chapel began to shake alarmingly with the tramping of the little feet on it, and it was condemned as unsafe. The year 1932 was that of Sister Berkeley's Golden Jubilee of vocation: fifty years a Sister of Charity. On all sides one heard, " A chapel must be built for this occasion." It was more easily said than done, for it was impossible to find space for it in the crowded compound. Mgr. Ou, Bishop of Haimen, solved the difficulty; when on a visit to Chusan, walking down the long entrance corridor, he said to Sister Berkeley, " Sister, your chapel must be built along the side of this corridor. You must pull down all those buildings there and make room for it."

Sister Berkeley had no fear of pulling down buildings; they were not trees, you could build them up again to-morrow. Down they came, and were transported, wholly or in parts, rebuilt, and miraculously fitted in somewhere. As usual in the pagan strong-hold of China, when a new work was proposed for the Glory of God, innumerable obstacles opposed it. In this case came the first Japanese offensive in Shanghai, the temporary outbreak in January 1932. The horizon grew very dark and uncertain for a time, so all new works were stopped. Suddenly the air cleared and hostilities ceased, and in the month of May Mgr. Defebvre, Bishop of Ningpo, came to lay the foundation stone of the new chapel and bless the ground.

Then work went ahead with a rapidity unknown in China; there was no " man-man chi " (go slowly) for Ta Momo's new chapel; it had to be finished for the Golden Jubilee Feast on September 8th, only three short months away. There was no time to be lost, and all hands were on the work; even in the great heat no one stopped. Fr. Chang of Podong received a band of carpenters on his premises to make the benches and other fittings. The altars, with their beautiful soapstone decorations, arrived from Wenchow. The new Stations of the Cross were given by the catechists of the islands; another group of country Christians gave the light fittings.

The gifts came in steadily from all sides, those from the poor being the most numerous. " For your chapel, Ta Momo," a

poor bamboo worker said, " a month's wages! " He slipped a little
red paper-covered packet into her hand, and hundreds followed
with the same.   England, Ireland and America all wanted to have
a share in the Golden Jubilee chapel of Chusan.   Cardinal
O'Connell of Boston sent a princely gift.   He was an old friend of
Sister Berkeley, and often when a donation came his way it
was for the needs of Chusan he sent it.   A Boston friend once said
that Sister Xavier Berkeley was the Cardinal's favourite Mission
Sister.

The climax came on the eve of the great Feast, when a cable
sent through a Shanghai bank brought the Jubilarian the congratulations of her American Sisters with a generous gift, which
paid all the debts and provided many necessary additions to the
equipment of the new chapel.

It seemed as if Almighty God were showering His blessings on
His much-loved child and faithful servant.   Gifts of beautiful
vestments, candlesticks, and altar furnishings of all kinds, including a new sanctuary lamp, poured in.   A gift which gave great
pleasure to Sister Berkeley was the lining of the new tabernacle; it
had been prepared by one who knew her great love and devotion
to the work for the children, and there was a beautiful picture,
painted on Chinese silk gauze, of Our Lord with the children
around Him.

Mgr. Defebvre from Ningpo, Mgr. Ou from Haimen, Fr.
Nugent, Director of the Major Seminary at Ningpo, a very old
friend of Sister Berkeley, Fr. Luke Yao of Sinkomen and many
other priests and friends came to rejoice with Chusan on Our
Lady's birthday, the Golden Jubilee Feast.   The Superiors and
Sisters from Shanghai houses and all those in the neighbourhood
were visitors for several days, and all agreed that there had never
been such a beautiful Feast; everything went off perfectly.

The new chapel was opened with High Mass sung by the Holy
Childhood children, who had a big share in the rejoicings, all in
their new clothes and gold-coloured shoes and stockings, the soles
of the shoes having been made by the prisoners.   It was beautiful
to see the chapel filled in every corner with the Christians of the
islands, among them old married Holy Childhood children of the
House, all pouring out their hearts in thanksgiving for God's
goodness, and offering their grateful prayers for the one who had
given so many years of loving service for them in God's name.

VISITING THE PRISON

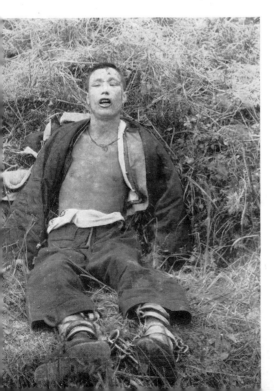

THE " GOOD THIEF "
Tze Paoding, famous chief of a brigand
band, was shot, but before he died he
was baptized, and the Miraculous Medal
can be seen round his neck

LORETTE, THE LITTLE SANATORIUM IN THE MOUNTAINS

CONVALESCENCE AFTER MEASLES AT LORETTE, 1932

Over 2,000 guests sat down to ' eat rice ', and as the mark of a great feast in China is the number of dishes provided to eat with the rice it must be told that there were twelve varieties at this Golden Jubilee dinner—meat, fish, and delicacies of all kinds. The Good Mother visited all the Houses in the compound during the meal, and distributed to the guests and her children beautiful pictures of Our Lady and the Divine Infant, together with a specially woven towel with a gold line in it to each one.

Later in the day entertainments were given by the children to the visitors, which were much enjoyed. After Benediction and a rousing sermon in Chinese by Fr. Luke Yao, the *Magnificat* was sung.

Every new feast day brought a special joy, since it was being celebrated for the first time in the new chapel. Christmas found the Divine Infant in His new home, then in 1933 came the Beatification of Blessed Catherine Labouré, followed by the Canonization of St. Louise de Marillac. For these great feasts, the new chapel was decorated with beautiful banners of pale blue satin, embroidered in gold, on which were painted by a Chinese artist pictures of scenes in the Holy Mother's life, and the Miraculous Medal visions. These banners were hung from the big columns of the chapel, which lent themselves well for decorations, the principal features of which were huge bamboos with their feathery green foliage.

The new chapel was a source of unending joy to Sister Berkeley in her last years; she would slip through the door at the back of her room and in one minute was in Our Lord's presence. One saw her smile at the Tabernacle as she entered, and if she were missing one always knew where to find her, wrapt in faith and adoration of the Holy Eucharist; all her troubles, all her joys, she brought there.

THE EUCHARISTIC CONGRESS IN THE PHILIPPINES

In 1937 Sister Berkeley was chosen to accompany the Sister Assistant of the China Province and three other Sisters to the Eucharistic Congress at Manila in the Philippine Islands. This was a joy and privilege which she greatly appreciated. One of the predominant features of the Congress was " Missionary Enterprise " and the presence of Missionaries, especially from the East, was greatly desired. It was good to see how the Western visitors

N

to the Congress were struck and edified by the fervent piety of the Eastern Christians, especially those from China and Japan.

The Spanish Sisters of Charity, working in the Philippines, had some years before been affiliated to the great family of St. Vincent under the Paris Superiors. They gave a warm welcome to their Missionary Sisters from China, and did everything possible to make their visit enjoyable. The headquarters of the visitors were at Concordia College, and the five short days which were passed at Manila were full from morning to night. Soon after four o'clock in the morning the call was given: " Come, we will go," and away went the Sisters in the Concordia motors to Mass and other ceremonies in the huge stadium arranged so beautifully for the Congress. In spare intervals, which were few, all the Houses of the Sisters in Manila were visited—the beautiful Hospital of St. John of God and the Orphanages, all very well arranged and efficiently carried on.

It was a full programme, and finished on the fifth day with a beautiful procession of the Blessed Sacrament, along the wide Dewey Avenue by the side of the sea, all carrying lighted candles and singing the Congress hymns.

On the passage to and from Manila Hongkong was visited, and Sister Mary Paul, the Superior of the Maryknoll Sisters there, gave her old friend Sister Berkeley a very warm welcome. She obtained a special permission from the Shanghai Superiors for her to visit a Maryknoll Mission in the interior, Kongmoon, one of the first given to them in China.

Here the Sisters were welcomed by Bishop Paschang, and after showing them his Mission works he took them to the Leper Settlement where Fr. Thomas Connor was working in the full vigour of his youthful strength and enthusiasm. The memory of him passing among his beloved lepers, dressing their wounds and attending to all their needs, corporal and spiritual, will never be forgotten. This devoted young Missioner was called to God the following year, when he returned home for a minor operation, which proved to be more serious than expected. He rests now in the Maryknoll Cemetery near his Venerated Father General.

The Sisters also paid a visit to Fr. Martin Burke's city Mission near Kongmoon. This zealous Maryknoll Missioner is especially gathering in the souls of the young men of the city, doing everything possible to make contact with them. There are interesting stories of these conversions in the *Field Afar*, and Fr. Burke maintains that the Chinese make the best kind of Christians, full of faith, piety and generosity, bringing many others to the True Fold after they themselves have entered. On this interesting visit to the Maryknoll Missions the Sisters were accompanied by Mgr. McKenna of Philadelphia, who was a most interesting and entertaining companion.

At Hongkong, on the way to Manila, the huge Japanese liner *Asa Maru* was met, also on its way to the Congress, carrying all the American pilgrims. There were many distinguished passengers on board, among them Archbishop Mitty of San Francisco. The Sisters went on board and found one of the largest first-class saloons arranged beautifully as a chapel in which was Exposition of the Blessed Sacrament. The memory rests with them of many Japanese pilgrims from Formosa kneeling in adoration in this chapel.

As the Sisters returned to their own Dutch liner in a little motor launch, Sister Berkeley pointed to the big Japanese boat they had just left, moored to the Kowloon wharf.

" Pagan Japan carrying Our Lord to the Congress! " she said.

XVII

SISTER PAULINE SOUEN

SISTER PAULINE was the devoted and zealous Chinese Sister at Chusan, of whom we have already spoken. No life of Sister Berkeley would be complete without a chapter on this holy old Sister, who was her right hand in the work for souls, especially among the extern schoolchildren and catechumens. It will also show the heights of sanctity and devotion to which many of the Chinese daughters of St. Vincent de Paul rise.

Sister Souen had an exciting childhood. She was born at Soochow, and when she was about seven years old the *Tchang Maos* (rebels) attacked that district. Her parents, with the younger children, escaped, but she remained with her grandfather, who stayed to guard the house. Sister Souen remembered that many rich people came to their house for safety, but on the arrival of the *Tchang Maos* they were all killed.

A woman servant seized the little girl by the hand, and they ran away together and hid in a river among the rushes, with water up to their waists. The *Tchang Maos* found them and dragged them out. Sister Souen remembered one with a red coat and big knife, who threatened to kill them. The pagan servant was screaming " *Oh-mey doh-mah*," the prayer to the Buddha, but the little Christian girl knelt down and prayed to God, offering herself and her life to His service if He would save her. The *Tchang Mao* said, " She is only a good-for-nothing girl, and so ugly, not worth killing! " Her life was saved and her uncle found her and took her to his house until her parents returned.

As a young girl Sister Souen studied in the newly opened school of the Helpers of the Holy Souls at Si-ka-wei, near Shanghai. She studied well and was much liked by the Mothers; she became one of the first Children of Mary of Mother St. Gertrude. Later she entered Carmel and stayed there seven years, but became unsettled when she heard of the Sisters of Charity, whose special vocation was the service of the poor. Sister Souen felt a strong desire to enter this Community, which was beginning to receive Chinese aspirants.

The Prioress and nuns of Carmel were loth to part with her, for they much appreciated her piety and virtue. It is interesting to know that in Sister Souen's ninety-first year, after sixty years' devoted service of the poor, she died peacefully on the Feast of Our Lady of Mount Carmel.

Two months after Sister Souen entered the Seminary (Novitiate) the Franco-Chinese war broke out, and she, with another Chinese novice, was quickly clothed with the habit and cornette of a Sister of Charity and sent to mind the Orphanage at Ningpo with an Italian Sister in the absence of the French Sisters, who were interned for safety at Shanghai.

After the war Sister Souen was sent to the Holy Childhood Orphanage, Hangchow. There she was very unhappy, often weeping, so she was called to Shanghai; but she still wept. In her old age, she said simply, " I was calumniated. They said that I had no vocation and wept because I wished to leave the Community." However, a kind French Sister, who spoke Chinese well, discovered the cause of her unhappiness. Sister Souen told her, " I was only a few weeks in the Seminary before I received the Holy Habit, and was sent to guard the House at Ningpo. I know hardly any French, so I don't understand the prayers and spiritual exercises. I have had very little instruction, so I know nothing of the spirit of my vocation. How can I serve God as a Sister of Charity if I only wear the habit and the cornette, and know nothing of the religious spirit ? "

The French Sister asked permission to give Sister Souen lessons in French, and instructions in Chinese on the spirit of her vocation. In her old age Sister Pauline said triumphantly, " I had a better Seminary than any of them."

One cannot but be edified at this beginning of her long life as a Sister of Charity, nor is one surprised that this first Chinese daughter of St. Vincent understood and practised the virtues of her state in an exemplary manner. With such a supernatural foundation she made an excellent Sister, after the hearts of St. Vincent de Paul and St. Louise de Marillac, for both of whom she had a real filial love and veneration, shown by her respect and obedience to her Superiors.

Sister Souen was next sent to the Mission of Chusan, where

she had the happiness of making her holy Vows. Named Sister Pauline, she was first put in charge of the kitchens, but she related that nearly all the Sisters went to visit the poor outside, her turn being in the afternoons when her kitchen work was finished.

A few years later Sister Pauline was given the charge of the extern school and catechumenate, and she continued this work to the end of her life. Besides the little Christian girls from the country villages and islands who come to be prepared for the Sacraments, there are always some pagan girls, engaged to Christians, who are prepared for Baptism, and also a number of women catechumens from newly converted families.

Sister Pauline, with much prayer and study, devoted herself to this new work. But she related that, looking back after some years, she found that some of her pupils had not turned out well, had become " lazy Christians ", as they say in China, while some newly baptized had apostatized. In her old age she said, " I was very pained and wondered what was wanting in my instructions. I prayed for help and guidance, for I felt it must be my fault. God showed me that I must speak more simply, adapt myself to their language; above all, I must appeal to their hearts so as to give my pupils a real desire for the Faith. I entirely remodelled my instructions and begged God to do the work Himself in His way, through me."

One is struck by the humility and sincerity with which the Sister took the blame to herself for the non-perseverance of some of her pupils. Also it reminds one of the " little method " of St. Vincent, which he was always recommending to his priests in their Missions to the poor country people, very simple words and manners to touch their hearts and lift them up to God.

Sister Pauline became all in all to these rough, sometimes coarse, country women and children; she loved them and they knew it. She saw their souls under the rough exterior, and she succeeded marvellously with them. Rarely was she heard to say, " Ah, that one, she never really had any Faith." Many said, " I was one of Sister Pauline's pupils and I have never forgotten what she taught me."

Those who fell away from their duties to God and came back were warmly welcomed by her; she called them " fishes ", the souls she was always trying to catch, and she spread her net in every direction to bring them into God's Kingdom. Sometimes

she would come to Sister Berkeley with a radiant face, saying,
" A big fish, Ta Momo, a big fish! " Perhaps it would be the
head of an apostate family come back to God, and his pagan wife
and children would be brought in to study with Sister Pauline.
Or it might be old Holy Childhood children, who had wandered
far from God, and in old age and sickness came back to their first
home. It is the experience of Missioners that Holy Childhood
children are seldom lost. Even after many years away from God,
when death approaches they say, " I am a Holy Childhood boy
[or girl]; I must die a good death."

The Sister in charge of the women's hospital often came to
ask Sister Pauline to come and see a " big fish ", a patient who
needed help in preparing to receive the Sacraments again. Sister
Pauline would go, patiently listen, perhaps make two or three visits
before she would say, " Now call the priest; she is ready."

On one occasion the Sister said, " Sister Pauline, there is a ' big
fish ' in the hospital," and she named the woman. " Will you
come and help her ? It is sixteen years since she went to Confession." After thinking a few minutes, Sister Pauline replied,
" Not sixteen years; oh no, it is twenty-four years! " The Sister,
rather surprised, said, " I was told she came here sixteen years ago
and went to Confession." " Ah yes," said Sister Pauline gravely,
" she did, but she did not tell everything! " How did she know ?
She had her ways, and the women appreciated it, for she went to
the root of the matter. They would often say, " Send Pauline
Momo to me; she knows how to help me."

Sometimes well-dressed women arrived from Shanghai or other
big cities and asked to see her. She would look at them closely
when they said, " Pauline Momo, do you remember me ? " Yes,
she remembered them, and their families, and their misdoings.
" What are you doing in Shanghai since your husband died ? "
she would ask one gravely, and the woman would hang her head
like a child ashamed. All had to come out into the light with
Sister Pauline, and she would pour forth on her favourite subject:
" There are two roads to eternity, the road that leads to Heaven
and the road that leads to Hell. We baptized Christians know
them, and each of us has the free will to choose which road to
take." Then she marked out clearly and gently to the strayed
sheep the way to come back.

An old Holy Childhood girl, after the death of her first husband, had married a rich pagan without a dispensation. He was a good pagan who would have accepted the conditions for it, but she carelessly let herself slip into sin. When death was approaching, remorse seized her; she went to Sister Pauline and said, " Pauline Momo, what shall I do ? " The Sister replied, " You must leave that man and come into the Sisters' hospital and die there. You must not see him again." She did it, and she died among the poor in the hospital, but with all the Sacraments and her soul at peace with God. The pagan man understood the situation, and did not come to see her, but he sent money for her coffin and for Masses to be said for her.

Sometimes it was the " little fishes " that Sister Pauline found when visiting the poor in the town or country—children of Christian parents, not practising their religion. She would make friends with the " little fishes ", give them Miraculous Medals on coloured strings, persuading them to take off their ugly pagan emblems and to come into her school. Many were brought in like that, and after Baptism, Communion and Confirmation she would follow them until they were safely settled in Christian homes or obtain dispensations if they were already engaged to pagans.

The extern school and catechumenate at Chusan are open for two periods in the year, the first, after the Chinese New Year, about the end of February, up to the end of June. First Communions are made on the Feast of the Sacred Heart and Confirmations at the visit of the Bishop. The second period is in the autumn after the rice crop is cut and the potato harvest is gathered in; this extends from September to Christmas, finishing on the Feast of the Epiphany.

The little country girls and women catechumens flock in, not only from the parish of St. Michael at Tinghai but also from that of St. Vincent of Podong and from Sinkomen, the fishing port on the other side of the island of Chusan, and from all the islands belonging to these parishes: Bougee, Kindong, Si-Hadgee, Tsu-ko-tsien, Taysain, etc.

Strictly speaking, Tinghai Mission is not obliged to receive in its school and catechumenate children and women from all these districts, but the parish priests always begged for their admittance. They said to Sister Berkeley, " If our Christian children and catechumens come to Tinghai, and live with the Sisters for some months, hear Sister Pauline's instructions, and have the Blessed

Sacrament in the house with daily Mass, they become fervent practising Christians, and we see the effects in their families."

The good Superior of the House of Mercy at Tinghai, Sister Berkeley, opened her heart and her house to them with zeal and generosity, as she always did when it was an affair of souls. It is true that there was no foundation or income for this extern work. The House of Mercy itself had no regular income, but lived on gifts from day to day. It seemed very rash, humanly speaking, to invite seventy to eighty extern children and women to come in and " eat their rice " for several months, twice a year; but this House was founded in 1868 on Divine Providence, and continued with the same confidence. One often heard Sister Berkeley say, " God will never let us suffer for what we do for the souls of the extern children and catechumens."

The dormitories and schoolrooms were often overflowing, and one heard afar off the shouting of the prayers and catechism, for hardly anyone could read. All had to be taught verbally, word by word, and, as we have already said, in Chusan everyone shouts; it is the normal speaking voice!

Sometimes the situation was overwhelming, even for Sister Pauline. One year numbers of women arrived from Dgiansain, a port farther down the coast, brought by the fervent convert widow of whom we have already spoken, Dgiansain Bo (the Grandmother from Dgiansain). With indefatigable zeal she brought in, unauthorized by the priests or Sisters, companies of women and children, catechumens, and somehow she always got her way; they had to be accepted if she brought them.

On this occasion a crowd of pagan women, most of them with babies in their arms, introduced into an already overflowing schoolroom, taxed even Sister Pauline's powers of adaptation. She had no facilities for the care of babies, and the babies cried, and no one, the mothers included, could learn anything.

The Sister in charge of the house nursery came to the rescue, and offered to receive these Dgiansain women to live there, and to leave their babies in the little cribs, while the poor mothers went to learn catechism and prayers. We say " poor " mothers, for they found it very hard to leave their precious babies in other hands.

It was difficult on both sides, for these rough country women made themselves thoroughly at home in the nursery, taking what they liked. The Sister in charge tried to follow in the footsteps of Sister Berkeley and Sister Pauline, whose rule was, " To gain souls, never mind a little disorder or difficulties; shut your eyes to everything that is not a mortal sin."

This first band of Dgiansain women and children all went home baptized. One of them, another widow woman, not poor, arranged a room in her house as a little chapel, where all could meet and say prayers together, and on rare occasions have Mass said when a priest visited them. Her little son wrote in big characters on a board " The Catholic Church ", and placed it over their front door. It was known at first with some amusement as the " Women's Church ", because nearly all the first members were women. Little by little their menfolk followed them, and there is now a flourishing Christian centre founded by Dgiansain Bo.

A Chusan Sister relates some interesting stories about Sister Pauline's " big and little fishes ":

" When I made excursions to the villages and islands to care for the sick people, I always asked Sister Pauline to tell me what Christian families lived in those districts, and if there were any children who ought to be called into her school. She would sometimes tell me of ' little fishes ' whose families were so poor that the children lived in rags, and they were ashamed to come in like that. So we prepared complete outfits which we took with us, shoes, stockings, pretty clothes, to try and draw the ' little fishes ' to come and study in the school and prepare for the Sacraments. This is so important, for there are some ignorant parents who think that if their children have not been to school they may marry them to pagans without sin.

" What was so wonderful about Sister Pauline was her readiness to ask advice and take suggestions, even from Europeans, which the Chinese find difficult. She only seemed to have in view the souls she was trying to save and train up in God's grace. Once she brought a little girl, eleven years old, to me saying, ' What is to be done ? Yudi says she must go home because the devil is tormenting her— Mokwey laike longsong gi.' These are common words in China. The devil is so strong in these pagan regions, and the people are terrified of him.

" This little girl was the child of apostate parents who were half turning back to their Faith and who had, with some reluctance, allowed us to bring in this child to prepare for Baptism. It would be sad if she left us and unlikely that we should ever see her again. It was the month of February and I noticed that her little arms were blue with cold (it was then the custom for women and girls to wear short elbow sleeves). ' Do you think, Sister Pauline,' I asked, ' that a pair of red knitted sleeves would drive the devil away ? ' ' We might try,' said Sister Pauline dubiously. I brought out some long red knitted sleeves, and the little cold arms were covered cosily warm; we heard no more of the devil.

" It must be said that Sister Pauline herself had a holy terror of the devil; indeed, all our Chinese Sisters have. To us in this pagan country he is a real personage with power to do great evil, though there are many striking cases in which the power of God intervenes and renders the devil helpless.

" In my first year in China I was sent with Sister Pauline to visit a sick pagan woman in the street near by, hoping to alleviate her sufferings, or perhaps to prepare her for Baptism if she was dying. When we entered the house, we saw all around the bed of the sick woman numbers of queer objects, branches of trees, etc., all decorated with bits of red rags. When Sister Pauline saw them, she gave a great start, and said in terror, ' Come away, come away; the devil is in strong possession here! ' She almost ran away, dragging me with her.

" As the confinement in a schoolroom was very trying to these country children, once, when the warm weather was beginning, I suggested to Sister Pauline that on Sunday afternoons I should take her pupils for a blow on the mountain side. To scramble about in the fresh air with a lunch of biscuits and fruit might freshen up their brains, and give them courage to attack the catechism and prayers once again.

" Sister Pauline looked at me with horror, ' You don't understand,' she said, ' they are not here to play. Every minute is valuable; there is so much to teach them.' I said no more, but the following Sunday she came to me and said, ' Perhaps you are right. It might do them good to go out for an hour; the present age is a dissipated one, and children must jump and play. We might try if it would help them to study better. But those five [she named them] cannot go, for they know absolutely nothing. I will keep them for personal instruction; the others can go to the mountain.'

" On Sunday afternoon a merry band got into line, carrying baskets of cakes and chunks of sugar cane to eat on the mountain top. Inside the schoolroom were five woeful faces, sitting before their books, and tears were falling. Sister Pauline looked at them, then at the happy faces outside. ' Shut your books and be off with you,' she said rather severely. They needed no second invitation. It was a happy party, and all came in with big appetites for supper and glowing faces. Sister Pauline acknowledged that it did them good. ' It is the dissipated age we live in,' she said, ' we must give in to it.'

" The way she trained these uncivilized country children was wonderful. Many of them came in like little savages, and yet, without any severity, in a week's time you saw them walking in order to Mass, reverently genuflecting before the Blessed Sacrament, saluting the priests and Sisters politely, quite changed and very happy. Sister Pauline read their characters, told them gently of their faults; they accepted anything from her."

Sometimes there would be a case of theft in the crowded dormitories. Was it to be wondered at? Some of them were poor little children who had never before seen pretty things, and they were sorely tempted to help themselves from the stores of their more fortunate companions. The Sisters tried to prevent this by providing the poorest with all necessaries, but if it did happen Sister Pauline dealt with it in a wonderful way. She always found out the culprit, and managed to get restitution made without " loss of face ", and she taught them the solid doctrine of the Ten Commandments.

In her Community life this Chinese Sister was an example of piety and virtue. Sister Berkeley said that naturally Sister Pauline had a very violent temper, and it had taken great efforts on her part to correct it. If she gave way to impatience or sharp words, she never failed to ask pardon before nightfall with great humility. Another striking quality was her love of work, which to her was the fulfilment of her fourth Vow. This was the more remarkable when one heard stories from a very old Sister, who had known her when she was a girl. She said, " In her home, she never left the house except when she was carried in a chair by four porters, and indoors she never picked up a handkerchief dropped on the floor. There were always servants around her to do such things! "

In Community Sister Pauline was never idle. During the holiday season, after she had put her classrooms and dormitories in order, she would go to Sister Berkeley and say simply, " Sister, what work do you wish me to do? " She went to visit the poor outside, looking up the Christian families, treating the sick people, and often bringing in a harvest of Baptisms, especially during the hot weather, and she took no notice of fatigue.

It was her work to buy the *ko* (unthrashed rice), and she would spend long days in the hot rice fields, weighing each sack and keeping strict accounts. Sometimes there would be a big catch of fish at the port, and it was Sister Pauline who went to buy and bring in large quantities to be dried and salted. She was Sister Berkeley's right hand for all difficult and distasteful work, especially for managing the Chinese business and correspondence. With her excellent education, she knew the right way of writing to people, and even at eighty years of age she still did this work for the House.

The priests found her invaluable because of her knowledge of all the Christian families. A Sister relates:

" Once I saw the parish priest arrive with members of two outside Christian families, and he asked Sister Pauline if she knew of any impediment against marriage between a boy and girl from these families. Sister asked a few questions, looked at the prospective bride and bridegroom, and said promptly, ' That cannot be; they are brother and sister. His mother [pointing to the boy] was his father's third wife, and she was also the girl's mother by her first husband! ' "

She knew such complications and even in her old age was capable of dealing with them.

Another task Sister Pauline always took over in her holidays was the renewal of the bedcovers, mattresses and pillows, etc. She would be seen working away at them in her school yard. But she was not satisfied if she had no direct work for souls, so Sister Berkeley would look through the Holy Childhood Houses, to find some blind, infirm or rather stupid children, who had only received Baptism and had got no farther, being given up as difficult cases. In the Old Women's Home, there might be some similar ones, or women servants, who were still catechumens and should be pushed on to Baptism.

This motley crew would be gathered together and presented to Sister Pauline as holiday work, and she was delighted. She would settle down with them, and very soon a happy band would be presented to Sister Berkeley and the parish priest, ready for the Sacraments. She liked difficult cases, and if they gave trouble later on they only had to be brought to Sister Pauline and she would put them right.

On January 25th, 1934, the Golden Jubilee of this holy old Sister was celebrated; she had been fifty years a Sister of Charity, working for the poor. From all sides came congratulations. Mgr. Defebvre, her Bishop, wrote a special letter, thanking her for all the work for souls she had done in his Vicariate. She was fêted on that day. A Vow song full of holy thoughts was sung by her companions, and then, for the lighter side, a huge gold-paper fish was presented, which opened as a little booklet, inside which were many incidents in verse, with pictures of Sister Pauline clasping a " big fish " in her arms, and a shoal of " little fishes " swimming after her! She accepted all with a quiet smile and " Merci, merci ".

Even at her advanced age she continued her active teaching until her enemy rheumatism made it impossible for her to use the stairs. So she was condemned to live in the Infirmary, but every morning she rose at four o'clock and was carried down to the chapel for Mass and Communion. Often alone, she followed all the spiritual exercises of the Community at regular hours, being very grateful when another Sister came to read with her. But sometimes she was found with tears in her eyes, because she had no longer any active work for souls; she could only " catch fishes " with her prayers. There were many enquiries for her from her old pupils and friends, so it was arranged for her to receive them in a little veranda room.

Then God gave her a special work for the last five years of her life, one which filled her with joy, and as she often said, " makes it possible for me to live ". During the years of war, the Sisters being prisoners in their House, there was more time to develop the intern works, so a little kindergarten school was organized for the Holy Childhood babies. Little extern Christian children also begged to be admitted; entering at the age of four or five years. It gave the opportunity for a good Christian formation, and even before seven years of age many were ready for First Communion.

The European Sister in charge needed a Chinese Sister to help with this important work. Sister Berkeley, seeing Sister Pauline's grief at losing her active work for souls, asked her to take on these " very small fishes ". She was delighted and a band of little ones stumped up the stairs daily, carrying their little stools, and sat round the eighty-five-year-old Sister. The children loved her and she loved them and adapted herself to them wonderfully. Even with the little extern boys she was a success, which amused her. " I have never had anything to do with boys in my life," she said.

Sister Berkeley related:

" Often I slipped in and listened; it was the same as with her bigger children. First she won their hearts and gave them a great desire for holy things; then she attacked their little faults, and roused up the will to correct them and prepare for Confession and Communion. They all spoke quite simply and openly to her. Once it was arranged for a little band of them to make their First Confession, but she left out one child, Ningvong by name. We said to her, ' Don't you think Ningvong can make her confession ? She knows her prayers well and her little sins.' ' No,' replied Sister Pauline, ' she must wait, for she has not yet *decided* that she *wishes* to go to Confession.' She was waiting for the decision of the will, and with it the resolution to correct the little faults. In a week's time Sister Pauline told us, ' Ningvong is ready; she *wishes* to go to Confession.' Little miss of six and a half years had made her decision."

Sometimes she put back a First Communion child to wait awhile, because she was not ' hungry ', as they say in China, to make her Communion. This did not occur often, for most of her little pupils were continually asking, " When can I make my First Communion ? I am longing for Our Lord to come into my heart! " On the great day, after their visit to Sister Berkeley, the children raced upstairs to see Sister Pauline; their faces and hers were beaming with joy, and she had a special word and gift for each one.

When the children acted scenes of the holy mysteries on Feast Days they always rushed up to Sister Pauline afterwards to " do it again for her." One saw Our Lady, St. Joseph, and the Angels flying down the passage, with their robes tucked up around them, tumbling up the stairs, to show all to her. She continued her work with them until her ninety-first year, and for the Feast of the Sacred Heart, 1944, three weeks before her death, she instructed her last band of First Communicants.

The soul of this holy old Chinese Sister passed to God very peacefully on the Feast of Our Lady of Mount Carmel. She had suffered much in the last few months of her life by the death of her beloved Superior, Sister Berkeley, who went to God on March 9th of that year. Sister Pauline was inconsolable and felt her loss keenly. The Sisters tried to console her, telling her that her turn would come soon, and this loved Superior would be waiting at Heaven's door to welcome and lead her to Our Blessed Lord, saying: " Here is my dear Sister Pauline, who gained so many souls for You." But the old Sister, weeping, would say, " Ah, but she was a great Saint and I am an old sinner."

Surely there must have been a great welcome in Heaven from all those " fishes ", big and little—souls who owed their salvation to this zealous daughter of St. Vincent and St. Louise. We can hear them saying in Heaven, " Pauline Momo is here."

XVIII

GOD'S ISLAND AND THE DEVIL'S ISLAND

" PRAY for the islands, convert the islands, and the gate to China will be opened," said Mgr. Reynaud, the old Bishop of Ningpo (1884 to 1926). " What islands, and where are they ? " even China herself asks sometimes. Letters addressed to Chusan Island, China, often wander up the Yangtse river, so little is known on the mainland of the Chusan Archipelago.

The country Mission of St. Vincent, outside the North Gate of Tinghai on Chusan Island, links up a chain of villages, until one comes to the fishing port of Sinkomen on the north side. At Sinkomen Bishop Reynaud planted a Catholic Mission, and here it was his dream to build a church in honour of Our Lady of the Rosary. The last blessing he received from the Holy Father in Rome, a few weeks before his death, was for Sinkomen, and who can doubt that he now prays for this Mission in Heaven ?

" God's Island " he called Chusan, but opposite to Sinkomen is the " Devil's Island "—Poodoo, inhabited by 3,000 bonzes (pagan monks) and covered with pagodas and pagan temples. At certain times of the year thousands of pilgrims come from all parts of China to offer sacrifices to the devil at the many shrines, the largest of which is dedicated to a goddess, Kwungying.

Bishop Reynaud's dream was to have counter-pilgrimages to Our Lady at Sinkomen, for all pagan pilgrims must pass this port on their way to Poodoo. Years ago, he bought the land, high up on the hill, facing the sea; the stone was blasted from the mountain side and a small chapel and residence built, but he was not to see the realization of his dream.

Years went by and alms were slowly gathered in for the Church of the Holy Rosary at Sinkomen; they came chiefly through the hands of Dom Arnold, O.S.B., of Buckfast Abbey, the majority being from American and Irish benefactors. In spite of China's troubled days, scorning human prudence, the work went steadily

CHURCH OF OUR LADY OF THE ROSARY, SINKOMEN, ON GOD'S ISLAND

"ELLA MARIS" VISITING THE ISLANDS   " SOFY BO "

WAR RELIEF WORK
Weekly distribution of rice and cracked wheat

TRANSFORMATION :   Right: A little deaf-mute beggar maid
Left: Later, in the " House of Mercy "

forward, and early in 1929 foundations were dug on the top of the hill for a big Church of Our Lady, with fifteen chapels of the Mysteries of the Rosary.

Later in the year a beautiful and touching ceremony took place, when Mgr. Defebvre, the successor of Bishop Reynaud, laid the foundation stone of the church and blessed the ground. It was a simple scene, high up on the hill above the fishing port, with the Christians of the neighbouring islands and villages gathered around, the priests from Ningpo and Tinghai, and the white cornettes of the Sisters of Charity, with a band of their Holy Childhood children, who came to sing the Mass.

Ten years before, Bishop Reynaud had asked the children to say ten " Hail Marys " daily for Sinkomen. In return he had promised them the first pilgrimage, and they held his successor to his word. Touched by their prayers, Mgr. Defebvre gave the invitation, and arranged for a special steamer to bring them to Sinkomen for the ceremony. A year later they came for the consecration and opening of the church, and then again for the Baptism and blessing of the big bell " Elizabeth ", whose god-mother was the aged Madame Chang.

A yearly pilgrimage was organized in the month of May to Our Lady of the Rosary at Sinkomen. The Sisters and their children would go round the island in the little steamboat, singing and chanting the Rosary on the way. At the Sinkomen wharf a procession was always formed, headed by four carrying the beautiful banner of the Children of Mary, and they climbed the hill to the church, singing the Lourdes hymn, " *Yavé, Yavé, Yavé, Ma-lee-ya* ".

Crowds of pagans watched them curiously in the streets of the fishing port; the " white-hat " Sisters some of them had seen before, for they went to be nursed in their hospital at Tinghai; but this band of happy, healthy children in their white coats and blue ribbons—were these the miserable, unwanted babies, so often sent round the island in the arms of old beggar women, to be received and cared for by the Sisters in the House of Mercy ? It gave them food for thought.

When the ceremonies were finished there was always time for rest and recreation, but the Sisters would slip down the beautiful hill into the narrow, crowded streets of the port with their medicine baskets. There they found plenty of misery to relieve and, among

o

their clients, many little "Thieves of Heaven". When the steamer whistled for departure they would arrive, breathless, and even on the boat still treated sore eyes and other ailments of those standing on the wharf.

The Christian children of the extern school had their pilgrimage, and the Union of Catholic Mothers also, all having their own banners. Lower down on the hill-side a Pilgrimage House was built, and soon from all the Christian centres at Shanghai, Ningpo, Dgiansain, Wenchow, etc., pilgrimages to Our Lady of the Rosary at Sinkomen were in full swing.

In 1933 the outstanding event was the visit of Mgr. Zanin, the Apostolic Delegate, to the islands. He arrived, with Bishop Ou from Haimen, at Tinghai at five o'clock in the morning, but Sister Berkeley and her Sisters were on the wharf to greet him. With his gracious smile, he said to them, " Ah, the Sisters of Charity got up at four o'clock this morning, certainly."

The distinguished visitor had a civic reception by the Mandarin and town officials, but what he seemed to enjoy most was the hearty welcome and smiling faces of the Holy Childhood children and inmates of the House of Mercy, which was decorated specially in white and yellow, the Papal colours. He was delighted with the Union of Catholic Mothers, and when the women knelt before him for his blessing he gave them a little instruction on their responsibilities towards their children, particularly the boys, in these days of piracy and brigandage, and especially told them that it was from their early training that he expected vocations to the priesthood.

On the second day of his visit Mgr. Zanin went to Sinkomen to celebrate the Feast of Christ the King in the Church of Our Lady of the Rosary. The Holy Childhood choir was invited to sing the Mass, and afterwards Mgr. Zanin sought out the children and complimented them on their singing. " You must never forget," he said to them, " that you sang the Mass of Christ the King at Sinkomen, with three Bishops in the sanctuary! "

. . . .

With the zealous parish priest, Fr. Luke Yao, there were many conversions at Sinkomen. He founded a branch of Catholic Action for the young men, who, in their zeal, went through the country villages and islands, carrying a portable harmonium, singing hymns to Our Lady and the Sacred Heart. Then one of them would jump on a chair and preach Faith in the One True God, Master of Heaven, and His blessed Mother, " Sing-Mo-Maleeya." New Christian centres were opened in the villages between Tinghai and Sinkomen. We give the history of one as it was written for friends in England and America:

HOW THE FAITH CAME TO DI-LUI-DGIE AND LAO-TCHI-DEUR.

" Some years ago, when passing round the island of Chusan in the little steamboat to Sinkomen, the Sisters noticed a landing place had been made at a fishing and salt-drying village called Di-lui-dgie, and small rowing boats took passengers to and from the steamer. This opened up a district which the Sisters had not yet been able to visit, as it was too far for a row or small sail boat.

" The first excursion there was not very encouraging; on the sea shore were scattered huts, difficult to reach because of the mud creeks. Farther inland were bigger villages, but the people were rough mannered and suspicious; they did not know the ' white hat ' Sisters. Suddenly a big man appeared in the staring crowd: ' Why,' he said, ' what are you thinking of, you people of Di-lui-dgie, not to be treating these Sisters well ? You do not know them ? I can tell you that they are very good and clever people. They have to pass through many years of study and examinations before they get one of those big white hats; indeed, that Sister looks very young to have got one already. These Sisters have come here to treat our sick people and do good works, and you must receive them with great respect.' The Sisters were much amused and the woman carrying their basket assured him that the Sister was not so young as she looked.

" The ice was broken, and afterwards at every visit the people poured out of their houses, welcoming the Sisters, bringing their sick people to be treated and often tiny wasted babies, to whom the grace of Baptism was given. Visits were made to many big villages inland at the feet of the highest mountains on Chusan. One of these, Lao-tchi-deur, was a *kali*, that is to say, a village with shops in it, a centre to which the country people come to buy their stores. It was to Lao-tchi-deur that Fr. Luke Yao sent his young men of the Catholic Action group to preach the doctrine of the One True God in Heaven.

" The seed was sown and flourished, bearing a small harvest of conversions, and in July 1936 a small chapel was opened at Lao-tchi-deur and fitted up with a simple altar and furnishings. The solemn opening and first Holy Mass were announced, and an invitation sent to the Sisters of Charity to be present with six of their Holy Childhood girls to sing the Mass.

" Early in the morning of that hot July day, two Sisters and the children arrived at Di-lui-dgie landing-place. They expected to walk through the rice fields to Lao-tchi-deur, but a big boat was waiting for them in the canal, and it brought them to the very steps of the Mission chapel, with its little white cross on the low roof. This meant a ceremonious arrival, and the fireworks went off on all sides, as the Sisters left the boat with their six favoured girls of the Children of Mary in white coats and blue ribbons.

" Crowds of pagans were watching the proceedings with puzzled faces until they saw the Sisters arrive, when their faces cleared and they pressed forward to welcome them. ' Ah,' they said, ' if the " white-hat " Sisters are in this new business, then there must be good in it.' They entered the little building, which was to be Almighty God's first sanctuary in this district: two small rooms, each about twenty-four feet square, one with a little wooden altar, crucifix, candle-sticks and rough kneeling benches. A statue of *Virgo Potens* and small Stations of the Cross pictures were brought by the Sisters as their offering.

" After a stirring sermon by Fr. Luke Yao, Holy Mass was cele-brated, and the fresh voices of the children's singing echoed far away to the villages inland. God came down on the altar; many visiting Christians received Him in Holy Communion, while the crowds of pagans watched in awestruck silence. After Mass, some catechumens and new Christians were brought to be presented. Then came the corporal works of mercy; the medicine baskets of the Sisters were carried outside to a low table and many sick people treated. A violent thunderstorm made the return journey very difficult for the Sisters and children, but they laughed and said, ' The devil wants to show his fury, because the Faith is planted at Lao-tchi-deur! ' "

Two years had passed since the opening of this little chapel. The Catholic Action men with Fr. Yao had been working steadily on and whole families were converted, baptized, their idols burnt, and the children sent in to study in the Christian schools at Tinghai. Large numbers of catechumens were enrolled, and hopes for the future were bright.

Again the Sisters were invited to visit the scene, and this time the presence of " Ta Momo ", Sister Berkeley, was specially desired. Sedan chairs were sent to bring the Sisters by the inland route, and as they entered the wide valley of Lao-tchi-deur, fireworks in the distance were heard, and a procession of children, carrying banners and flags, chanting prayers, awaited the Sisters under a big decorated arch in the middle of the valley. These children were new Christians, catechumens and even pagans, studying in the school attached to the chapel, directed by a young schoolmaster, also a new Christian.

It was difficult to enter the little chapel, the crowds were so great, and the Sisters were called on all sides by Christians, proudly introducing their catechumens. Gaily coloured holy pictures were distributed with explanations of doctrine on the back, then came, as usual, the care of the sick. The time was very short, as it was a long journey home by the inland route, but promises were made for a quick return. With the charming Chinese goodbye salutation, " Mey-mey-chi, kwa-kwa-lai " (" Go away slowly, come back quickly "), the Sisters got into the sedan chairs, the porters lifted them with their usual " Hey-ho ", and with the last of the fireworks blazing, away they went, smiling faces saluting them on all sides at Lao-tchi-deur and in the villages. What a difference from the first visit eight years before!

Of course the chief object in inviting the Sisters this time was that they might see the necessity of building a big chapel in this district. All think they are fairy godmothers, who have only to wave their wands and gifts arrive. The daily struggle to keep their own works going was little understood, especially when the first year of war had begun and the horizon was dark and uncertain.

But the planting of the Faith in a new district and the harvest of conversions is God's work, and we, His humble instruments, must not be lacking in zeal; so we hope and pray that one day soon this new chapel will be built. The benefactor would choose the Patron Saint.

It is this district which was particularly terrorized by Tze Paoding, the famous brigand, and his band, but it must be said to their credit that they would never allow to be touched the house or person of the chief Christian man there, a certain Ko Siesang, a very zealous preacher. They used to say, " Let him alone, he is good to the poor."

Sinkomen being so close to Poodoo, the devil's stronghold, there are many cases of " possession " in this district. After having spent huge sums of money unsuccessfully with the bonzes, some of these cases came to Fr. Yao to be cured. He would invite them to come and live for a time in the Pilgrimage House under the protection of Our Lady of the Rosary, and he would teach them Christian doctrine and prayers, and the use of Holy Water; also he gave them Miraculous Medals. Many were cured, continued their instructions as catechumens and became fervent Christians.

It seems strange that the devil should give up his prey in this way, but it shows the power of Our Blessed Lady and her Divine

Son. One could tell many extraordinary and interesting tales of the devil being conquered by Divine Power. Once he said by the mouth of a possessed man, " I hate those ' big white bonnets ' [the Sisters]; I can do nothing when they are there." Another time the pagan monks were praying at the side of a possessed man and the devil's advocate was also called. Suddenly he said, " There is something in this room which prevents me from working, something Christian." It was found to be a rosary in the pocket of a Christian man, who had come to see if he could do anything for the poor man. The pagans drove him out.

In Fr. Cyprian Aroud's *Mission Letters*[1] (from Wenchow) there are many remarkable tales of the activity of the devil. There was one very extraordinary case in a village served by Fr. Yao near Sinkomen, an account of which was sent to England and America, and from which we quote:

" Fourteen years ago there was a flourishing Christian centre at Keu-san, a village on the coast of Chusan Island, halfway between Tinghai and Sinkomen. Sad to say, the catechist of Keu-san fell into grave sin, and he and all his family became apostates. They destroyed the crucifixes and holy pictures in their homes, and put up pagan idols over the altar in the little chapel. As they were the principal Christians in that district, many others fell with them into apostasy.

" The Sisters of Charity, in their country visits, passed to that side of the island to treat the sick people, and give the cholera injection in the village of Dong-awe. Since the apostasy of Keu-san, a nice little chapel had been built there, dedicated to St. Thérèse of the Infant Jesus.

" One day the Sisters felt inspired to pass over the creek, and visit the apostate village of Keu-san; they had a fruitful expedition, many baptisms of sick babies, and they were struck by the number of people who ran to meet them, bending the knee in salutation (an old custom of the Christians). They confessed themselves to be apostates, but they gratefully accepted Miraculous Medals, which the Sisters offered them with encouraging words. In some houses, the inmates hid themselves. It was a sad sight, but the Sisters begged Our Blessed Lady to bring back these wandering souls.

" Early the next year a strange thing happened. In the house of the old catechist, now dead, fires began to break out in all sorts of queer places, sometimes in the corners of beds, inside cupboards or under chairs or tables. The members of the family had to be prepared day and night with buckets of water, for they never knew at what moment or where a fire would break out, sometimes in two or three places at the same time.

[1] Published by " Maison des Missionaires," Vichy, France.

" They thought that the devil, whom they served, was angry with them so they called the bonzes to come and pray. They paid them huge sums of money, and night and day the gongs were banging and the prayers to the devil being recited with burning of joss sticks. But the fires grew worse and worse and the members of the household were terrified; they could not understand the reason.

" One day they heard that in a neighbour's house was the good Christian man from Dong-awe, Ko Siesang; he had heard of the fires, everyone was talking about them, and he thought he would go to see, and prayed that he might do some good to, the unfortunate apostate family. They were delighted to see him and asked his advice; he at once told them that it was the Hand of God punishing them, and perhaps offering them the grace of repentance. He advised them to burn all their idols; they agreed and he, with great delight, helped to do it. The fires became much less, but still continued.

" Ko Siesang saw a fire break out ten times; he then suggested that they should call Fr. Luke Yao, the priest from Sinkomen. They did so, and when Fr. Yao arrived all the apostates of the family knelt before him and begged him to help them. He spent three nights in their house. The first day he saw the fire break out eight times, and he said that though he took some of it in his hands, it did not burn him. It had a peculiar colour, blue like alcohol, with a smell of sulphur.

" After Fr. Yao had blessed the house and said Mass there, there were no more fires; one of the women members found at the bottom of her box an old picture of the Sacred Heart, which she had kept secretly all these years. This was put up over the altar in the room which was formerly the chapel. All those who could do so went to Confession, and small children were baptized.

" The men of the family sent in their pagan wives, ' big fishes ', to study with Sister Pauline for their Baptism; the children came to the extern school, and with this family came many others from Keu-san and the district around. Over the entrance door is now a large badge of the Sacred Heart, and a white cross has been placed on the roof. The Sisters brought pictures of the Stations of the Cross, which were blessed and erected; the Christians in China have great devotion to making the Way of the Cross. During their visit, the Sisters saw the marks of the fire in different places all over the house."

Sad to say, the terrible war years stopped many developments, but one prays and hopes that with peace Our Lady of the Rosary at Sinkomen will do great things for the islands. At the side of Poodoo is the beautiful island of Tsu-ko-tsien, on the ocean side of which one sees the blue sea and beaches where bathing is safe. There is a chapel and residence on the Sinkomen side of this

island, and a fervent Christian village, where many of the Chusan
Holy Childhood girls are married.

It was another dream of Bishop Reynaud to put a Trappist
Monastery on this island of Tsu-ko-tsien, for there is much good
arable land which could be cultivated, and he wanted, above all,
the prayers of a contemplative Order to destroy the power of the
devil, and convert his beloved islands to the True Faith.

When the Pilgrimage House at Sinkomen was built, the Sisters
of Charity at Tinghai received permission from their Superiors to
pass one night there from time to time, so that they might visit
the islands around the port, also the inland mountain villages.
These expeditions do much good, not only through the medical
service given to the poor, and the baptisms obtained, but through
the contact which the Sisters make with the country people, thus
preparing the way for the Missioners and their catechists. We
give some interesting details of them, for Sister Berkeley had great
devotion to this work and encouraged it in every way.

Sometimes the Sisters would walk ten miles to the other side
of Chusan Island, passing over two or three mountains, and tour
the villages there, sitting down in the little courtyards of the farm-
houses and holding a dispensary to which the people flocked in
large numbers. Once they were welcomed in a village visited for
the first time, very far away, by a woman who ran to meet them
and begged them to sit down in her house. " For many years, I
have wondered when you would come here," she said. " My
grandmother used to tell me about you when I was a child. She
lived in a village near your town, and she said that a very tall Sister
[Sister Berkeley] used to come and treat the sick people. I always
hoped you would come here one day. Sit down and I will go and
cook the rice for your dinner, and you must stay the night."
The Sisters smiled at this warm welcome, but were only able to
stay a short time with the hospitable woman, treating the sick
people in her courtyard, so that she had " great face "; then they
passed on to another village.

Sometimes it was to the neighbouring islands that they went in
a rowing boat, or, best of all, in a sailing junk. The tides had to
be carefully watched lest the Sisters should be cut off on the return
journey. Tamao was an island not really far away, but had a very
difficult passage to it, and one never seemed to be able to hit on
a day when the tide was right to go to it, with its high peaked

mountains. One day the Sisters arranged to catch the little Sinko-men steamer and drop off it at one of the landing places for the seaside villages. When they arrived at the port, the steamer had left, for boats at Chusan go at ' any old time '; when you hear the whistle, you run!

Once an expedition is decided on, it is a rule at Chusan not to abandon it for any obstacle that arises, for the Sisters say that it is the devil who wants to stop them because of the many little souls which would be saved for Heaven. On this occasion they at once decided to take a boat to another island, but for no place was the tide right. " Very well," they said, " then we will walk inland to one of the villages."

As they were leaving the port, a man on a big junk hailed them. " Do you want to go to Tamao ? " he called. " The tide is only right to-day for sailing to Tamao." The Sisters quickly got on the junk, and in a few minutes were sailing merrily to the much-longed-for island of Tamao. They jumped ashore on the rocks, and visited the seaside villages first, where they found many friends, who said, " Why have you never come to Tamao before ? "

They passed over the high mountains to other villages and met a man with a stiff leg, who hailed them with delight. He had had his leg saved from amputation by weeks of care in the Sisters' hospital, and now he had " great face ", leading them through the villages as his friends. Finally they returned to a headland from which they could hail their junk; they jumped on it and sailed home. A big harvest of baptisms was gained that day, and they brought back with them for the hospital a very sick man, who was arranged comfortably in the hold of the boat.

In the pagan atmosphere of Chusan, the Sisters feel the power of the devil to be very strong, but they fight it with fervent prayer and scorn! They say that he always seems to be trying to make mischief in some part of their House, shown by quarrels, accidents and tiresome things happening. He certainly hates the House of Mercy and its work for souls. All of a sudden he disappears, and there is calm and peace again, and the Sisters, laughing, say: " The devil is gone; where will he come next ? "

Another feature of the outside expeditions is the visiting of the Christian families in the mountain villages and islands. The Sisters make their headquarters in their houses, while treating the sick people, thus giving them " great face " among their pagan neighbours. Much good can be done by stirring up the " lazy " Christians, making friends with them, and helping the very poor ones.

The pagans' houses are full of gaily-coloured pictures of their idols, so the Sisters take pretty holy pictures to be put up in the houses of the Christians. They sometimes take little wooden altar shelves to be nailed to the walls, and candlesticks with candles. They tell the Christians to say daily prayers before these altars and also to light their candles before the Sacred Heart and Our Lady when they are in trouble or have sickness. Their pagan neighbours make burnt offerings to the devil when they are in trouble; the Christians can show their Faith in the One True God by human means. The poverty of many of the country Christians is very great. They live from day to day, and Sister Berkeley was their " Good Mother ". She had great sympathy for them, and helped them in a delicate way as much as possible.

.   .   .   .

Sometimes there were big epidemics in the villages, particularly the terrible Chinese measles, which kills so many little children through its septic complications. When the Sisters heard of a measles epidemic, they would hasten to that district to care for the sick children and baptize the dying. On one occasion they were on their way to a big village called Djiao-Mien, a two-mountain expedition—that means two mountains to climb going and returning. The Sisters were at the foot of the second mountain when they saw two men hastening towards them, calling them. " Come quickly! " they said; " how fortunate that you received our message." " What message ? " the Sisters enquired. " We sent to tell you early this morning of the big epidemic of measles in our villages of this Mo-yang-tiou district and to beg you to come and treat the children, some of whom are very ill." The Sisters had received no message, but they felt the Hand of God leading them to that valley of Mo-yang-tiou, with its many big villages. That day they baptized many little dying children, attacked by the terrible disease of *Cancrum oris*, which is a common complication of measles in China. Two days later they returned, bringing more special remedies, and spent a long day caring for the sick children and baptizing the dying.

Often a malignant fever attacks the poor country people, especially at the time of the cutting of the rice harvest. They thrash the grain in the fields between bamboo wind-screens, and then leave the cocks of straw to dry. If rain comes, this straw rots, dries in the hot sun, gives off a bad smell and fever attacks the people. They call it the " straw sickness ".

When the country people develop any kind of sickness they are in a sad condition, for no one nurses them. Very few have the means to come in to the town and see a Chinese doctor or buy medicines. The grown-up people may recover, but the children and babies die by hundreds.

Once the Sisters were called to a big valley of many villages, Mo-aw, by the sea, involving a ten-mile walk over three mountains. The straw sickness was raging there. As soon as the Sisters arrived, the people poured out of their houses and followed them, begging for medicines. It was pitiful to see their white drawn faces, blue lips and shaking hands. Big men trying to work in the fields came, saying, " Momo, I have no strength; help me." It was anæmia following the fever; the children were even worse. Mothers, hardly able to walk themselves, carried dying babies, leading by the hand little wasted children with white faces.

It was sad that the Sisters could do so little for them. Quinine and aspirin were dealt out generously to those with fever, packets of cinchona powder and iron pills as tonics, while heart tablets and injections were given; and they were invited to come into hospital or send neighbours to fetch bottles of medicine. The Sisters said to them: " Kill a pig; eat fresh meat, liver especially, to strengthen your blood." The people looked at them in amazement, saying, " We never kill pigs, except for the Chinese New Year and a wedding! " Their food was of the poorest, with little nourishment in it.

Four times the Sisters made the long journey over the three mountains, twice to Mo-aw and twice to Sio-soh, another big valley close by. In these four visits over 300 dying babies and little children were baptized, and there would have been many more if the Sisters could have stayed longer. They heard afterwards that in these epidemics of straw sickness hundreds of children and grown-up people had died. That year was a record one for baptisms, for over 2,000 were offered to the Divine Infant in the Christmas Crib.

Some of these baptisms were gained by fervent Christian women, trained for this work. They can go farther afield, passing a week sometimes in the distant islands and isolated country districts. These women, many of whom are members of the Union of Catholic Mothers, give invaluable aid to the Mission, not only as *Médecins Baptiseurs* but also in visiting Christian families where there are disputes and difficulties to be put right.

One of the best known of these helpers during Sister Berkeley's life at Chusan was an old lady known as " Sofy Bo " (Grandma Sofy). She was a great-grandmother of the Holy Childhood and passed her last days with the Sisters. How many miles she trudged even in her old age with her little medicine basket on her arm, welcomed in all the villages and islands and consulted specially for sick children!

There are wonderful tales of her work for the poor; she cared for their bodies as well as their souls. Once she found a poor dying woman with a newly born babe in a beggars' shelter in the country. Sofy Bo began her ministrations by baptizing the baby, which seemed to have hardly a breath of life in it; then the old lady went to beg of the neighbours a bedcover, a pillow and hot food. She arranged the poor woman comfortably, fed her and instructed her in the necessary truths of Faith in the One God. She eventually baptized her, stayed with her, helping her until the last moment of life. Then she arranged for her burial, and finally carried the wee baby to the Sisters' Orphanage.

During her long life Sofy Bo must have baptized thousands of little dying pagan babies, and when, at the age of eighty-seven, she was dying in the Sisters' hospital, she smiled and said several times, " So many little children here; how beautiful they are, all around me! " They were surely the angels, the happy little souls to whom she had opened Heaven by Baptism, and who were waiting to lead her to God's presence in the glory of Heaven.

.   .   .   .

Sometimes people wondered that Sister Berkeley allowed her Sisters to go on these long country expeditions in such a brigand-infested island as Chusan. It must be remembered that the brigands were the special friends of the Sisters through their care of them in prison. It was often heard that word was passed to all the bands to respect and help the " white-hat Momos ".

A Sister relates: " If, on a mountain or any lonely place I met very rough-looking fellows who were surely brigands, I at once smiled at them and said, ' Oh, I did not know that you lived over here; we, the Sisters, have come to visit the sick people and do good works.' The rough faces would soften at this friendly greeting and the men would ask for remedies for sore eyes or 'dobie tong', and the meeting would end amicably."

Once on a homeward journey to Sinkomen from the inland villages, the Sisters were taking a little lunch at the top of their third mountain, in a sheltered hollow. Suddenly, one of them caught sight of a man with a gun, looking at them from behind a tree. She warned her Sister quietly; the two packed up the lunch basket, and, with their women, took to their heels and raced down the mountain side to Sinkomen.

When the night was passed in the Pilgrimage House after visiting the villages or islands, it was the custom of good Fr. Yao to prepare supper for the Sisters with his cook, who had been trained in a French restaurant but had broken down in health and was now doing light work with the priest. The Sisters would beg to be allowed to prepare their own modest supper in the Pilgrimage House, but Fr. Yao always waved them aside, saying, " I know how I ought to treat the Sisters, especially when they come to do good works for my people."

On this occasion on the supper menu were roast pigeons; the next morning after Mass and breakfast the Sisters went to thank the priest and say goodbye. He replied in the usual polite Chinese way. " I am sorry you had such a wretched supper; there was nothing fit to eat. Yesterday afternoon I sent one of my Christians up the mountain to see if he could shoot some wild pigeons; he managed to bring in two." The Sisters turned, and there was " the brigand with the gun " smiling at them! They had a hearty laugh with Fr. Yao, telling him of their fright.

On another occasion, they were visiting seaside villages on the island, to which they had come in a small rowing boat. One Sister went inland, the other passed along the shore to the scattered huts of the fishermen. She saw a big Fokien junk anchored not far off from the land. Presently a small boat from it arrived at the shore, and the men in it called the Sister. She thought they probably wanted some remedies and approached them, but they asked her to come out to their junk to see a very sick man in it.

The Sister was just going to step into their boat when she realized that she was doing a very imprudent thing. If it were a pirate junk she would probably be kidnapped and no one would know, as it was a very isolated spot. She smiled at the men and told them her doubts quite simply : " Perhaps you are pirates and will kidnap me ? "

The men looked at her with pained surprise, not a word of expostulation or assurance. " You think that of us ! " they said. " Then there is nothing to be done," and they turned to row back to the junk. " Wait," said the Sister, " I will come. You have good faces, I trust you." " Who would injure the white-hat Sisters ? " they said reproachfully, then quickly rowed out to the junk. The man was very sick but the Sister treated him, left medicines for two days, and told them that if he was not better to bring him to the hospital at Tinghai.

Talking of Fokien junks, one must not leave the Sinkomen stories without speaking of the Fokien Catholic fishermen. At certain times of the year they brought their huge gaily-painted junks to Sinkomen port, and went up the hill to the Church of Our Lady of the Rosary and gave Fr. Yao large sums of money for Masses. They all went to the Sacraments, in spite of the difficulties of their strange dialect, and they always invited the priest to come out to their junks and see the little altars to Our Lady arranged in their cabins.

These Fokien fishermen are the spiritual children of the Dominican Fathers in South China, so they have a great devotion to the Rosary, and always ask for white rosaries, which are not often liked by the Chinese, as white is their mourning colour. Whenever white rosaries arrived in parcels, Sister Berkeley always put them aside for the Fokien fishermen and the Sisters would sometimes visit them on their junks.

.   .   .   .

We must also speak here of one who gave invaluable aid to the active Mission works of the Sisters at Chusan, and was a much-loved friend. This was Reverend Mother Nourry, the first Superior of the Sacred Heart nuns in China. In her first year in China she had passed the summer months with her Mothers at Chusan in the Sisters' little sanatorium house of Lorette. The paganism around her had stirred her great missionary soul, and not only by her prayers but with constant generous gifts she helped the missionary works of the Sisters at Chusan.

She sent quantities of big coloured pictures of the Sacred Heart which were presented to country chapels, put up in the houses of

Christians, and were always among the wedding presents of Holy Childhood girls. Every Christmas came big boxes of treasures to the House of Mercy at Chusan from the Sacred Heart Convent, just the things needed for the children, hospitals and outside works.

Sometimes there were country chapels in need of repairs and refurnishing and an appeal to Reverend Mother Nourry was never refused; she showed her joy at being asked to share in a work for souls. She and Sister Berkeley were kindred spirits and very warm friends. This great Missionary Mother of the Sacred Heart went to God on May 31st, 1946. R.I.P.

XIX

SPECIAL CHARACTERISTICS

IN her beautiful Life of the Foundress of the Sisters of Charity, St. Louise de Marillac, Lady Lovat speaks of the triple supernatural action in her soul, as in those of many Saints, by which the soul first empties itself entirely of self-love, then is filled with God, and finally gives God to the world.

In her English Missionary daughter we see the same process. One cannot say that she was a spoilt child in her family life at home, for the wise Catholic training of her parents prevented that; but it was a life of great natural happiness, with every want supplied, and nothing to suffer from those around her. When, as a young girl, she faced her vocation, she knew that suffering and hardship lay before her, but her generous soul welcomed them.

As a Sister of Charity, during her early years in England and then in China, we see by her spiritual notes the efforts she had to make to subdue her imperious temper, her strong will, which urged her to follow and develop her own ideas without consideration of others. Obedience and renunciation were hard to that energetic nature, but she kept them ever before her, seeing so clearly her faults and shortcomings. This self-knowledge brought her to the feet of God in humility and simplicity, before the Blessed Sacrament with strong faith and loving confidence.

A Missionary priest in China, who knew Sister Berkeley well for many years, said of her: " She was contemplative as well as active; her activity received its power from her dynamic supernatural life. She was a seriously minded Sister on the road to perfection, and that all the way from the beginning with a straightforward intensity which must have rejoiced the heart of her holy Father St. Vincent. Our Blessed Lord was always present to her; she saw His Will in all the events of her life, and His work to do in all souls with which she came in contact."

When she arrived at Chusan in her fiftieth year she was calmer. The wilful nature was in hand, her humble efforts, blessed by

God's grace, had emptied her soul of the obstacles to His life within it. Difficulties and sufferings she accepted calmly and generously. " His Will only and in the way He wishes ", we read so often in her notes. His loved filled her heart. " Love God, oh my soul, love God, and with a light heart go thy way," she writes.

Of the third process, the giving of God to those around her, one might truly say that with her it was always in action throughout her Missionary life, but now, self being banished from her soul, there was a greater store of Divine Love to give to others. Like her Holy Mother, St. Louise, her love of souls was the natural consequence of her love of God. In every work before her, she always saw souls, and the help she could give them on their way to Heaven.

She excused their faults; a wonderfully wide-minded charity made her shut her eyes, as she said, " to all that was not a mortal sin ". She said that the poor were so ignorant and suffered so much that God surely forgave them the many " queer " things they did. She would say to the Sisters, " Pray for that poor woman " (one who had received great injury from another); " she has been to Confession, she forgives, but she cannot yet go to Holy Communion, for she says her heart is not right." How patiently the " Good Mother " helped that poor wounded heart to get right, and to approach the Holy Table without scruple.

Her Sisters relate that Sister Berkeley could not scold; she did not know how to do it. When there was some big disorder to be put right, she would say rather severely, " Such a person must be spoken to seriously, and I think, my dear Sister [turning to a companion], that *you* had better do it." The Sister smiled and accepted it, but if the scolding simply had to be done by " Ta Momo " it was amusing to see how she prepared for action. She would perhaps go to the pharmacy and make up a good bottle of tonic, or send a woman to buy a pound of dried prunes (supposed to be very strengthening in China). She would lay her hand caressingly on the shoulder of the " naughty one ", begin by telling her that she looked run down and needed a tonic. This would lead to a gentle reprimand and good advice; the victim would leave her, saying with a sniff, " Ta Momo understands me "! The Sisters often said that the next state was worse than the last! It was no good, " Ta Momo " could not scold. Yet it must not

P

be thought that her government was weak; no, when she announced firmly what had to be done and in what way, the most rebellious obeyed though they might murmur under their breath, " These *nakko ninn* [foreigners] are very difficult ", but they followed out her wishes like obedient children.

With her Sisters, and especially with the Chinese, there is only one remark to make; she was their " Mother ". In her spiritual notes after her nomination as a Superior one reads at every retreat: " Resolution, to be a Mother to my Sisters, first by my own good example, in regularity, and by great kindness." Even now, some years after her death, the Sisters, children and poor still say, " She was our Mother, she loved us as a Mother would." Especially to her Chinese Sisters she gave this maternal love lavishly. A European Sister once said to her laughingly, " You love your Chinese Sisters more than you do us, the Europeans." Sister Berkeley looked surprised and then said simply, " Of course I do; I came to China for them."

She thought so highly of them, because they had followed their vocation so generously. " They have not had the early training or the graces we have had in a Christian country," she would say. " It is heroic the way they live under rule and work from morning to night. They must be very dear to Our Lord's heart for their loving and generous service of Him in the person of the poor."

Some of her Chinese Sisters visited the sick people in the city and country, trudging for long hours on their little bound feet. One little Sister said to Sister Berkeley, " My mother died when I was very young, and my eldest Sister did not know the right way to arrange my feet; they were never done properly and there are always big corns on the soles where the foot is turned back! " And this little Sister was often out for hours walking on those " corned feet ", visiting the poor and sending little souls to Heaven.[1]

Sister Berkeley often said that the Chinese Sisters were capable of great things, and her words came true in the summer of 1945, when the foreign Sisters were expelled from Chusan and the Chinese were left alone in one half of the compound, the Japanese soldiers occupying the other half, with only a low bamboo fence between them. The Sisters remained at their post, caring for the children and old people with great devotion, and when the

[1] The feet of Chinese women are no longer bound.

bombardments began they refused to leave them. " We will die with them," they said. " Who will look after them if we go away ? " They lived in fidelity to their rule, observing all the Community customs and spiritual exercises. They were real heroines of the war.

The maternal care of Sister Berkeley for the health of her Sisters was very marked. " We make a vow to work for the poor," she said, " and it is our duty to keep our Sisters fit for this work." She had no patience with self-imposed mortifications, which weakened health and strength, or want of common-sense precautions against excessive heat and cold. She said to a newly arrived European Sister, " Try never to be ill through your own fault; it throws back the works and the poor suffer for it."

For sick and delicate Sisters, of whom she had many, sent to the good air of Chusan, she could not do enough in her kindly care. A Chinese Sister relates, " When you were ill and suffering, Sister Berkeley nursed you as your own mother would do. Several times a day she was at your bedside, and provided everything possible to relieve you. During convalescence she delighted to bring you your meals herself, arranging them with such delicate attention." Another says: " During a long and fatiguing illness, night and day Sister Berkeley was at my side, and a quarter of an hour before midnight she would come to give me hot food, feeding me herself, so that I might not find the fast too long to receive Holy Communion the next morning." She was over seventy years of age at that time.

With nervous Sisters she was so patient and gentle, never laughing at or scolding them for fears and fancies. On one occasion a Chinese Sister was visiting the poor on a big island near Chusan, when a savage dog rushed out from a farm and bit her. This was a great shock to the Sister, who was naturally nervous, and she became convinced that the dog was mad, and that she would die of that terrible disease, rabies. This fear affected her health and she grew pale and thin, and could not sleep or eat. After trying many remedies Sister Berkeley had the idea of sending a gardener and a woman to the island to find the dog and learn its history. They went, and on arrival the same dog rushed out and bit them both! The farmer was full of excuses, saying that he was obliged to keep a savage dog because of the many pirates and brigands around him. This news soon cured the Sister.

Sisters broken down in health, dying of tuberculosis, etc., were often sent to Chusan to pass their last days. They said, " It is like dying with your mother to be with Sister Berkeley ", and they died in her arms, after having received every possible care and delicate attention. We have spoken of the welcome she gave to convalescent Sisters sent to rest at Lorette. One of them relates: " I arrived at Chusan tired, sick and discouraged, having been only a short time in China and feeling that I was no good for Mission life and had better go back to Europe. I was not half an hour in the house with Sister Berkeley before I felt different; she received me with such maternal joy, assuring me that I should get strong and work for souls in China." When Sisters returned to their city houses, strengthened, their Superiors would write and thank Sister Berkeley for the good it had done them, physically and also morally. It was like a tonic to live with her for a time.

Bishop Walsh, the founder of Maryknoll, wrote once to her, saying, " I wish I could send all our newly arrived Mission Sisters to stay with you for a while; you would infect them with real Missionary zeal. Your House is my ideal; simple, modest buildings for the Sisters and with the poor Chinese around you all day long. It is real Mission life such as I wish our Sisters to live."

Poverty was practised at Chusan very closely, which was remarkable when one thinks of the life of luxury and comfort of Sister Berkeley's youth, but, as we have seen in her early days as a Sister, she studied the obligations of the Vows very closely. A Sister who lived with her many years said: " Sister Berkeley lived as a poor person would live, from day to day, rarely making big purchases, but little by little as she had the means." She sometimes said, " So many of the benefactors of our House are poor, working people, they make great sacrifices to be able to send us gifts; we should use them as poor people would do, with great care, always remembering our Vow of Poverty."

She had a great horror and dislike of " show " and was almost severe sometimes with her European Sisters if they wanted to make a " little Europe " around them with everything in exquisite perfection. " In China," she would say, " God does not like things to be done too grandly. See how often He lets beautiful buildings and organizations be destroyed by floods, war, etc., and all has to be begun again more simply and modestly." She often spoke of the poverty practised by our Holy Mother, St. Louise, and the first Sisters, as well as the hardships endured by the early Sisters in China. She herself remembered the poor equipment and want of many things in her first years of Mission life, but she would say with a smile, " God gave us many souls to reward us."

Yet it must not be thought that Sister Berkeley had a low standard for what was needed in the rearing of the children and care of the poor. Far from it! Nothing made her happier than to see improvements carried out for the simple, homely comfort of her big family. She would say, " Every year we should try to do things better than last year," and she would urge the Sisters to prayer and effort that the works confided to them should be more efficient. A Chinese Sister relates: " Sometimes Ta Momo asked you to do something new and difficult, which you did not think would succeed, and would greatly add to your work. When you hesitated and made objections, suddenly she would jump up and say, ' Come along, we will go and do it together,' and away she went with her quick step and you had to follow."

A kindergarten school was proposed for the nursery babies, but for many years Sister Berkeley would not give her consent, because she was afraid that the European Sister would make a grand school, full of expensive apparatus, and have no more time or taste for the rougher service of the poor and for saving souls.

However, during the war years, when the Sisters were interned and could no longer go out to visit the poor, Sister Berkeley herself proposed that the kindergarten school should be organized, especially as a gift destined for education was waiting to be used; otherwise the diminished resources would not have permitted the opening of a new work. With Sister Berkeley you must never stand still. If God took away one work, you must open another with confidence.

The little school was planned and organized as a Montessori school, and it was a great success, doing immense good in the training of the Holy Childhood children. It gave great pleasure to Sister Berkeley and she was completely won over to its value; she said one day to the Sister in charge, " Thank you for making my little children so happy." In the famine days of sickness, in the difficulties and sufferings of the Japanese occupation, she would sometimes go and sit amongst the children working at their little tables. " It makes me forget the troubles," she would say.

" I love to see those happy busy faces and they give me such a welcome."

Sister Berkeley had a great devotion to the standard of " every day ", she detested having cupboards full of feast-day clothes while the children went about in shabby ugly attire every day. " My children are not beggars," she would say indignantly, " and I won't have them look like them." She liked them to be dressed in pretty well-made clothes every day, though this was not Chusan custom. If you had pretty clothes, you kept them carefully in cupboards for very special occasions and wore any old rags every day; but in the House of Mercy the children had to be prettily dressed every day to suit Sister Berkeley. She said that it gives a sense of superiority and confidence to a little child, who says to herself, " I am loved, that is why they give me pretty clothes."

In the hospitals and hospices she liked the beds to be covered with gay bedspreads; there must be a look of comfort and beauty. Every House had to be ready at any moment to welcome visitors, showing the life and customs of every day. Even in the war years the Japanese officials, in their constant visits of inspection, could find nothing to criticize. They watched the happy family life of the children, the dancing, chattering babies, in their gaily-coloured overalls, going to school. Certainly reserves of clothes were getting very low, and one heard continually, " There will soon be no more left ", for nothing could be renewed; but somehow they held on until peace came. The " Divine Providence " of Sister Berkeley and her dear old Sister Pauline always brought what was necessary from day to day. She said, " At Chusan we are especially the children of Divine Providence; He never fails us."

We have spoken of the kindness and care received by sick priests, who were often sent to her for rest and change of air. Once Mgr. Ou sent her a tubercular priest, hoping that some months' rest at Chusan would enable him to continue his apostolate, but it was too late; the disease was too far advanced. Sister Berkeley, however, kept him for two years, nursing him like a good mother to the end. She often told him that his prayers and sufferings gained for her and her House many graces and blessings.

Sick and delicate seminarians from Ningpo were often received at Chusan and built up for the long and arduous years of training before them. The Directors of the Seminary, Fr. Nugent, C.M., and Fr. O'Hara, C.M., were old and devoted friends of Sister Berkeley. She mothered them and often spoke of the privilege it was to help them in every way possible to carry on their splendid work in the Seminary. Their standard of training was high and they sent out serious devoted young priests, some of whom were accepted for University studies in Pekin.

.   .   .   .

Did she practise personal mortification ? She led the common life of the rule, never complaining. A Sister in charge of the kitchen said: " Sister Berkeley was very easy to please; she took simply what was placed before her, bad or good." It was known that she liked milk, and when possible a small jug was placed at her side in the refectory, and one would see her breaking bread into it, and eating bread and milk like a child. She once said, " I like to drink milk because it makes you strong; when I was a girl in the schoolroom at home, milk used to be served to us in the middle of the morning. My elder sisters refused it, saying, ' Milk is for babies to drink ', but I always took it, for I thought it would make me strong, and I felt that in my future life I should need to be very strong." The young girl in her teens was always thinking of that vocation, and in her simple, common-sense way preparing for it.

On one occasion in later life a package in a disused cupboard was found, containing a discipline and some spiked chains, instruments of penance. Sister Berkeley said quickly, " Oh, those belonged to Sister Feilding [her cousin]; after her death all her things were sent to me." But after Sister Berkeley's death a letter was found from the Father Director of the Province, renewing his permission for her to wear the spiked chain, though not in the hot summer, which of itself was enough penance.

To the end of her life the great heat of summer tried her intensely, especially when she had attacks of asthma and could not breathe; but she always bore it patiently with a smile and lived the common life in all points. She always came smiling to recreation and enjoyed it, though her deafness of later years was a great trial to her. She hated people shouting at her, and always spoke herself in a low tone.

In the private memoirs of her father we read: " His Catholic habit of confidence in the intercession of the Holy Mother of God moved him more and more to turn to her who helps her clients now and at the hour of death. How often his fingers passed over the beads of his rosary the Angels only know." It was the same with his daughter, the Sister of Charity; her rosary was constantly in her hands, and she had ever before her the imitation of her heavenly Mother. At the side of her desk were two books into which she often dipped. "When I feel worried or inclined to be upset," she said, "a few minutes' reading calms me." Those two books were *L'Humble Vierge Marie* and *The Apparitions of Lourdes.*

One cannot omit to speak of Sister Berkeley's great devotion to Holy Mass; we could truthfully say that, from her early childhood, she never missed her daily Mass, except inevitably on journeys or in sickness. When Sisters were convalescent, she would always gently propose to them to rise for Mass and Communion, even if it were necessary to rest again afterwards. "One Mass is of incomparable value," she would say. "We should never miss Mass through our own fault."

Entering the chapel, she smiled at the Tabernacle and knelt before the Blessed Sacrament with her hands joined like a little child. The Sisters, the children, the poor said, "If Ta Momo is in the chapel and you go to call her, she does not hear you; if you stand before her, she does not see you; she has so much business with God."

XX

WAR COMES TO CHINA

THE autumn of 1937 found China plunged in the horrors of war. It came suddenly, and all hoped it would finish speedily, as before; but this time it dragged on for eight weary years.

Shanghai was the first battlefield, and on both sides of the Foreign Settlement huge districts were bombarded and laid waste, and thousands of working homes destroyed, with misery and suffering on all sides. The well-known universal charity of Shanghai rose to the occasion as usual, and huge refugee camps were established, in which thousands of homeless people were cared for. Foreign Relief Committees were formed, big sums were donated from America and England, and China's own people gave generously to their suffering compatriots. Personal service was given by doctors, nurses, and all those who had time and strength to devote to this work of charity.

In the early years of the war all was peaceful in Chusan, though the people lived in constant terror of the bombing aeroplanes which passed continually over them. Hundreds of poor refugees poured in, many of them those who had relatives in the islands. Women and children arrived half dead with fright, and they found it difficult to live the poor and rough life of the country after Shanghai.

The House of Mercy was overflowing; little refugee babies and young children were brought in, while sick and suffering men and women filled the hospitals. Alas, these refugees brought with them an enemy from which Chusan had been free for many years —the cholera! A sharp epidemic broke out and there were many victims.

After the experiences of this terrible scourge in her early days at Chusan, Sister Berkeley had refused to take cholera cases into her hospitals, because of the big orphanage of children so near to them. But she found it heartrending to turn the sick and dying from her door, and she obtained permission from the Mandarin to arrange a little cholera hospital outside the West Gate, in the rice fields. It was a beggars' shelter, but she had it cleaned up, bamboo walls built on the open sides, doors made, and rows of plank beds arranged, with one side screened off for women. It was equipped with everything necessary and a Sister went several times a day to nurse the patients. A devoted Christian woman offered herself as nurse, and two Christian men also gave their services.

The town followed by opening a hospital in a large pagan temple on the east side, but the poorest of the poor came to the Sisters, besides women who could be nursed there more modestly and comfortably. There were many good cures, and also many baptisms of dying patients, some of these being convalescent men, who persisted in going out to take forbidden food, which caused hopeless relapses.

Among the refugees were many negligent Christians, apostates who had wandered far from God. Here was work for old Sister Pauline, who knew many of them, and she spread her net for " fishes ", big and small. The ignorant were instructed, children baptized, marriages put right; through their country's humiliations and sufferings many wandering sheep came back to the fold. It was in this first year of war that China lost her great apostle of charity, Mr. Lo Pa-Hong, who was cruelly assassinated. He was greatly mourned by Christians and pagans alike.

Long before this outbreak of war, Sister Berkeley had foreseen that it was coming and she was heard to say, " We have some bad years before us." The commander of a British gunboat who visited Tinghai in 1936 said to her, " There is going to be something big up with Japan soon; be prepared! " She began to buy small quantities of extra rice during the harvests so as to have some reserves. Although actual war did not touch the islands in those first years, the blockade of the Chekiang coast affected them. All boat service was stopped, trade was at a standstill and stores and post could only come through by roundabout routes in junks.

A strange incident took place at this time. In the country districts of Chusan were many so-called guerrillas. To whom they belonged, no one was sure, and certainly many brigands joined their ranks. On New Year's Eve, 1938, a party of these soldiers approached the town of Tinghai. They seemed to have peaceable intentions and were on good terms with the Mandarin and town officials. The latter gave them food and lodging, and they, in return, caught a band of brigands who were giving trouble to the neighbourhood. Then there was some dispute over the payment they demanded and suddenly they turned on the Mandarin, drove him and his officials out of the town, and took possession themselves. They looted the shops, and opened the prison doors, setting free over 300 prisoners, most of them brigands and pirates.

There was great excitement in the prison, men knocking off one another's chains with big stones, smashing doors and windows, and taking all the belongings of the Governor and warders; these latter had taken refuge in the Catholic Mission. The sick prisoners in the little hospital rose up and went out with the others, with the exception of one paralyzed man. They left in their hospital clothes, with the Red Cross mark on them, for their own were stolen by their comrades below; but it was very striking that nothing else belonging to the Sisters was taken, not one bedcover, coat, thermos flask, or even cup or towel.

One poor boy, nineteen years old, who had been shot in the abdomen, managed to drag himself to his home at Sinkomen, eighteen miles away. He wrote from there to the Sisters, asking pardon for going away in the hospital clothes, and saying that his mother was washing them and would return them. This lad was caught again and brought back to the prison; he died in the hospital after being baptized. Most of the patients, who were very sick men, had had enough of their liberty by night, and dragged themselves into the Mission hospital. The Sisters had sent men to investigate the conditions in the prison; the great gates were wide open, furniture smashed, and the paralyzed man lay in the hospital, quite calm, saying, " I know the Sisters won't forget me." He was carried off on a plank to the Mission.

Already the island of Chusan had had one false alarm of a Japanese attack. A gunboat arrived one afternoon at the port and the people took up their bedcovers and small possessions and bolted into the country villages. Large numbers came into the House of Mercy and filled the corridors and empty spaces. In a few hours' time the gunboat went away and the people returned to their homes. After two days' possession of the town the guerrillas heard that Japanese gunboats were coming to see what had happened, for Shanghai reported that " Chusan Island was taken by pirates " !

The guerrillas disappeared, the Mandarin came back, and the town was quiet. Suddenly two Japanese boats arrived at the port and again there was a big exodus of people into the country. Every corner of the House of Mercy was filled with refugees, and there were rumours that the Japanese were going to attack the island and take it. All night long searchlights played over the town, especially on the white crosses and foreign flags of the Mission Houses.

The very morning the attack was expected a marriage had been arranged for one of the Holy Childhood girls. The events of daily life had to go on, and the young bridegroom had arrived the day before from a village three mountains away. The wedding preparations were made and the " pig was killed "; it was impossible to stop this important affair. The little bride walked over to the church and came back, passing down the long entrance corridor between lines of refugees sitting on their bedcovers. They forgot their fright and misery in admiring her, and were struck to see one of the Sisters' girls dressed in red satin bride's clothes and pearl head-dress (always hired for the occasion) like girls in families outside.

There had been trouble the night before because the young bridegroom had counted on buying the wedding ring in the town, but all the jewellery shops had been looted by the guerrillas and gold wedding rings had especially taken their fancy; there was not one left. However, as usual, the Sisters came to the rescue, being well accustomed to extraordinary mishaps on these occasions. They always keep a wedding ring to lend, in case the flustered young bridegroom has forgotten or lost it. The pair were happily married with the ring borrowed for the occasion. The bridegroom then went home, according to custom, to finish the preparations there. Two days later the little bride followed in the red marriage chair, but her trousseau boxes were kept behind for safety until there should be less danger from the brigands and guerrillas in the country.

About midday the Japanese gunboats went away. They had only come to survey the situation this time, and the people went back to their homes. But on the fourth visit the Japanese bombarded the big pagan temple at the port, Tong-Ou-Kong. They continued until many parts of it were smashed, also several houses and one of the quays of the port.

The people, as usual, had rushed to the country and to the Mission for refuge. The bombardment ended, the Japanese boats went away. As many of the big idols in the temple had been broken, the pagans went to consult the devil as to what was to be done. He replied through his advocate, " I must jump out of my house ", which meant that the remaining idols should be removed. They were taken to a big temple at Sen-kang on the other side of the island.

When bombardments began, Sister Berkeley called all the children and old people to the chapel to say the Rosary, and it was surely their prayers that kept them safe. The children took it as a joke, saying, " Bombardments do not hurt you; they only shake you up a bit." Even the babies in the nurseries became accustomed to flinging themselves on their knees and chanting prayers at the first bang; though at the same time expecting the Sister to come and give them biscuits as reward for their bravery.

The third year of war approached and still Chusan was fairly quiet, with the exception of occasional bombardments at the port. The blockade of the coast brought great suffering to the people—there was no commerce, no food coming through. As Chusan Island can only grow sufficient rice to feed its population for three months of the year, it was serious. The port was deserted and hundreds of men out of work.

In Shanghai the Foreign Relief Committees were in full action and Sister Berkeley appealed to them for help to feed not only her own large family but the starving poor outside. They responded generously with money gifts, and also offers of cracked wheat and rice, if means could be found to bring them to the island. Though all Chinese steamers were blockaded, occasional Portuguese, Swedish and even English merchant ships came and went, bringing post and stores. Sister Berkeley made friends with the captains of these ships, and all offered to bring the food given for the poor, free. Mr. Chang, head of the Tax Department in Tinghai, also helped to pass it through. He became a very good friend to the Sisters and later took refuge with his wife and family in the Mission when the Japanese occupied Chusan.

Here we must speak of the famous Heyko house. Next door to the crowded compound of the House of Mercy is a large property on which are several good Chinese houses and courtyards. They belong to a rich pagan called Mr. Hey, who never lives there, having other houses in Shanghai and Hongkong. This property, always called Heyko (the house of Hey), was a real Naboth's vineyard to Sister Berkeley and her Sisters. They sometimes visited it, as the old caretaker was very friendly, and they would wander through the houses and courts, dreaming of their over-crowded poor people in those big empty rooms.

On the side facing the Sisters' houses is a two-storied European building on the same property, having fine rooms with glass fronts and wide verandas. This house Mr. Hey built expressly for the " spirits of his ancestors ", and twice a year he sent some relatives to offer sacrifices in it to these spirits. Twice Sister Berkeley had made a personal appeal to him to give this property or part of it for his poor compatriots in the House of Mercy, but he indignantly refused.

However, in the war emergency days the Mandarin and Town Council informed him that they were taking possession of it for the installation of a temporary hospital in preparation for the Japanese attack. This was put into the hands of the Sisters, who with great joy entered into Heyko, tucking many Miraculous Medals into corners to ensure lasting possession. Appeals were made to the British and American Red Cross Commissions in Shanghai, and generous medical supplies and equipment, money and more cracked wheat arrived. The wheat was much appre-ciated by the children of the Orphanage, and mixed with the rice it added greatly to the nutritive value. Mr. Fong, the Director of Education in Tinghai, lent beds from the American school, and everything was soon ready in the big " House of the Spirits " at Heyko.

On June 23rd, 1939, came the attack and capture of the island by the Japanese. As early as five o'clock in the morning planes were seen circling over the town; lower and lower they came, dropping small explosives but not big bombs. During the 5.30 a.m. Mass in the Sisters' chapel all were shaken by the bombardment at the port; several big gunboats were there. The refugees came pouring into the House of Mercy by hundreds, and were also sent into the Chinese houses of Heyko.

By nine o'clock the town of Tinghai was completely deserted; the Japanese had landed at several points and were making their way unopposed into the town. The Chinese soldiers had all retreated into the country by the Mandarin's orders, as he wanted to save the town. About ten o'clock the Sisters saw the Japanese soldiers raising their flag on the city walls at the West Gate, about three minutes' walk from their front entrance, opposite the Church of St. Michael, and a few minutes later they came marching up the street. Sister Berkeley and another English Sister were waiting at the door to receive them.

Though still the month of June, it was one of the hottest days of the year, so the Sisters had placed a table outside the entrance, with big pots of tea and basins of hot water and towels, to help the contact to be an amiable one. With the soldiers came an interpreter, the General's secretary, who went into the church residence to see the French priests, while the soldiers broke ranks and waited. Though not showing any friendliness, they accepted the tea and hot water, passing the bowls to the Sisters to taste first, evidently fearing poison. The menservants drank to reassure them.

The Japanese then passed into the town, breaking open the doors of the houses, and looting the little shops; there was no sign of the inhabitants. Presently a fresh regiment arrived, dragging cannons, which were taken to the country to hunt the Chinese soldiers. Two young officers sat down in the Sisters' porch to check the passing cannons. They took tea and presently one of them said to Sister Berkeley, "Where are all the Englishmen in this English city?" She smiled and replied, "There are no Englishmen on this island, only two English Sisters of Charity." The officer said, "Not you, the Sisters, but the Englishmen and English houses in this English settlement?" The Sisters said again, "This is no English settlement; it is a little Chinese island with only nine foreigners here, two English Sisters and some French Sisters and priests, all belonging to the Catholic Mission." The officers looked puzzled and passed on, following the cannons into the country. Machine-gun fire from the aeroplanes wounded many poor people in the villages and the French priests went out with their bands of stretcher bearers to bring them into the Mission hospitals.

Soon the needs of the refugees became pressing, for, alas, a gift of rice promised for this emergency had not arrived. The Protestant minister, an excellent man, who had taken refuge with his family and flock in Heyko, said that he had some rice for the poor in his house and would go to bring it in if two Sisters would accompany him. It was about ten minutes' walk, and they started off, the Sisters putting up their umbrellas to shield them from the hot midday sun.

The town was deserted; doors of shops and houses were wide open, and loot was lying in the streets. Bang went the cannon in the country, and the wails of a house in the street fell with a crash! Then came a spattering of machine-gun fire from the planes above. Mr. Chen, the minister, begged the Sisters to close their umbrellas so that the white cornettes might be seen and respected, but it was a perilous walk. However, the rice was brought in safely, and, mixed with cracked wheat, made a good meal for the hundreds of refugees.

It was a disturbing afternoon, for Japanese soldiers came strolling in, wandering where they liked, which was not pleasant in a house of women and children. More refugees came creeping in from hiding places; poor things, one was full of pity for them; many were people of good position, others were very poor. The next day two regular meals daily were arranged; the relatives of a very rich merchant, absent in Shanghai, sent to beg the Sisters to take out of his house all the rice and other stores before the Japanese took possession of them. As his property had one of the city canals running through it, the food was brought in quickly and unobserved in the Sisters' boat. Soon there were nearly 1,000 refugees in Heyko and many parts of the House of Mercy.

On June 24th the visit of the Japanese General was announced. He came with many soldiers and Red Cross officers, riding in a small armoured car, the first automobile ever seen in Chusan. He visited all parts of the House, children, old people, etc., and the refugees in Heyko. He seemed fairly friendly, and, to the great relief of the Sisters, gave a big printed notice to be put on the front door, forbidding soldiers to enter. For this, all said a fervent " Thank God ".

With the General was a Red Cross Commander who wished to visit the hospitals and report on the sick people. This was rather alarming, as many important men refugees were hiding there; however, they were not recognized and the visit passed off satis-factorily, though the Commander was a very fierce, disagreeable man, who sneered at the poor people, especially the aged, and

WAR RELIEF WORK : Daily feeding the starving people
—and the little beggar boys. CHUSAN, 1939-42

WAR RELIEF—CHUSAN
Fishing net workrooms.

THE CHILDREN AT WORK

insisted, suspiciously, on taking blood specimens of all the fever cases. He spoke of the Japanese taking full charge of the medical work, which was a disturbing prospect.

During the first few days of the occupation the Sisters were constantly receiving agonizing messages begging them to go and rescue women, many of them ladies in rich families, with their girls, who were hiding in different parts of the town. One poor lady was hidden in the roof of her house, where she was nearly suffocated. The Sisters, headed by Sister Berkeley, went out in rickshaws, accompanying the person who called them, generally an old woman, for whom there was less danger. They brought in these ladies and girls, walking between the rickshaws, and they were not interfered with by the Japanese.

These were busy days, but there were many good lay helpers, including the devoted Dr. Gni and his wife. The latter took full charge of the maternity rooms which had at once to be arranged for the refugees. On June 27th there were more visits from Japanese Red Cross Commanders, but these were elderly, genial men of the old style in Japan. They praised the organization of the House of Mercy and the good care taken of the children, old people and sick. One of them confided to the English Sister in a whisper, " I did most of my training in an English hospital in London." Evidently they represented to the higher authorities that it was ridiculous to waste their time taking charge of a House of Good Works which was well managed by the Sisters, for no more was heard of it.

In a few days the gunboats and Red Cross ships went away, but the General stayed as Commander of the town, with a regiment of soldiers. The latter scoured the country villages, looking for the Chinese soldiers, and there were more wounded civilians brought in to the Mission hospitals. Little by little life became more normal, and some elderly Chinese notables were called to form a council under the Japanese.

For many months the town of Tinghai was like a dead place, with streets of empty houses and shops. Some people came back, but the many regulations, passes, photographs and injections required frightened them and they slipped away again. There were only Japanese gunboats, transports and cargo ships running for their own needs; no stores or post could get through from Shanghai except by junks from the other side of the island.

Q

In the House of Mercy life went on as usual, the children at school, the big girls busy in the workrooms. For the latter the difficulty was to get the finished work away to Shanghai for sale. A rather amusing incident occurred. A young Japanese lieutenant presented himself one day with a gun, asking permission to come in and shoot birds in the gardens. This request could not be refused, and day by day he wandered about, occasionally shooting birds. Of course the real reason for his presence was to survey closely all that was going on; in plain words, he was a spy. Everyone treated him very amiably, only imploring him not to shoot too close to the babies' nurseries. Often the older children left their places in the workroom to go to him and say, " Look, there is a nice big bird up there. Don't you want to shoot it ? "

The Sisters made friends with this lieutenant and explained to him their difficulties about sending the embroideries to Shanghai. He gave valuable help, taking charge of boxes of work which were sent on Japanese naval boats to Shanghai and delivered to the Sisters' Central House. This young officer also obtained permission for a very sick Sister, needing urgent surgical treatment, to be taken to Shanghai on an Army transport ship. The journey was an interesting and amusing one. The Sister in charge of the patient was brought back to Chusan on the same ship and treated courteously.

In those days of the occupation the Sisters were treated politely by the officers and those in high position, as long as they conformed to all the regulations and " did not hold their heads too high "! They devoted themselves to their children and their poor and sometimes received gifts for them from the Japanese Commander—confiscated food, salt fish and dried vegetables which the poor country people were always trying to smuggle in without paying the heavy taxes demanded. The second-in-command of the town was a genial elderly man, Captain Kisima, who visited the Sisters and took interest in their works of charity, though he did not seem to have any power to help them in their constant difficulties with the common soldiers.

An amusing incident took place at that time with regard to a captured brigand in the country. When the Japanese took the town of Tinghai, for some unknown reason they opened the prison doors and set free over 300 prisoners. On the second day of the occupation a Sister, accompanied by men carriers and women, went to the prison; she found it empty, and the hospital equipment thrown about in disorder; evidently it was used by the Japanese soldiers at night. Guarding the door herself, her men gathered up everything, beds included, emptied the cupboards, and, in several journeys, carried all to the Mission by back streets, unobserved. The Japanese were in the country all day, and the town was fairly deserted in the daytime. The hospital equipment came in useful for the refugees in Heyko.

A few days later a brigand in the country was caught, brought into the town and shut up in a temporary lock-up. He had been shot through the knee, the bone being smashed, and for six days no treatment had been given, so the stench from his wounds was insupportable and they were full of worms! The Japanese were told that it was only the " white-hat Momos " who could deal with such cases, so they sent for them. A Sister came with one of her men nurses, dressed the man's wounds, and asked that he should be sent to the Mission hospital, as such dressings were too difficult to do in the prison courtyard. All were delighted to be delivered from the brigand in that state, and he was carried off to the Mission.

One day Captain Kisima invited the Sisters to visit him at the naval headquarters. While there, the conversation turned on this brigand and Sister C. gave the Japanese Commander a graphic account of his wounds and the worms! Captain Kisima turned to Sister A. and said, " I am sorry you had such dirty work to do." " Oh," she replied, " it was my duty." " Your holy duty ? " he asked, with a smile. " Yes," she said, " my holy duty."

Meanwhile the work of caring for the refugees went on in Heyko. The rice of the rich merchant, Mr. Gno, mixed with the American cracked wheat proved sufficient for the daily food of these poor people. Gradually some of them went out to relatives in the country, but there was no work and the poor in the town and at the port were faced with starvation. Sister Berkeley organized a weekly distribution of portions of cracked wheat, according to the numbers in families. With this help, more of them went out and began life again, but the women and girls stayed with the Sisters for many months.

In the early days of the occupation the island of Chusan Meng was threatened. A young Japanese lieutenant, who was in charge of making signalling stations at the port, wanted to take possession of it for this purpose, for it certainly is in a strategic position. Hearing it belonged to the Sisters, the Japanese called them to a council, and asked at what price they would sell the island to them. Sister Berkeley gave a characteristic reply: " I cannot sell China's land to Japan; that I will never do. If you take it from me, I cannot prevent you, but I beg that my gardeners may continue to cultivate the island, as its produce is the food of my orphan children and poor."

A few days later the Japanese sent to ask for the deeds of purchase of the island to examine them, but Sister Berkeley was prepared. At the time of the occupation she had sent all her deeds of land purchase to Shanghai with her compradore in a junk from the other side of the island. She referred the Japanese in all important business to the Bishop at Ningpo or the Superiors of the Sisters at Shanghai. She told tnem, " We Sisters are like you soldiers, under obedience to our higher authorities, and we can give no decisive answers without reference to them."

There seemed, however, little hope of keeping Chusan Meng, for the Chinese Governing Council said that they would take it in the name of China. Influential friends told the Sisters there was nothing to be done, they must accept the loss; but somehow it never happened. It was said that the island was too low for a signalling station, and so the high mountains on Bougee, the neighbouring island, were taken instead. From time to time Japanese soldiers landed on Chusan Meng and told the gardeners they would have to leave soon. They stole large quantities of vegetables and fruit, and in the autumn of 1944 cut down all the big trees to build an aerodrome. This was after Sister Berkeley's death. It would have been a great grief to her. We have, however, come through to the end of the war and Chusan Meng, by a real miracle, is still in the hands of the Sisters.

Many Japanese gunboats visited Tinghai, and their commanders, officers and sailors came frequently to the House of Mercy, showing great interest in the children. The officers treated the Sisters politely, often gave gifts of money for their poor, and more than once made the following remark, " We understand you Sisters leave your homes, forget your nationalities and unite together to do good works for the poor in any country; it is very beautiful."

On one occasion it was announced that an admiral of very high

rank was coming to visit the House. He was brought by the
Mandarin with great ceremony, but when he arrived at the front
entrance he waited there until Sister Berkeley and her Sisters came
to invite him to enter. He was a very tall man, with a severe
expression, but when surrounded by the happy faces of the
children, especially the babies, he broke into smiles, and in excellent English said to the Sisters, " I cannot tell you the great
pleasure it gives me to visit your children and see them so happy."

He was very interested in the kindergarten school, and watched
the children working busily at their little tables. One little girl,
about five years old, drew out of her work bag a knitted duster,
which she had just finished making. She had not yet decided what
she wished to do with it. She brought it to the Sister and said,
" Do you think the Japanese gentleman would like to have this
duster, which I made myself ? He could wipe his table with it."
When this was translated to the admiral, he made a low bow to
the little Chinese child, and taking the duster with great pleasure,
he folded it carefully and put it away in an inner pocket.

It was always supposed that the water around Chusan Island
was too shallow for big gunboats, but the Japanese brought very
big boats there and often held naval councils at Tinghai. They
liked the Chusan islands very much, said that they reminded
them of Japan, and from the first they announced their intention
of keeping them after the war was finished.

XXI

WORK OF THE RELIEF COMMITTEE

GRADUALLY more communication was opened up between Chusan and Shanghai, though under very strict supervision by the Japanese. For a long time there were no passenger boats, only cargo steamers, which ran very irregularly. Sister Berkeley had appealed to Dr. Hylbert, the head of the American Relief Committee in Shanghai, for more help, especially for cracked wheat and rice, not only for her own household but also for the starving poor outside.

Hearing of the organized weekly distribution to the latter, Dr. Hylbert responded generously with money, gifts of food and medicines. He proposed to Sister Berkeley that she should form a local committee in Tinghai for outside relief, she and her Sisters serving on it with Mr. Chen, the Protestant minister, Dr. Gni, and others willing to help. Dr. Hylbert offered regular monthly allocations from his committee for such a work. He had great confidence in Sister Berkeley and the Sisters, and proved himself a very kind and valuable friend to them.

With the permission of the Shanghai Superiors, this committee was formed. Sister Berkeley was elected president, with three of her Sisters, Mr. Chen, Dr. Gni and three elderly Chinese gentlemen filling the other offices. For two and a half years it did very good work for the relief of the outside poor, not only in the town and port of Tinghai but also in the country districts and neighbouring islands where there was famine.

Families making application for help were visited to find out their needs, then given tickets to present each week for portions of cracked wheat and rice, according to their numbers and needs. Many of those asking for help were wives whose husbands worked in Shanghai and who had not been heard of since the outbreak of the war so no help came through for their families. In some sad cases the husbands and brothers were never heard of again; probably they had been killed in the Shanghai bombardments.

Others had lost their employment or had no means of sending money. Sister Berkeley arranged to pass money through the Sisters' Central House for them.

The number of outside poor receiving relief grew to over 1,000, and as the winter set in other works of charity were added. In Chusan, and indeed in most parts of China, it is the custom for the poor and middle-class people to put their bedcovers and winter clothes in the pawnshops during the summer months. The reason for this is that they have little space in their small, badly arranged houses; moreover, they live from day to day.

A Sister relates that she once saw one of her hospital nurses, a respectable woman, going out of the front door with a large bundle. When asked what it was, she replied quite simply, " Oh Momo, all my winter clothes are in it. I am going to put them in pawn so as to get enough money to buy an oufit for my boy who is going to be apprenticed." The Sister asked, " But when the winter comes, where will you find the money to take them out ? " She replied, " It will turn up somehow; I can pawn my summer clothes or borrow." The result is that they are rarely without debts.

In the winter months of the Japanese occupation of Chusan hundreds of families had no money to take their bedcovers and winter clothes out of pawn. The Outside Relief Committee came to the rescue and helped in this charity, but it needed very close supervision. Winter clothes were made for the suffering poor; much of the material used was that of the sacks in which the wheat and rice came. This was dyed black, dark grey, or blue and made excellent clothes; by washing the sacks very vigorously the red dye of the Red Cross printed name washed out, making the sack a pale pink colour. Little girls who came for clothes asked eagerly for a " pink coat ".

Another work taken on by the Relief Committee was the provision of coffins for the very poor, but this was only in the early days. Later it was stopped, for there was no wood to be procured, and eventually the poor and middle-class people had to be buried without coffins—a terrible grief for them!

The Mission hospitals were always full, and many of the patients were those suffering from " hunger sickness." They would be brought in almost dead with exhaustion, having been many days without food. After being nursed back to life, fed well and strengthened, they would then be put on their feet to begin life again with regular help for a time. Money was given by the Relief Committee for this purpose; it is called *siau sangi*, selling things from door to door.

Very soon it was found necessary to provide a daily meal, such as is done in soup kitchens for the poor. In Chusan it was the good cracked wheat, which was cooked with fresh vegetables and salt, and served every morning at the door to those who brought their bowls and old tins to receive it. But this manner of serving her " Lords and Masters, the Poor " did not suit Sister Berkeley, and she soon organized a better service.

Early in the morning tables with benches were arranged down the two sides of the entrance corridor. Bowls and chopsticks were provided and at a certain hour a Sister let in at the door first the children, then the old women and men, among whom were many respectable people who were dying of hunger. No longer receiving their little monthly pittances from relatives in Shanghai, they were literally starving, getting thinner from day to day. They often told Sister Berkeley with tears in their eyes, when served with the good wheat porridge, " Ta Momo, this is the one real meal I have in the day." Many of these old people eventually came in to the Sisters' hospices, so that sometimes there were several waiting for an empty bed. Soon the professional beggars heard of the daily meal, and presented themselves; they were not refused, but they came and went, often being absent in the country, where they found better rice to eat!

At the top of the corridor, near the statue of the Sacred Heart, was the serving table, and it was good to see Sister Berkeley seated before the steaming buckets of wheat porridge. She insisted on it being thick and substantial, with fresh vegetables mixed with it. She served it herself and welcomed these poor guests, going amongst them, making friends, and hearing their sad tales with sympathetic interest. Very soon she decided that one bowl was not sufficient, and that a second half-bowl portion should be given, but her half-bowls were never far from the brims.

For serving this meal the Good Mother called daily some of her children, and even the little kindergarten babies took their turn with great joy. It was delightful to see them carefully carrying the hot bowls of porridge, then dancing back to the serving table. Sister Berkeley remarked one day with a smile, " Our waiters are very full of springs and jumps! " She was pleased to teach them this act of faith, " to serve Our Lord in the person of the poor ". Portions of the cooked wheat were carried by the Sisters and their women to those who were sick or infirm in their houses, and many interesting tales could be told of this work.

The little beggar boys must not be forgotten. Alas, many children in the town, country and islands, with formerly respectable parents, were turned out to beg, and soon there was a real army of them, especially boys. Naturally, these little rascals all turned up with beaming, dirty faces for the daily meal at the Sisters' House, and many an effort was made to convert them to better ways. They were presented with towels and clean clothes, made from the empty sacks, and they were invited to go and wash themselves in the river before coming in to eat; this they took as a huge joke.

Later on the Mandarin collected these little boys and made a municipal orphanage. When Sister Berkeley heard of this, she said with a smile, " You will see, it will end by them all being turned over to us." Her words came true, for in the winter of 1944, a line of dirty, neglected, little boys was marched into the House of Mercy corridor, with a request from the Mandarin to take them in. His orphanage had failed; he could find no one trustworthy to care for the children. So, in the last year of her life, Sister Berkeley, though weighed down with the anxieties of feeding her own big family, opened a new work—an orphanage for boys. She took in these little lads, mothered and educated them; her words had come true.

Week by week, the numbers applying for relief grew larger. One heard on all sides, " We should starve if the Sisters were not here to help us "; better still, " It is not the *poussahs* [idols] in the temples who are helping us, but the One True God, the Master of Heaven. Let us thank and adore Him." Many of these poor people began to come to Mass on Sundays and listen afterwards to a little instruction. The climax came at Chinese New Year when hundreds of the people came to the Catholic Church to thank God for the past year, instead of going to the pagan temples to thank the devil, as is the custom.

On one occasion shipping difficulties prevented the supplies of wheat and rice from arriving, and, also, the monthly allocation of money was delayed in the post. Sometimes when there was no food in hand to give, money would be distributed instead, though faces would grow sad on seeing it. " Money buys so little," they would say. " It is food we need."

A day arrived when there was neither food nor money in the hands of the Relief Committee, though help was expected daily. What would happen with those hundreds of people arriving with their relief tickets ? Would there be a riot at the front door ? All were a little anxious, but to their surprise the people took it very quietly, and went away at once, saying, " The Sisters say they have nothing to give this week. It is no good waiting or talking; we know and trust them. If they had it, they would give it to us."

From the British Relief Committee in Shanghai came welcome gifts of medicines, especially much-needed quinine for the constant epidemics of malaria in the islands, and big tins of cod liver oil. Sister Berkeley welcomed this especially for her Holy Childhood children; for many years before the war, it was her devoted mother, the " Chusan Grandmother ", who sent a barrel of cod liver oil every winter. Dr. Bernard Reed, of the British Relief Committee, was a kind and valuable friend; he was much interested in the food question of those war years and made many good suggestions.

Through the Lord Mayor's Fund in London came also generous gifts, and another organization which was always ready to help poor hospitals was the British Women's Hospital Aid Department in Shanghai. Big sacks of bandages, babies' clothes, etc., came regularly to Chusan from their members, who will be pleased to know that their last gift before the 1941 outbreak, forty rolls of thick white muslin, was a valuable standby in the following lean years of war, and it saved the situation again and again.

From the American Red Cross came cracked wheat and good rice; the weekly portions given to the poor contained half rice, half wheat. Sister Berkeley had many urgent requests from rich people to give or sell to them the American rice and wheat which the poor people were receiving. With great difficulty she stood firm, representing to the rich that she had signed her name as a guarantee to the Red Cross that the food given by them should only be passed to the poor and not sold to anyone. This was the condition on which it was given, but many people in Tinghai failed to understand this, and the Sisters were pressed on all sides to sell or give it to those who were not in need. Sister Berkeley used to say, " What is given for the poor must go to the poor, and the honour of the Community is at stake."

The prisoners in the town prison, the special friends of the Sisters, were not forgotten. They were on very short rations, therefore once a week Sister Berkeley served a generous lunch of wheat and vegetables to over 300 hungry men. She went herself to supervise it, and when her tall figure and smiling face appeared in the corridor between the cells the men behind the iron grilles hailed her with delight. " Ta Momo, Ta Momo." The big, steaming buckets of wheat porridge were brought in, and she served on one side. It was no good saying to her, " Ta Momo, if you give such big helpings, there won't be enough to go round for the others." " Never mind," she would reply, " we will make some more to-morrow for those who have not enough to-day." The men on that side thought they were lucky to be served by her.

It seemed as if Almighty God in His Divine Providence were laying in stores for the coming famine years. Like the oil in the widow's cruse, many things seemed to multiply miraculously and kept the works going in the House of Mercy. In September 1941 the Red Cross granted to Chusan fifty sacks of Farina, a kind of fine semolina made from white flour, as well as fifty sacks of rolled oats. These were specially given for the babies and sick people, but unfortunately the shipping of these stores to the island became more and more difficult and costly.

On December 8th, when the news came of the break with England and America, all hope was abandoned of receiving this last valuable shipment of food. That afternoon the last steamer to leave Shanghai before the bombardment arrived at Tinghai port and in it were the rolled oats and Farina. They were received with great joy and thanksgiving to Our Lady, who had managed that difficult affair on her Feast Day. During the next three years the Farina made bread for the foreigners, by being ground back into white flour in a hand mill.

.   .   .   .

Another work of the Outside Relief Committee was the establishment of special workrooms for women and girls. Many were taught lace-making and embroidery and soon earned wages. Others, who were not capable of such fine work, were gathered together in a " fishing net " workroom. This was a very interesting venture and the Sisters devoted much time and thought to its development, for it was to supply fishing nets to the islands. Unfortunately, it is a very badly paid work, normally done by a rough class of men, who live in boats.

A " Head Professor " was found in the person of an old Wenchow woman who had made nets in her youth on the seashore, and who still possessed one of the roughly made bamboo machines for winding the hemp into fine cord. She was one of the Sisters' poor guests who came to dine daily and she was delighted to help with this new workroom.

The great difficulty was to find the hemp needed, although the Sisters began at once to grow it on their mountain land. But a superior, stronger kind was needed for the nets. This had always come from ports farther south, but these were now closed, as Chusan was in Japanese hands.

The fishing-net workroom was placed under the patronage of St. Peter, and a big picture of him in his boat, with nets around him, was hung on the wall. It is remarkable to relate that on his Feast Day large quantities of hemp arrived, smuggled through from another port. Profits at first from this new work were poor, as a large part of them went into the hands of middlemen. So one day the Sisters made a dash in a junk to a big fishing island, Heysan, hoping to escape Japanese gunboats or pirates on the way. While they visited the sick people on the island, their compradore discussed nets with the fishermen and sold several. Finding the work good, orders began to come in direct from the islands.

To all workers in the embroidery and fishing-net workrooms two good meals were served daily, a dinner of rice and wheat mixed, and for supper wheat porridge. Sister Berkeley was often seen letting in many of her poor friends outside to share these meals, for she could not refuse the hungry. Later on, after December 1941, when the Red Cross supplies stopped, then only one meal a day could be given to the workers. Eventually, when there was real famine in the House of Mercy, these outside workrooms had to be given up. As for the fishing nets, it is a work which will be taken up again in peace time, for it gives employment to women in their own houses, preparing the hemp; moreover, it is useful for the blind in the orphanage.

The prisoners' weekly lunch had also to be given up, because of the lack of supplies of relief food. A rather striking incident took place on the day the last lunch was served. It happened to be the anniversary of the fall of Singapore, and the Japanese made great celebrations. They called all the school children of Tinghai to their naval parade ground in procession, carrying flags and banners on which were written, " Down with foreigners "—" No more English imperialism ", etc., and there were speeches of anti-foreign propaganda.

Sister Berkeley was returning from the prison in a rickshaw, with another Sister, when they met this procession of school children going home. To make way for them Sister Berkeley had her rickshaw drawn to the side of the narrow road, and she sat there, smiling at the children. They knew her well, a very old friend, and as they passed all broke out into salutations, shouting " Ta Momo, Ta Momo ", with smiling faces and waving their flags! Their masters and mistresses did the same, all being highly amused. Fortunately no Japanese were with them to see this demonstration of affection for one of the hated English.

XXII

THE LAST YEARS OF SISTER BERKELEY

DURING the first years of the war the children and occupants of the House of Mercy had not really suffered. They were fed by the good cereals of the Red Cross and Relief Committees, though all extras had to be cut down. There was need of strict economy, for no more gifts came through from Europe. Many little abandoned babies were brought in from famine districts, and one often heard, " Eight babies are waiting at the port, brought from the island of Kindong [or another]; please send women and rickshaws to carry them in." Bands of starving children came, especially from the big island of Taysain, where there was severe famine. A stalwart countrywoman would arrive, swinging from her bamboo shoulder-pole two baskets, in each of which would be two or three or more babies. Walking by her side would be little hungry children aged from three to ten years, those who were too small or weak to beg for themselves outside.

These children picked up marvellously with the nourishing food still available, but when real famine days came they were the first to fall again and develop beri-beri and anæmia. Sister Berkeley with her great experience said, " Children who have once suffered from famine in their early years have no constitution to stand it a second time."

The Sisters spoke of some of these little ones as " those who came to us for a year or two, received five sacraments and went to Heaven "! They took their places in the family, grew fat and happy, studied, received Baptism, prepared for First Confession and Communion, and then soon afterwards fell ill and went to Heaven, having received the five Sacraments, Baptism, Penance, Holy Eucharist, Confirmation and Extreme Unction. The pathetic part was that they did not want to go to Heaven. When lying in the infirmary, with their swollen legs and puffed faces, they would say pitifully, " Yes, I know Heaven is a very nice place. I believe all you tell me, but I don't want to go there. I am very happy here; everyone is so kind to me. Don't let the priest come and pray over my hands and feet [Extreme Unction] as he did to Tseydi and Amao [little companions] for that would mean I am going to Heaven and I don't want to go. I like being here."

It was a great grief to the Sisters, especially to the good Mother, Sister Berkeley, to see these sick and suffering children dying from the want of good nourishment. She had always given the best of everything to them, and now her hands were empty she could do so little. One often saw her face drawn with pain when she came away from her constant visits to the infirmary. From thirty to forty children died of beri-beri and anæmia in those famine years.

.   .   .   .

In 1943 regulations tightened for the foreigners in Chusan. Already Allied nationals were being collected into concentration camps in Japanese-occupied territory. It was extraordinary that Sister Berkeley and her English companion were not called to Shanghai to be interned in the camp there. Perhaps it was her great age that saved her, for she was over eighty years old; moreover, she was known to be a person of distinction, for whom, with her Orphanage and House of Good Works, special protection had been asked in high quarters. Her cousin, Lord Denbigh, in the early days of the war in the East, had made friends with the Japanese Ambassador in London, whose wife and daughter were Catholics, and had obtained a promise from the Japanese naval and military authorities that Chusan Island should not be bombed if there were no Chinese military activities there.

An amusing rumour passed among the Chusan people that the " Ta Momo " of the " Tzong-ze-dong " (House of Mercy) was related to the English Royal family!

Indeed, one of the notables, a good benefactor of the House, announced that she was the King's aunt!

God spared her the great blow of having to leave her beloved Mission, but she and her Sisters were interned, prisoners in their own House; even the Chinese Sisters, the foreign costume being given as reason for this. The supervision was very strict, and surprise visits were often made by the Japanese. To the end they were convinced that somehow the Sisters were in communication with the British and Americans. They constantly searched the Houses for radios, although the Sisters assured them that they were not allowed by their Rule to use them.

" How do you carry on your House and works of charity ? " they often asked suspiciously. " Where does the money come from ? " Sister Berkeley would reply, " We live from day to day, very poorly, on gifts. Our Chinese friends help us; they are very kind and good." One day the Japanese officer said angrily, " And are not we, the Japanese, also kind and good to you ? " She replied calmly, " But it is not your duty; it is their duty to help their poor."

One morning there was great trouble in the House of Mercy, two of the large iron stoves in the Chinese kitchens broke, and no food could be cooked there that day. Sister Berkeley gave orders that each House in the compound must find means of cooking its own dinner in the small kitchens. This meant an increase of work for the Sisters, and in the middle of it came a peremptory summons from the Municipality for all the foreigners to come at once.

Being on very friendly terms with the Mandarin, Sister Berkeley sent to tell him of the kitchen disaster and to beg that the interview might be postponed to the afternoon. At two o'clock, the foreigners —five Sisters and three priests, English, French and Canadian— went to the Municipality; after they had waited an hour the Mandarin arrived and assured them with a smile that it was a mistake; he had not called them.

Later in the afternoon another peremptory call came, but the foreigners refused to go, saying that it was a hoax. The next morning a terrified secretary rushed in, saying, " Momo, it is the Japanese who are calling you. Come quickly, they are furious." When the Sisters and priests arrived there was a stormy interview. They were scolded and abused for their disobedience to the Japanese orders. " They did not understand how kind the Japanese were to them . . ." etc. " America and Britain were treating the Japanese very badly and they deserved the same treatment," etc., etc.!

The Chinese interpreter, a friend of the Sisters, translated it all with a twinkle in his eye. He explained to the Japanese the affair of the kitchen stoves, saying, " You do not understand these

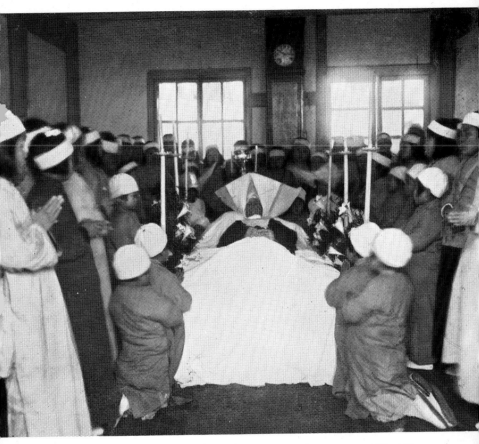

THE LYING-IN-STATE OF SISTER BERKELEY, WHO DIED AT
CHUSAN, MARCH 9th, 1944, AGED 83 YEARS
" The Mandarin of the Poor."

SISTER BERKELEY'S GRAVE AT THE "HOUSE OF MERCY"

ladies; they do everything themselves for their children and poor, even to the cooking and serving of meals. They could not leave such an important affair as the dinner." "Yes," thought the English Sister with an inward smile, " even the ' King's aunt '!— if they could have seen her, in her white apron, rushing from House to House to see that the dinner was properly cooked for her beloved children and poor! "

In 1943 the food supplies became very scarce and poor. The Mandarin, who said that he had taken charge of the House of Mercy to save it from the Japanese, sent no more rice, only a very inferior kind of brown flour, said to be the ground husks of sorghum. Illness among the children increased and many died; moreover, there being no milk or country nurses, the tiny babies could not be reared, and most of them died.

In the autumn of 1943 Sister Berkeley herself had a very severe illness, from which she slowly recovered. It seemed a miracle that she did regain health and strength; it was largely due to the devoted care of her doctor, Dr. Gni Tsatse, a very kind friend to the Sisters and their children. Also gifts were brought from the country by the married children and Christians for their Good Mother. Though their poultry yards were constantly stripped by the Japanese, they managed to smuggle in chickens and eggs for her convalescence. Often poor people in the town would bring an orange or a pear (almost priceless in those days, bought at the cost of their own meals). They would offer it at the door, saying, " For Ta Momo, to grow strong." She did recover and, with her strong will, forced herself to lead the common life again, though those around her saw what efforts it required.

Christmas of 1943 passed, a happy day, for the Sisters had the privilege of Midnight Mass in their own chapel in spite of the official black-out. Two tiny candles were burned, a luxury, for Mass was celebrated with a saucer of vegetable oil on other days. For Chinese New Year celebrations, a kind friend in the town gave a dinner of fresh meat for the children and poor, a luxury they had not tasted for many a long day. Though it had to be done secretly, because of the Japanese, the Chusan people constantly brought gifts in money and kind for the children. Employees in a shop, clerks in a bank would make collections, and several times substantial gifts arrived from some old lady or gentleman—money given to them by their families to celebrate

R

their sixtieth or seventieth birthday with a big feast. They made a sacrifice of the feast and sent the money to feed the children of the House of Mercy.

February of 1944 came in with icy weather and there was no means of heating nurseries or hospitals; many little babies died of the cold. One poor little mother, living close to the Sisters, found her baby dead in her arms in the morning, a poor little undernourished war infant, who had not yet been seen by the father working in Shanghai.

When Sister Berkeley heard of this little mother, sitting weeping at home, she called a companion and said, " Come, we will slip across the road and go to see poor little Siagnoh. No Japanese will be about at this time." She comforted the little wife as a mother would do and persuaded her to take food. It was her last act of charity in this world, for during the following night she was taken in the grip of double pneumonia. The next day her condition was so serious with heart failure that in the afternoon she received the Last Sacraments. The Sisters knelt around her; she was very quiet, joined in the prayers, and renewed her Vows in a steady voice.

The next day brought hope, for all the household were praying; it was February 9th and in two days would be the Feast of Our Lady of Lourdes. Surely she would obtain for them this miracle and keep their beloved mother with them a little longer. The prayers seemed answered, and with good care the alarming symptoms passed, and on Our Lady's Feast, February 11th, she seemed to be making a miraculous recovery. She said, " I knocked at the door of Heaven, but Our Lord sent me back. He had something more for me to do, but it will not be long."

She was soon convalescent and the family rejoiced to see their mother gaining strength daily. The little kindergarten children gathered round the Grotto of Lourdes just below her window one afternoon and sang hymns to Our Lady and the Sacred Heart. She smiled and said, " Oh, I'm being serenaded! How beautiful it is! "

Alas, the icy March winds set in, and the unheated rooms caused another cold to seize her, bringing complications of bronchitis and her old enemy asthma. She suffered terribly from breathlessness, and could no longer lie in bed, spending the last days in a long rest-chair, her eyes never leaving the big crucifix on the wall in front of her. She spoke little, only smiled at those who visited her, and took no further interest in the government of the house and daily events.

The nights seemed long, and she often asked, " When will it be time for Communion ? " Through the day, with her rosary beads always slipping through her fingers, she seemed only half on earth. Her sufferings were great physically, one could see, but she did not suffer spiritually, for her will was united to Our Lord on the Cross; her eyes never left Him. Were these days of suffering the " something more Our Lord had for her to do " ? Perhaps it was the last purification necessary before she entered straight into the glory of His presence.

At midnight on March 8th she threw up her arms towards the Crucifix, saying, " Oh, I am so weary, so weary. I can do no more! " It was like the cry of an old warrior who had fought to the end, and God permitted that she should die " with her weapons in her hands ". She had often asked a prayer for this intention. A little later she put her arms round her Sister infirmarian, saying, " God bless you, God bless you; you have been so good to me." Then she seemed to sleep quietly, but just after five o'clock the breathing changed. The priest was quickly called, and it was hoped that she could again receive Holy Communion, but she was gone in a few minutes—no agony, no struggle, with a look of perfect peace on that noble face. R.I.P.

> " For ah, the Master is so fair;
> His smile so sweet to banished men
> That those who meet it unaware
> Can never rest on earth again.
>
> Praise God, the Master is so sweet;
> Praise God, the country is so fair;
> We would not hold them from His feet,
> We would but haste to meet them there."
>   (Lines found in an old English Missal.)

When the news reached the villages and islands that their beloved " Ta Momo " had gone to God that morning, there was no hesitation. Old and young, grandmothers, mothers with babies in their arms, and children, all set out on foot or by boat, the many sons-in-law accompanying them.

Owing to the Japanese occupation it was often difficult and disagreeable to pass the sentries at the city gates. Many had been prevented for a long time from coming in to visit their old home, but that day no one was stopped. Those grief-stricken men, women and children passed the sentries with determination; they were on their way to offer their love and respect for the last time to their " Mother " and to pray by her side.

This humble Sister of Charity, eighty-three years of age, lay peacefully, surrounded by lilies, in the room where she had so often welcomed her children, and for a day and a half hundreds came and went, praying beside her and in the garden before the open door. Night and day they watched and prayed, newcomers constantly arriving from far-off districts.

The children of the house knelt around her, turn by turn; most of them were calm, hardly realizing their loss, chanting their prayers and looking at that dear face under the white cornette, the big form, so still now—a contrast to her never-ceasing activity in life. Many pagan notables and friends came to pay their respects and they brought a beautiful pale-blue, brocaded satin coverlet to be laid on her as a mark of their esteem and veneration of the " Mother of their Poor ".

When the gong sounded, according to Chinese custom, for her to be placed in the coffin, there rose up a wail of sorrow from those around her and the hundreds kneeling in the garden. It was difficult to clear the room, for the children flung themselves down beside her, and a cry came from outside, " We want to see that dear face again. It is our right to see her in the coffin, for she is our mother." That was true; it is the custom in China, so they were allowed to pass in singly for a last look, but it was very difficult to control them for all wanted to stay and weep beside her.

Gradually they were all moved into the chapel, the beautiful chapel built for her Golden Jubilee twelve years before and for which so many of them had brought their humble offerings. It was packed with them now, four generations of her children. When the coffin was carried in to be placed on the catafalque, the scene was heart-breaking, children sobbing, and young and old wailing: " Our Mother, our Mother is gone, no one will ever love us as she did, our Mother, our Mother."

Requiem Masses were celebrated in the Sisters' chapel and the Parish Church. The Mandarin and his officials attended the latter, heading the procession which carried the coffin to the church. It was brave of them, in those days of Japanese occupation, to show honour to one of the hated foreigners, but no official notice was taken; all passed off quietly.

The Mandarin had already paid his respects to this English Sister of Charity early in the morning, a few hours after her death. After saluting her three times solemnly in the Oriental manner, he said, " This was a fine Momo who had great merit; we must honour her." He sent the coffin, the most magnificent one he could find, and he paid all the funeral expenses, sending candles, rice, and white cloth for the mourning caps and shoes. To one of his friends he said, " Sister Berkeley was a Mandarin as I am, she was the ' Mandarin of the Poor.' How many years she did good works for the poor and orphans of Chusan! Now she is gone, I must follow her example and help them as she did."

The European Sisters being interned in their own house, prisoners, it was not safe or prudent to ask to go to the Sisters' cemetery outside the city gates. So the Mandarin sent men to build a small temporary tomb in the garden of the House of Mercy. All were happy to keep their dear one with them. The children often lined themselves up in a long corridor at the side of the garden and chanted their harmonious Chinese prayers. The babies played in their garden close by and they often looked at the little tomb and said, " Ta Momo is in that little house." Sometimes they cried and threw out their little arms, calling, " Ta Momo, come back to us."

One of the blackest of black sheep among her many sons-in-law, but one who would have cheerfully given his life at any moment for Ta Momo, came back to his duties to God with many others on this occasion. He constituted himself the master of ceremonies at the funeral, directing all: the carrying of the coffin from chapel to church and church to garden, which office was claimed as their right by the many sons-in-law of the house, and the band (Oriental custom) for the procession. Nothing was too good for Ta Momo.

When all was finished the black sheep said: " Ta Momo was the same to everyone, gracious, smiling; to the Mandarin and the notables, to the beggar at her door asking for a dinner, to the sick and homeless dying who sought a refuge in their last days, to the prisoners, and above all to her beloved children. All received the same smiling welcome and were treated like kings."

Even her enemies paid respect to her. One day two Japanese officers of high rank marched in, visiting the different houses as they often did. In the nursery they saw a photograph on the wall, and the babies said to them, " That is Ta Momo; she has gone away." The Japanese said to the women, " Berkeley, Berkeley ? " They nodded their heads and pointed to the little tomb in the garden. The officers made them a sign to open the door, whereupon they marched out solemnly to the tomb, took off their hats, and saluted with three deep bows.

The House of Mercy had received a big blow, and that dear presence was sorely missed. It was hard to pass the open door and see the empty chair at her desk. Even the elastic spirits of the children seemed as if they could not rebound. Then one of the Sisters had a very beautiful dream. She was sitting in her workroom at the designing table, the bigger children around her working at their embroidery frames.

Suddenly Sister Berkeley came into the room, but oh so straight, strong and beautiful as in her younger days. The children all sprang up to greet her, " Ta Momo, Ta Momo! " She went among them, examining their work as she used to do, the beautiful gold-embroidered vestments, the Venise lace, praising the industrious ones, encouraging the lazy ones. Then she turned to the Sister and asked her what new work she was preparing. " Oh, Ta Momo," said the Sister sadly, " I have no heart to prepare anything new; we are all so sad because you are no longer here."

" Oh, no-no-no-no-no," said Sister Berkeley in her quick way (she often used the little English ' no ' like that), " that will never do. You must not be sad, and don't say that I am no longer here. Why, I am always here; you cannot see me, but I never leave you and I watch over you and help you. I will always do so."

The Sister related this dream to the children, and although it brought floods of tears, as always when that dear name was mentioned, yet they were comforted. Word went through the houses to all, " Ta Momo is always here with us, although we cannot see her; she is helping and watching over us."

She is surely enjoying the reward of her long life of service for God and the poor and we would not wish her back, for she was growing very tired, bowed down at the age of eighty-three years with the heaviest burdens she had borne in her long life, but always smiling and courageous, an example to all. Though we miss her sorely we look up with a spirit of faith and believe she will help us still. In the many letters and messages from friends we read the same words. "Yes, I will indeed pray and I have had many Masses said for her, but I feel and believe that she has no need of them. She surely went straight to the glory of Heaven."

Fr. Nugent, C.M., the Director of the Ningpo Major Seminary, wrote:

"I am so grateful for the photos, especially the one of her at her bureau. I have it here on my desk and I often ask her to help me. You know the interest she always took in the Seminary and how she rejoiced with us on Ordination days and prayed so much for my 'Boys', as she always called the Seminarians. Well, do you think she will be less zealous for the Seminary now that she is near the centre and fountain of all graces?

"I have just finished fifteen Masses for the repose of her soul, and I shall have all the Masses you ask for said in the Seminary, but I feel she does not need them, for the purification of the sufferings of these past years was sufficient Purgatory for such a saintly soul. She is surely now 'with Christ,' as St. Paul so beautifully expresses it, the recompense of that dear soul who so loved Him in His Person and in the poor.

"What a wonderful welcome she must have had from her own dear ones who have gone before her and from the countless Chinese who owe to her, after God, their eternal happiness. There, besides Our Lord and His Blessed Mother, she will take great care of you and the House of Charity at Chusan, all the children and the poor, for she is now nearer the fountain and source of all and she will know how to plead for the cause. I feel myself that the maternal interest she always took in me will be infinitely more effective, and that I have now for myself and the Seminary a powerful advocate in Heaven."

Many European and Chinese priests wrote in like manner. One said, "How much I owe to her! She nursed me through a long illness when I was a Seminarian. I shall never forget her." Another, "She cared for me when I was run down and discouraged; she put me on my feet again and gave me new zeal and strength to work for souls."

Many spoke of the help she had given them for their poor Missions, putting them in touch with benefactors, sending new vestments, etc., for their chapels. Passing through Chusan, what a welcome they always received from her; above all, how she prayed for their apostolate.

When the soul of this Sister of Charity, daughter of St. Vincent de Paul, went forth from the world into the presence of God, we may think that He did not say to her, " You have practised this virtue, this mortification," but " I was hungry and you gave Me to eat, thirsty and you gave Me to drink, harbourless and you took Me in, naked and you clothed Me, sick and in prison and you visited Me. Amen I say unto you that as often as you have done these things to the least of My brethren, you have done them unto Me. Come, you blessed of My Father, possess the kingdom prepared for you from the foundation of the world."

XXIII

CHUSAN BEFORE AND AFTER THE JAPANESE SURRENDER

AFTER the death of Sister Berkeley the poverty and suffering in the House of Mercy increased. Day by day it was necessary to sell anything which would bring in money to buy food—iron heating stoves, beds and furniture not actually needed at the moment. Even the beautiful microscope in the hospital laboratory had to be sacrificed when a large sum of money was offered for it. This microscope was a very valuable instrument, a family gift to Sister Berkeley, and it cost the Sisters much to part with it. The Japanese cut down all the trees on their mountain lands to build an aerodrome, and bombs were expected daily from the American planes which were often seen flying high over the island.

In March 1945 the Japanese Commander of the town arrived one morning, accompanied by the Mandarin, who looked very worried and uneasy. The Japanese announced that the foreigners, priests and Sisters, were to be expelled from Chusan and taken to Shanghai, also that the House of Mercy must be entirely evacuated as the Japanese soldiers were going to take possession and live there. The Chinese Sisters and the children and old people were to go to the little North Gate village of Podong.

This news filled all with consternation and alarm and for the moment had a paralyzing effect. No one knew where to begin! How was a family of nearly 300, many of them babies and infirm and bedridden people, to be moved out into the country to a few village huts and the little house of Lorette? Happily in the afternoon of the same day the Mandarin returned to say that he had persuaded the Japanese to leave half the houses in the compound to the Chinese Sisters and the children.

At once the moving of furniture and equipment began. Many of the elder girls were sent to Christian families in the country

243

for safety, and some of the younger children were given shelter by kindly neighbours to reduce the numbers. Suddenly in the evening, at seven o'clock, Japanese soldiers arrived to take the foreigners to the port. Four Sisters and three priests were hustled out in the dark and put on board a Japanese gunboat. Two days and two nights they were in the hold of the boat, with constant attacks from American planes overhead. At last they arrived at Woosung, the mouth of the river, where they were put on a motor launch and brought up to Shanghai; then they were taken first to the Japanese police station, and afterwards to the Naval Bureau. Finally they were rescued that night by the French Consul, and allowed to go to their Shanghai Houses. The next day the Canadian priest and the English Sister were sent to concentration camps.

A few hours after the foreigners had left it the Japanese gunboat was sunk. This news went through to Chusan, where all thought the Sisters and priests had perished on it. An even worse tale went to Ningpo to the Bishop. Two separate individuals, who seemed trustworthy witnesses, brought a report that the foreigners had been shot at the port of Tinghai and their bodies thrown into the sea—the white cornettes of the Sisters had been seen floating on the water! For a whole month in Ningpo this tale was believed to be true and Masses were said for the victims.

During seven months of isolation the eight Chinese Sisters at Chusan carried on with great courage and devotion in the Houses left to them by the Japanese, with only a low bamboo fence between them and their enemies. The Japanese often came in and took what they liked—furniture, fittings, fresh-water pumps, etc. There was a daily fear of American bombs, and such of the elder girls who still remained were sent to a pagoda in the country for safety.

The Mandarin, doctor and other friends implored the Sisters to accompany them, but they firmly refused to leave the younger children, babies and old people. " If they are to die," they said, " we will die with them. Who will care for them if we go away ? Besides, the babies have measles now. They must be nursed. How can you ask us to leave them ? " The epidemic of measles added greatly to the difficulties in the overcrowded houses; many little ones died of that terrible disease, so fatal in China with its septic complications.

The provision of food for the children and poor was a daily problem. The Mandarin sent very little and that was of poor quality, so that the Sisters had often to send to him and say, " There is nothing for dinner to-day! " They went out daily to beg from door to door, and were well received, though the Chusan people were themselves in want. Some pagan ladies invited one or two little orphan girls to dine and sup with them every day. The Bishop made arrangements for thirty of the younger children to be taken to Ningpo; it was a difficult journey by junk and land, but great charity was shown by all to the children on the way.

God in His Divine Providence watched over the little family at Chusan, though the Sisters were in great danger. To the joy of all, the piece of garden with Sister Berkeley's temporary tomb was on their side of the compound. This comforted them, and they often said, " Ta Momo is taking care of us." She surely did so, and specially guarded her Sisters in their dangerous position. They lived the regular life of the Community, omitting none of their spiritual exercises and duties, though terribly cramped for space, surrounded closely as they were by the children and the poor.

A small classroom was arranged as a temporary chapel, and here came all the outside Christians, for the Parish Church and residence were occupied by the Japanese. A letter came through secretly from the Sisters, by junk, describing how they had spent the Feast of the Annunciation. " On the Eve, we made our Retreat in preparation for the Renovation of the Vows, piously but sadly, and in the morning we renewed our Holy Vows, thinking of you and praying for you." They never failed to make their Monthly Retreats.

The Japanese aerodrome, just ten minutes away, was heavily bombed by American planes several times. The Sisters described it as being " like hell fire all around them ", their houses shaking, glass falling, etc. All lay flat on the ground in terror. It was amazing that the buildings were not injured, but American airmen, in later visits after peace, told the Sisters that their orphanage was marked on the map for protection.

Towards the end of August news of the surrender came slowly through, but it was some time before the Japanese left the Sisters' Houses. Those who were in the country villages were chased out with spades and forks by the inhabitants, and they took refuge in the House of Mercy. Early in September an American boat came to Chusan. The doctor and officers visited the Sisters and were horrified to see their white-faced undernourished children! They gave them injections of blood plasma and large cases of their own rations and medicines, with a collection of money from all on board.

As soon as transportation was possible the foreign Sisters returned to Chusan, and what a welcome they received. But, alas, they were almost empty-handed and penniless, for the relief organizations were not yet working in Shanghai, and no money could get through from foreign countries. Day by day the Sisters went to the country villages and begged from door to door for a little rice and potatoes to feed their children. The generous Australian Red Cross had given them some cases of milk and rolled oats which saved the situation for the babies, together with some tinned food; but with a family of over 200 this was soon finished. For the first two months of the return only two meals a day could be served through lack of food and wood for cooking.

The houses which had been occupied by the Japanese were in a sad state: floors taken up, doors and windows missing, all covered ways torn down, the zinc and wood taken, furniture stolen and some buildings demolished. The kitchen, wash-houses and drying verandas of the babies' nurseries were all gone; the pharmacy was stripped of its white tiling and special equipment. It was a scene of desolation and it required great courage to attack the work of rebuilding, though the first problem to be solved was the finding of daily food.

Then, five days before Christmas, came splendid supplies from the British Red Cross, brought on an American ship by the kind Lieutenant Stokes and his officers. They carefully explained that it was Lieutenant Bulley of H.M.S. *Tyrian* who had collected all the stores and sent them to the American ship, as the British could not get permission from Chungking to come themselves.

Sacks of good U.N.R.R.A. flour and foodstuffs of all kinds, medical stores, leather for shoes, blankets, etc., were brought ashore piled up on Japanese lorries, and carried in on the backs of Japanese soldiers! The children cheered the kind American officers as they went away, and piled up their car with beautiful Christmas holly, for which Chusan is famous. Christmas was celebrated in the old pre-war manner, the children and all the household eating *mi* (Chinese macaroni) with many other luxuries not seen for years.

At the end of January came H.M.S. *Hind* with Lieutenant-Commander White, and Fr. Nugent was on board. This time permission had been given for a British ship to come, and big supplies were brought ashore of prisoner-of-war food parcels, full of good things, together with medicines, soap, towels, and clothing sent by General Myers of the British Red Cross, who proved himself to be Chusan's best friend.

The Holy Childhood children had the time of their lives. Sixty of them went aboard the *Hind* and had a memorable tea-party; they were the envy of the town. Dressed in their gayest clothes, they chugged away in the British motor boats to the big ship, and climbed up the side, the younger ones being carried by the sailors, who made great pets of them. It was a day never to be forgotten, and they well deserved it after eight years of war sufferings. The Sisters were also remembered, and every possible kindness was shown to them by the kind Commander White and officers of the *Hind*.

At the end of June H.M.S. *Lagos* brought Captain Unwin and Dr. Rankin of the British Red Cross, who came to visit and report on the Mission conditions. Another generous supply of prisoner-of-war parcels arrived, with cases of medicines, again through the kindness of General Myers. The little Chinese children learnt to munch chocolate with great delight. It was very nourishing, with the good " Klim " milk which came in the food parcels. One heard the babies saying, " Shoh-ko-lah, Momo, shoh-ko-lah, pa ala " (" Give us some chocolate, Momo "). Canada had " great face " in Chusan those days, for so many of the good things in the parcels came from the Canadian Red Cross, and they were of the finest quality.

One greatly appreciated gift from the British Red Cross was a money donation to enable the Sisters to make a proper tomb for their much-loved English Superior, Sister Berkeley. When, however, they spoke of taking her to the cemetery on the mountain outside the city, there was an outcry and tears from all at the idea of her leaving them. So permission was given by the Bishop to lay her to rest in a little piece of ground at the east side of the chapel.

With the help of the British Red Cross the simple tomb was

made, but then the Chinese stepped in and said, " This is not
your affair. We are going to do the rest. She was our ' Mother ',
the Mother of our orphans and poor for so many years; and you
cannot prevent us from honouring her in our way."

They formed a Head Committee in the town, and branch ones
in the country districts and islands, and with the permission of
the Bishop a great ceremony was planned for April 29th, 1946.
All the Christians in the islands were invited, also old friends from
Ningpo and many pagans. A little Chinese booklet was published,
an appreciation of this English Sister of Charity who had given
fifty-four years of service to China. One remark in it was striking:
" She forgot that she was English; she became Chinese, and lived
and worked among us for our orphans and poor! "

Knowing the poverty of the House of Mercy, and that the old-
time hospitality could not be offered, all visitors brought their
" own rice " and generous contributions; even the poorest
brought eggs, fowls, fish, etc., as their share. Some days before
the ceremony, the little brick tomb was opened and the big red
and gold coffin (presented by the Mandarin in 1944) was carried
reverently to a little room prepared as a chapel. It lay there,
surrounded with lilies, and the old married children came to weep
and pray at its side.

Mgr. Defebvre, the Bishop of Ningpo, was unable to be present,
but Mgr. Ou, Bishop of Haimen, took his place. He was an old
Chusan boy and a great friend of Sister Berkeley. He told an
interesting story on the occasion of this visit, which we relate.
About fifty years ago, when he was a schoolboy studying at
Ningpo, one day the boys heard the music of a big band and they
all rushed out of school to see it. It was the band of a British
man-of-war, on a visit to Ningpo, and the Commander and his
officers were marching at the head with great ceremony. They
were on their way to the House of Charity of the Sisters, " Maison
Jésu Enfant," in the city, and they wished to show honour to
their compatriot, the English Sister, who was working there amongst
the Chinese poor (Sister Berkeley).

Bishop Ou said that he and his schoolfellows knew the tall
English Sister well, for they sometimes went to watch her dressing
sores and nursing the poor sick people in the dispensary. That
day the thought struck home to him, " That Sister has left her
home, her country, to care for those poor people for the love of

God, and to try to win their souls for Heaven. Could not I also give my life to the service of God for souls ? " It was the birth of his vocation, and he always said that he owed it to the Sisters, especially Sister Berkeley.

Fr. Nugent, the head of the Ningpo Seminary, was also present. As a young Missionary at Ninghay he had been mothered by Sister Berkeley and she always followed him with maternal care. Every hole and corner in the House of Mercy was filled with women and children, and the men and boys filled the church residence and schools. On the Sunday afternoon, the day before the funeral, all gathered in the Sisters' chapel, which was beautifully decorated for the occasion by the special request of the Chinese. Many Christian and pagan friends rose to give their appreciation of the life and service of this " Mother of the Poor ".

That evening the coffin was carried to the Parish Church and placed on the catafalque before the high altar. Early the next morning the church was packed with Christians, pagans and town officials. The Bishop and priests, in procession, entered by the big south door, preceded by the town band reverently playing the music of an English hymn. The Requiem Mass was sung by the Holy Childhood children, and at the Elevation small cannon were fired outside and fireworks let off.

After Mass the coffin was carried to the glass hearse, with its red and gold roof, and now came the only dispute and difficulty in the whole affair. It was among the many sons-in-law and grandsons of Sister Berkeley for the honour of carrying the hearse; it required twenty strong men, ten at a time changing. This procession through the town was much against the will and taste of the Sisters, but they had to give way, because special permission had been granted for it by the Bishop to the Christians. They said, " The town wish to honour the Mother of their Poor."

First came the big Cross, then three flags—Chinese, French and British (the latter had been presented by the British Navy in Shanghai). These were followed by big Chinese lanterns and Church banners, the town band, the photograph of Sister Berkeley carried by the Orphanage boys on a *brancarde* draped with silk hangings and flowers, the altar boys in red cassocks and white surplices, carrying lighted candles, and the boys of the Catholic schools in uniform.

Then came the banners, most of them presented by pagan

friends. There were twenty-four of these—huge banners of silk and satin in all colours, red, blue, green, purple and gold, with inscriptions in big gold lettering: " The Mother of the Orphans and the Poor "; " She led a good life and died a good death "; " She was the model of all virtues "; " She gave her life and strength to the Poor "; " She faded away like a flower but is now glorious in Heaven "; " Her example will always live and remain with us ", and many others with similar appreciations. Among them were some plain white cloth banners with inscriptions written in ink. These came from the inmates of the town prison, appreciations of the charity shown to the sick and suffering prisoners.

The clergy walked in front of the hearse, and the Sisters followed it. After them came the Holy Childhood children of the House, about 200 of them, carrying their banners of the Children of Mary and the Angels. The elder girls wore long blue robes, with white mourning bands round their heads, and the younger school children, also in blue robes, wore little round white caps (Chinese mourning fashion). Even thirty of the babies, five and six years old, marched valiantly, dressed in the gold-flowered coats made for their " Mother's Jubilee " twelve years before, with little white caps; and not one of them slipped in the mud. For it must be told that the rainy season had begun, and though the rain kept off for the procession and the sun came out, yet the muddy street made walking a real penance.

The children were followed by the old men and women of the hospices, the able ones, and with them came mutes, cripples, idiots, and most of the blind, led by kind companions. Lastly came the Christian women and girls of the different parishes, the members of the Union of Catholic Mothers carrying their beautiful banner of St. Louise de Marillac and the Holy Family. Many pagan friends followed in respectful silence.

When the procession entered the House of Mercy the coffin was carried to the place prepared for it. As it was lowered into the tomb, the priests sang the *In Paradisum* and Fr. Nugent gave the *Absoute*, but their voices were drowned by the wails and sobs of the women and children. It is the custom of the Chinese to bewail the dead at this moment, but here it was genuine emotion, children mourning their much-loved Mother. A newcomer, lately arrived, said to them, " But it is two years since she died, and you still mourn her ? " They replied sadly, " Ah, you never knew her;

she was our Mother, no one will ever love us as she did. We shall never forget her."

From above she surely looked down on them that day with indulgent compassion, though shaking her head in horror at the honour paid to her. Her remains rest peacefully in the little tomb with its cross at the head and *Spes Unica* engraved on it. All who come and go look at it with affectionate remembrance, and even the pagans say, " It is good you keep her with you here."

She sees around her the ruins of so much that her patient toil for years had built up and arranged, but she will gain help and courage for those who carry on her work, to lift it up again with the same love and devotion for the children. Above all, this great missionary soul surely makes the same appeal before the Throne of God that the sons and daughters of St. Vincent do, in the prayer they say daily,

" The harvest is indeed great but the labourers are few. We pray Thee, therefore, who art the Lord of the harvest, to send labourers into Thy harvest."

END

INDEX

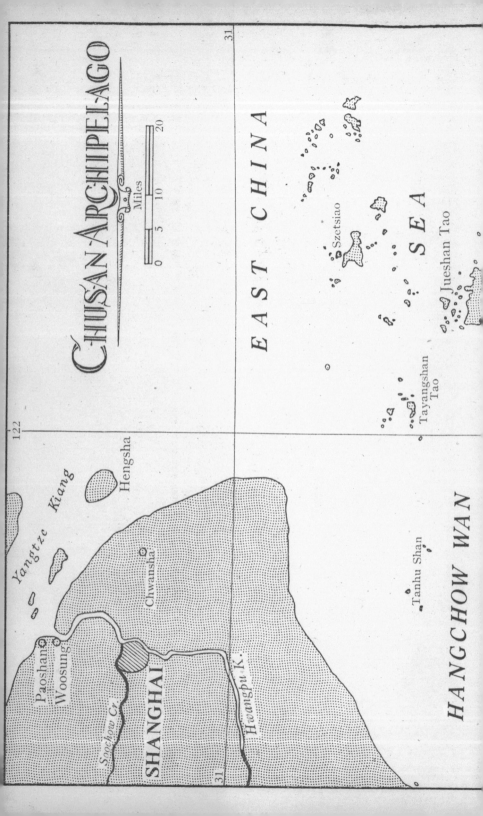